THE MAGICAL QUEST

To the memory of
Professor Geoffrey Shepherd

Anne Wilson

THE MAGICAL QUEST

THE USE OF MAGIC IN ARTHURIAN ROMANCE

Manchester University Press
Manchester and New York

*Distributed exclusively in the USA and Canada
by* St. Martin's Press, New York
Room 400, 175 Fifth Avenue, New York 10010, USA

Published by Manchester University Press
Oxford Road, Manchester M139PL, UK

*Distributed exclusively in the USA and Canada
by* St. Martin's Press, Inc.,
Room 400, 175 Fifth Avenue, New York, NY10010, USA

British Library cataloguing in publication data
Wilson, Anne, 1934–
   The magical quest: the use of magic in
   Arthurian romance.
   1. Arthurian romances — History and
   criticism
   I. Title
   809'.93351   PN57.A6

Library of Congress cataloging in publication data
Wilson, Anne.
   The magical quest.
   Includes index.
   1. Arthurian romances — History and criticism.
2. Magic in literature.   I. Title.
PN686.M33W55   1988   809'.02   88–5281

ISBN 0–7190–2373–4 *hardback*

Typeset in Hong Kong
by Graphicraft Typesetters Ltd

Printed in Great Britain by
Billing & Sons Ltd., Worcester

CONTENTS

Truly, Sir Priest, my own experience tells me that so-called books of chivalry are very prejudicial to the commonwealth; ... even though the principal aim of such books is to delight, I do not know how they can succeed, seeing the monstrous absurdities they are filled with .... What beauty can there be, or what harmony between the parts and the whole, or between the whole and its parts, in a book or story in which a sixteen-year-old lad deals a giant as tall as a steeple one blow with his sword, and cuts him in two as if he were made of marzipan? And when they want to describe a battle, first they tell us that there are a million fighting men on the enemy's side. But if the hero of the book is against them, inevitably, whether we like it or not, we have to believe that such and such a knight gained the victory by the valour of his strong arm alone. Then what are we to say of the ease with which a hereditary Queen or Empress throws herself into the arms of an unknown and wandering knight? What mind not totally barbarous and uncultured can get pleasure from reading that a great tower, full of knights, sails out over the sea like a ship before a favourable wind, and that one night it is in Lombardy and by dawn next morning in the land of Prester John or the Indies, or in some other country that Ptolemy never knew nor Marco Polo visited?

Miguel de Cervantes Saavedra, *The Adventures of Don Quixote*, Part 1, Ch. xlvii, translated by J. M. Cohen (Harmondsworth, 1950), pp. 424–5.

PREFACE

The writing of a book such as this is made particularly solitary by its unusual subject, but I am indebted to many people, specialists and others, for their advice as to how to present my material. I have also taken up suggestions as to texts I should investigate, and I have had helpful discussions with a number of specialists in areas I have invaded. Not all these people were fully aware of the kind of argument I would eventually produce, and I must, in any case, take entire responsibility for my extraordinary thesis, and for the mistakes I may very well have made as a result of casting my net in waters other than my own (I am an English specialist). So I shall not mention unsuspecting scholars by name, but simply record my gratitude here for the friendship and generosity I have met with in many universities, colleges and libraries. Of those I shall mention by name, Dr David Blamires of Manchester University must come first: he has given me moral support throughout my pursuit of my unusual subject, and, in the case of this present book, invaluable help with publication. I must also thank Mr Bernard O'Donoghue of Magdalen College, Oxford, and Dr Neville Davies of the Shakespeare Institute, Birmingham University, for reading some chapters at an early stage of the book, and giving me advice and much encouragement. Mrs Margaret Spencer, of the Institute of Education, London University, took particular trouble in advising me over how *not* to present my introductory material, when she saw an early attempt, and my daughter Frances Wilson advised me on the preparation of this material in the light of current critical approaches. Meanwhile, my friend Elaine Turner, an English specialist like myself, has supported and advised me over many years, and I would not have investigated the 'All's Well' story had it not been for her insistence. At two stages when there were problems unsolved over the presentation of many of the chapters, my friend Lindsey March gave much time to reading the book and giving me invaluable advice on style and the clear presentation of my arguments. My son Kenneth Wilson also read the book and advised me from the point of view of the general reader. I am also grateful to the readers of Manchester University Press for their helpful guidance over the presentation of my material and for their suggestions as to studies which might be included; in particular, I owe my chapter on Ywain to one of them. My editor John Banks has shown much kindness and patience during long delays caused by illness, and it is a great pleasure to publish with the Manchester University Press, the press of my *alma mater*. Finally, I wish to remember Professor Geoffrey Shepherd, under whose supervision I made my initial investigation of the magical plot. Professor Shepherd also gave me invaluable advice when I was preparing my second book. I am sad that he has not lived to see my studies of the Perceval and Ywain romances, and am dedicating this book to his memory.

A. D. W.
University of Birmingham

ACKNOWLEDGEMENTS

The author's thanks are due to the proprietors of the copyrights in the following works quoted in the text: *Perceval: The Story of the Grail*, by Chrétien de Troyes, translated by Nigel Bryant (D. S. Brewer, Ltd.); *Parzival*, by Wolfram von Eschenbach, translated by A. T. Hatto (Penguin Classics, 1980, copyright © A. T. Hatto, 1980); *Yvain, the Knight of the Lion*, by Chrétien de Troyes, translated by Tony Hunt, and *Chrétien de Troyes' Arthurian Romance 'Yvain'*, by Tony Hunt, from *The New Pelican Guide to English Literature: 1. Medieval Literature Part Two: The European Inheritance*, edited by Boris Ford (Pelican Books, 1983, copyright © Boris Ford, 1983); *A Reading of 'Sir Gawain and the Green Knight'*, by J. A. Burrow (Associated Book Publishers (U. K.) Ltd.); *What 'Sir Gawain and the Green Knight' is About*, by G. V. Smithers, from *Medium Aevum* XXXII, No. 3, 1963 (Basil Blackwell, Ltd.). She is also grateful to Gwyn and Mair Jones for permission to quote from *The Mabinogion*, translated by Gwyn Jones and Thomas Jones, 1948, and revised by Gwyn and Mair Jones, 1974 (J. M. Dent & Sons, Ltd.).

INTRODUCTION

Why is it that so many medieval romances show moral contradictions? In one romance, the narrator declares the hero innocent and, almost immediately, the hero finds himself unbearably guilty.[1] In another romance, the narrator presents the slaying of one person by another as both a deed of honour and a sin.[2] In a third, an innocent knight is accused of infringing the knightly code while another who infringes it grossly is rewarded with honours.[3] In none of these texts does the author appear to have noticed the contradiction.

This kind of moral contradiction is found in works where the author is making use of a plot of traditional origin. These works also show contradictions in the author's handling of the characters: the characters' behaviour is often inconsistent with their behaviour elsewhere in the text, and incongruous in relation to their characterisation. Sometimes the hero engages in a series of adventures which are presented as relating to the rest of the material in the text and yet there seems to be no evidence as to what the relationship is. There are, thus, occasions when studies of works containing a traditional plot are checked by the problem that the relationship between the author's art and the plot he is using is too enigmatic. All that can be discerned in the text is the presence of distinctive contradictions and inconsistencies.

Recently, a critic pointed out these very problems in the case of Chrétien's *Yvain*. What 'is the moral value of Yvain's undertaking and his conduct of the adventure?', this critic asks; how are we to understand Yvain's aggression against the fountain knight? He continues, 'Nothing could be more ambiguous than the apparent marriage of convenience which takes place between Yvain and Laudine' (the fountain knight's widow). He also comments on the succeeding adventures that 'It is anything but clear how the adventures relate to the rewinning of Laudine'; 'it is difficult to divine the hero's intentions'. After an investigation of Chrétien's irony and an illuminating discussion of the possibility that Chrétien dismantles the courtly 'co-ordination of chivalric and amatory pursuits', the critic concludes that 'This leaves every major issue open'; Chrétien's *Yvain* 'is a puzzle'.[4]

This critic of *Yvain* looks for solutions in the subtlety of Chrétien's art, while a critic of another text presenting these problems, the play *Pericles, Prince of Tyre*, notes, 'The play is about people who suffer unaccountable misfortunes and gain equally unaccountable good fortune ... we are not offered a clue to any meaning lying in the progression of events'.[5] Its plot, the time-honoured Apollonius of Tyre story, shows a remarkable degree of incoherence in character, action and moral vision, while authors who make use of it fail, it seems, to notice that their characters are behaving with puzzling inconsistency, and, without irony, they treat as noble a character who appears infamous.

Critics of *Sir Gawain and the Green Knight* have commented on inconsistent treatment of the magic, of the Lady and Morgan le Fay, of the Christian material and *courtoisie*. They have asked questions about the incongruous part played by Bertilak: his characteristics are not consistent with his having consented to Morgan's spiteful scheme, and he is strangely confused with a hermit, associated with a 'chapel' in desolate country and hearing Gawain's 'confession'. The problems over the close proximity of two confessions have been pointed out, and also contradictions between them: the poet assures us emphatically that Gawain is 'clene', when the priest has heard his confession, and yet Gawain does not find himself clean at the Green Chapel. Moreover, Gawain there confesses to covetousness, although the Lady's belt has not been wrongfully acquired; she has given it to him.

The studies in this book address these problems in a number of medieval texts. The problems are not always so glaring as they appear to be in the Ywain, Apollonius and Green Knight texts, but they can nevertheless be present in the

same way. When they are not so obvious, it is easier to fall
back on our knowledge that inconsistencies and inexplicable
features are characteristic of some traditional stories, and of
medieval works making use of them: we are aware that
traditional stories tend to be about a great deal more than
those concerns which we find sensible in the world outside
art, and that medieval authors did not usually choose to
make radical alterations to material well-known to audiences, preferring to develop its potential and enrich it in the
retelling through their own additions in thought and language. But I am interested in pursuing patterns and consis-
tencies which I see in the contradictions and irrationalities,
not in order to rationalise them by having them make sense
in relation to established, familiar systems of knowledge or
ideas — whether those concerned with authorial treatment
or those explaining traditional material: I am interested in
the anatomy of the problems themselves and, while I find
form and meaning in the plots and their treatment, these are
as crazy to the rational mind as the nature of the problems
suggests they will be.

In my introductory study of the Apollonius story, and in
my studies of the Ywain and Green Knight romances, I seek
to show that the plots concerned have a concerted purpose
beyond the reach of an author's transforming art. I do not
wish to say that the authors are unconscious of what is
taking place, for there is no proving whether this is so; all I
can show is that an author will re-create the purpose with
power, even while it contradicts his own themes, and that a
variety of interesting situations arise in a text where an
author, on the one hand, and one of these strange plots, on
the other, are going about their separate business.

These plots I call 'magical plots' (in previous books I called them 'fantasy structures'). While this collection of studies is a quite fresh attempt to tackle this subject, it is a
subject I have explored and struggled to define over a period
of fifteen years. Magical plots are common in the traditional
Western European literature I have studied, but I would not
be surprised if scholars find that they are not always common elsewhere; my own limited excursions into traditional
stories of other parts of the world have led me to suspect

that there may be an exceptional number of magical plots in the tales of medieval Europe. Since European authors of stature have made use of traditional stories, a small number of texts regarded as important include a plot which I would define as magical. Chaucer's texts are not among these (he made use of one magical story, for his Wife of Bath's tale, and totally transformed it, eclipsing its magical purposes),[6] and Shakespeare used only three magical plots (the stories of Apollonius, Hamlet and *All's Well*), but I find the plots of a great number of medieval romances magical, including those of the early Tristan romances[7] and other of our most compelling and enduring works. In this book, I seek to show that Chrétien's Grail story is among them.

What do I mean by 'magical'? Briefly, I mean that the plot is a series of mental rituals, through which participants bring about desires (in the mind, of course) and dispel fear or guilt. Participants are members of an audience (or the storyteller) identifying themselves with the story, especially with its chief character, and I therefore call these participants 'the hero' or, where the chief character is female, 'heroine'. Such magical devices as exorcism, ritual punishment and magic words are employed. Because of its ritual character, the magical plot has a very decided form, this being a series of steps in the hero's (or heroine's) struggle to achieve desires and solve their conflict with fear or guilt. Herein, I believe, lie the clues to the 'meaning lying in the progression of events' and to 'how the adventures relate to the rewinning of Laudine'. The inexplicable decisions of the characters are magical decisions, and the problems over the relationship between the author and his plot are consistently the kind of problems which arise when two entirely different levels of thought are at work without acknowledging each other's presence — for example, an author's moral vision and the solipsistic, irrational concern with desire and guilt in the magical plot.

Used as a model, the 'magical plot' directs the investigator to take up the notion that there is only one point of view in the plot under investigation, that of the participant 'hero' or 'heroine', who is using all the characters as figures in the rituals. It also imposes other disciplines. The steps in the magical structure, which I call 'moves',[8] are related to each other very closely, making use of 'repeat' characters, and this is an important guide in the struggle to understand a series of adventures. The many characters in a plot will represent only a few characters in the hero's mind. The model also helps the investigator to concentrate on understanding form, rather than meaning, and it directs the investigator to examine how the details relate to each other, forbidding any resort to ad hoc interpretations taken from somewhere outside the text. Our difficulty with the irrational is that we are prone to rationalise it all the time, giving explanations for it which make it conform with what the reasoning, conscious mind knows about, and such explanations leave many details and problems in the text unaccounted for. Any meaning eventually unearthed will be confused and ambivalent because that is the situation in the mind beneath our organising powers of reason, but, while the model cannot give us any final answers as to meaning, it can help us to explore a highly organised linear structure with two or more — sometimes ten or more — moves, which come to an end when the desired state of mind has been achieved.

Before I go on to a general discussion of the magical plot, I will give a brief example, choosing the romance of *King Horn*[9] because it shows the morphology of these plots particularly clearly. The moves are divided by sea journeys, the chief character arriving after each journey at a court where there is a king and a princess. Beginning as the son of a king killed by pirates, he crosses the sea in exile, to arrive at the court of King Aylmer, disguised as a thrall. There he loves Rymenild, the king's daughter, but his low-born companion Fikenild tells the king that he has seduced the princess and intends to destroy the king. Horn crosses the sea in exile once more, and arrives at another king's court. He calls himself 'Goodmind', and saves the king from a monstrous giant threatening him. The king offers him his daughter, but he refuses her. Next, he returns to King Aylmer's court as a beggar, but he is now no longer afraid of the king and calls himself 'Horn'. He kills the king to whom Rymenild has been promised. After this, he returns home, becomes king and restores his mother to her position. Finally, disguised as a harper, he returns to King Aylmer's court, and finds that Fikenild has built himself a castle and is seeking to take Rymenild by force from her cowed father. Horn defeats Fikenild and marries Rymenild.

Among the curious features of the story is the absence of an explanation as to why Horn should be a thrall rather than a king in exile, at Aylmer's court. Nor is it explained how the low-born Fikenild could gain such power over Aylmer at that king's own court. But it is the name 'Goodmind' ('Cutbeard' in one text) which is the chief clue indicating a decided meaning in the progression of events in *King Horn*. 'Horn' and 'Goodmind' are contrasting names in parallel contexts where there is a king, a princess and an adventuring hero. Horn leaves King Aylmer and goes to another court, there to play out a role which is precisely the reverse of that which he is accused of at Aylmer's court. During these reversing events he calls himself 'Goodmind' (or 'Cutbeard'). Then he returns to King Aylmer, no longer afraid of him, and calling himself 'Horn'. As 'Goodmind', eliminating the monster threatening the king, and renouncing the princess, the hero is being good. It can also be seen that in defeating Fikenild, who is threatening King Aylmer, the hero is being good. Fikenild is threatening the king in order to seize the princess, and this is what he has accused Horn of doing earlier in the story. The hero's being 'Horn' must include thoughts of the behaviour in Fikenild's accusation, and his acting out the 'Goodmind' roles is clearly important in his progress towards his marriage with the princess: he begins to get bigger in relation to King Aylmer after being 'Goodmind', and he marries Rymenild after removing Fikenild.

It emerges that the plot makes best sense as a series of rituals whereby the hero achieves his aspirations by means of a successful struggle against an idea that they are wrong, being a threat to one seen as occupying the position to which he aspires. This position is not conceived in strictly political terms: it is a state of mind achieved after the removal of guilt. This, put very simply here, is the kind of way in which a magical plot works. It is evident that such a plot is one that is used by storyteller and audience in a special way: the hero is a different kind of hero from the chief character in other fictions. This is not a hero who has a companion called Fikenild: this is a hero who appears in two characters for his own purposes — in order to resolve an inner conflict by performing rituals. There is no detached point of view: the critic cannot here be concerned with the author's tone, but instead must address the hero's mood.

The conflict at the heart of this popular old tale appears to be of an Oedipal nature, but it is important not to allow ready-made interpretations or blunt, reductionist methods of analysis to intrude and distort the study of texts containing a magical plot. A careful analysis of such texts could bring more to light concerning the workings of the primitive mind. Meaning is extremely slippery in a magical plot, but analysis of the magical arrangements for dealing with conflicts can be carried out with a great deal of exactness, bringing to bear the tools of the literary specialist.

The level of thought which creates a magical plot is entirely distinct from the levels of thought with which literary specialists are generally concerned. The words 'fantasy' and 'imagination' have been given a variety of uses, and to explain my point about the level of thought in a magical plot I have had to draw distinctions between magical thought and imaginative thought, and between magical fantasy and fantasy which has been contrived by the conscious, 'rational' artist. The imagination is a power of the mind which can separate itself from solipsistic desires and fears to reflect on the world and step into the shoes of other people. Magical thought is, by contrast, entirely concerned with the feelings of the solipsistic inner world. While the imagination is essential for the efficient conduct of our lives in the world, magical thought can have no practical efficiency in the world beyond the self, although it can play a useful part by bringing about desired states of mind and thus providing a sense of well-being which has a practical value. The magical plot plays such a role.

However, I believe it could also be claimed that stories which are not magical play a role in creating desired states of mind. W. H. Auden argues that the detective story addict restores himself to a state of 'innocence' by means of having a genius from outside remove the suspicion of guilt, giving knowledge of it and expelling it,[10] and recent studies of Mills and Boon romances suggest that they are narratives in which their millions of female readers alter prevailing situations in heterosexual relationships, taming the dominant male character and having him provide nurturing love.[11] Similar roles may also be discerned in the plots of more considerable novels, but a magical plot is distinguished by its use of magical devices, in a distinct ritual structure: a magical hero does not use stratagems which would work, even in ideal circumstances, in the world beyond the mind; instead, he uses a ritual. In the case of many a novel and story, the reader identifies with the chief character and may bring about desired states of mind, but the concerns and decisions of the characters appeal directly to the rational — if not always very sensible — mind, even in Fantastic fictions. Attention is given to the points of view of all the characters, as we find, for example, in the encounter between Jim Hawkins and Israel Hands in *Treasure Island*: both characters are engaged in anticipating moves, outwittings, trickery and the planning of strategies.[12] Similarly, Tolkien's *The Lord of the Rings* appeals to the reasoning powers we use for our everyday tactical and moral decision-making, and Tolkien creates for his magical world a set of laws coherent to our rational minds — for example, the laws by which the Ring's powers work — these being explained to the reader as Frodo learns them.[13] In *King Horn*, on the other hand, the point of view of King Aylmer is absent, and no explanation is offered for the extraordinary reversal of power between this king in his own kingdom and the low-born, exiled Fikenild; no explanations are needed at the magical level.

The magical plot can be illuminated by a judicious consideration of its similarity to dream and day-dream material, in spite of the obvious problem that these are personal, original material, rather than 'ready-made', shared material which is adopted by participants. Nocturnal dreams are, in addition, too elusive and much too idiosyncratic in content and imagery to be of great assistance in describing the thought in the magical plot, and they do not have the striking organisation of its ritual form, honed by long use in tradition. But, in the dream, we see magical thought in action: we see how the content is about the feelings of the creator of it (the dreamer), and that these feelings bring things about, while the dreamer may resort to some kind of additional magic in the attempt to get control over the magical power of such feelings as fear and a sense of powerlessness.

In a previous study, I cite the seven-year-old dreamer Martin, who used the magic word EMIN to restore his head after his fears had led to its being cut off.[14] I will give the most relevant details again here. The dream began with a car journey in which the dreamer's father crashed the car into a wall and had to go back to buy a new car. Many frightening adventures followed, the beheading scene coming as the culmination.

The girl peeped through a small little door and called us all to come because a man wanted our heads. The boys went into a house and I followed them in. I saw a pair of shoes and a pair of hands and a head. In his hands was an axe, and above the axe, on the wall, was written EM and two letters after that; I called the word EMIN. The man made us vanish and then he took us all and put us on two blocks with our necks over the gap between them. He chopped off our heads, and then he made us come back to life again without any heads. He put our heads back on us and stood us up. There was a line round our necks, but the axe had no blood on it. We walked down the corridor very slowly so that our heads wouldn't fall off. When we were quite far I remembered the magic word EMIN, so I said EMIN to make our heads come back to life again.Then our heads were fixed on again so that we could run back to the place where Daddy had a new car. And then we went home with Daddy.

Nightmares such as this can make a particularly interesting study, because the magical nature of the thought is more evident. Six months later, this child dreamed that he and his friends were attacked by some men: 'We got a spear off one of the men and we killed a king who was so powerful that when you touched his blood you would be the strongest in the world; so we touched his blood and so we were the strongest in the world.' The dream continued with the boys' making a den in a wood and building a wall round it 'because lions and tigers were around. Some aeroplanes came to attack us from the air so Nisse made a roof on the den. Only small animals could get through the door we made. Nisse was magic so that no men or animals would come and attack us. He made a magic sign [demonstrated to the recorder by the dreamer as being a pressing movement made with arms folded] while he was building the walls and roof.' The dreamer was so frightened at this point that he woke up.[15] This child resorted to the magic word and gesture in his attempts to get control during his nightmares, and also to a primitive identification ritual ('we touched his blood'). He told himself that these particular words and actions had special power.

Day-dreams are not, in general, unconscious, directly magical material, as are these dreams; their thought and content are affected by a consciousness of the external world, even though amazing things can happen in them. But the contemplation of day-dreams helps one to grasp what is meant by the hero or heroine being one and the same as the creator of the narrative, and there being only one point of view, that of the day-dreamer/hero. Sometimes day-dreaming can take a form similar to that of the magical plot's moves, there being repeated enactions of a scenario — for example, a confrontation with someone — until the day-dreamer feels satisfied with one of them, or has, indeed, gained satisfaction from all of them. The more the day-dreamer explores the point of view of the other person, the more useful this day-dream is for an actual confrontation, while, if there is only one point of view present — that of the day-dreamer, the other person being placed in a variety of postures dictated by the feelings of the day-dreamer — then we have a 'narrative' closer to that of the magical plot. The stratagems may still not be magical: tricksters stories such as those of Uncle Remus show how our need for the underdog to be victorious can be satisfied by stratagems which, far from being magical, are keenly enjoyed for their cunning and ingenuity.

It is a golden rule that the function of the magical plot is to bring about the participant's wishes, a rule important to

bear in mind because content such as the successful removal
of fear or guilt can appear in the form of events which, to
outward view, are far from desirable and even tragic. No
problem is presented by the opposition of fear or guilt in
some plots, such as that of *Jack and the Beanstalk*: the wishes
can have full reign within the magical powers and safeguards provided by the plot. Other plots, such as those of
Hamlet and Apollonius of Tyre, are chiefly concerned with
dispelling fear or guilt from the participant's mind, the desired state of mind being the feeling that certain desires
entertained by the participant are free from evil. The majority of the plots I have studied are somewhere between these
two extremes: the progress towards the triumph of wishes
(wishes usually expressed by the image of a kingdom) involves conflict with opposing feelings, most commonly those
of guilt. Rituals to dispel the opposing feelings may take
place concurrently with the progress towards the triumph,
as they do in *King Horn*, or they may take place in rituals
following the triumph, as they do in the Ywain plot and *Sir
Perceval of Galles*. Two plots I have studied, one of them that
of *Sir Gawain and the Green Knight*, fall into yet another
category: they are concerned with neither triumph nor
purification, but with the enjoyment of certain experiences
felt to be forbidden, within a great number of safeguards
placating the powers-that-be. This last category I shall discuss in my chapter on *Sir Gawain and the Green Knight*; the
others I shall attend to further here.

Jack and the Beanstalk* provides a pleasurable ritual in
which the hero's thefts and defeat of the giant can be enjoyed with the single aid of the disguises found in every
magical plot (the participant need not confront the nature of
his feelings or even his participation). If the hero experi-
enced conflict between his wishes and opposing feelings, he
would have much less control over what the giants do, because his opposing feelings would have the same magical
power as his wishes to bring things about in his story. As
it is, the hero can enjoy the easy defeat of a formidable
giant without the sometimes desperate measures of Martin's
dreams.[16] In plots where there is conflict, it is part of the
plot's function to resolve this conflict, because opposing feel-

ings prevent the attainment of the desired state of mind. Thus, we find, in these plots, that such a triumph as Jack's is preceded or followed by events which tend to appear extraordinary, such as the hero's having to kill and mutilate the fox in *The Golden Bird*[17] and the heroine of *The Goose-Girl*'s having her right to be queen declared by her talking horse after (not before) it is beheaded by the usurper.[18] The fox and the horse, in each case, take the chief character to the brink of sovereignty (the kingdom) and then there is a hitch, different in each plot and yet with striking similarities. I find evidence that these particular extraordinary events are ritual punishments dealing with guilt: the hero of *The Golden Bird* has been a thief and the heroine of *The Goose-Girl* feels she is a usurper of her mother's place. In each case, the hero or heroine gains control over the feelings preventing the happy ending in the same way that Martin gained control over the fear in his beheading dream — by using some magical device invested with the power to eliminate the feeling. The heroine of *The Goose-Girl*, like the hero of *King Horn*, deals with her guilt concurrently with her progress towards her kingdom; the plots differ in that she uses a cleansing ritual punishment, while the hero of *King Horn* uses rituals which remove (exorcise) the idea that his wishes and actions are evil. This form of plot can be interchangeable with the kind of plot I find in *The Golden Bird*, where two moves to deal with the guilt follow the hero's seizure of the attributes of sovereignty: the plot of Chrétien's unfinished *Perceval* is evidently engaged in dealing with the guilt concurrently, while Wolfram's *Parzival* and *Sir Perceval of Galles* (in very different ways) deal with the guilt after the seizure of the attributes of sovereignty.

As I have already surveyed, in *King Horn*, the type of plot which deals with the guilt concurrently, I shall now devote attention to the type which deals with it subsequently. The plot used for the Ywain romances is remarkably similar to that of *The Golden Bird*. Both have four moves. In the first, initial arrangements for the theft of sovereignty are made: a vision of the theft — in, respectively, Calogrenant's tale and the golden bird's thefts of the king's golden apples — leads to the next move and its strategies. In the second move, the hero uses a magic formula which propels him to the seizure of the attributes of sovereignty, these being, respectively, Calogrenant's tale, sanctioned as an adventure by King Arthur and his queen, and the rides on the fox's tail from king to king to fetch the attributes. Then follow, in each plot, two final moves to deal with the guilt. The plot of *Sir Perceval of Galles* reaches this point in a different way, since it takes the hero to the seizure of sovereignty in six moves rather than two, but its two final moves for the expulsion of the guilt take exactly the same form as those in the other two plots. In all three plots, these two moves are two steps to a solution, the first move using surrogates, while the second deals directly with the guilt, though it uses heavy disguises. For example, the hero of *The Golden Bird* at first refuses the fox's request that he be killed and mutilated, and turns his own brothers into the thieves of the royal objects. He declares the thefts to the king, who punishes the brothers, gives the hero the princess (one of the stolen attributes of kingship) and makes him his heir. At the fox's second request, the hero kills him and cuts off his head and his feet; the fox then turns into the brother of the princess. The relationship of the moves is, in part, that the first involves an evasion and the second an acknowledgement of guilt, albeit disguised (the hero using the agent he employed for his thefts). But the first of the moves has another function: it creates a situation in which the king gives the hero what the hero has stolen; the seizure is legitimised and completed. The relationship between these two moves in *The Golden Bird* provides a useful guide to the other two plots, but the critic has to be ready to spot differences in the relationship: in the Ywain plot, the first of the two moves is engaged in exorcising the theft and the second, the treachery.

It can be both useful and dangerous to make these comparisons between plots. There are certain recurring patterns, but the use to which the hero or heroine puts these varies greatly from one plot to another, and the critic has to examine the thought and mood of each plot in strict isolation from other plots. Awareness of the recurring patterns helps the critic to use the magical plot effectively as a model for the detection of function, but this detection, and the accompanying work of interpretation are delicate interrelated processes, requiring meticulous concentration on the text concerned.

The rituals which deal with the opposing feelings in *The Golden Bird* are punishments, while, in the Ywain plot, they are exorcisms, and, in *Sir Perceval of Galles*, they are exorcisms followed by a penance. Most remarkable of all resolutions must be that of Wolfram's *Parzival*, which the author himself invents. The moves are less distinct because of the presence of a great deal of additional material, but the methods are clear: magic words, involving the Christian religion, are organised into the Grail prophecies, the second of these, announced by Cundrie, being the most powerful magic spell I have come across. The magical plot always deals with its conflicts magically; in no magical plot does the hero or heroine use rational means, such as coming to terms with guilt or ambivalence, or realising the true status of the fantasies. Guilt and fear have to be eliminated (dispelled), and they may be eliminated by magic words, which give the hero's wishes special power, or by a cleansing ritual punishment or penance, or — most commonly — by rituals which remove (exorcise) the idea that the hero's wishes and actions are evil.

The discipline that the magical plot always brings about the wishes of the hero, and that the conflict must be resolved, was one I found essential when dealing with the difficulties of the Hamlet plot. My bearing in mind that the death of Hamlet was likely to be the solution bringing the plot to an end led to my grasping the startling character of the revenge theme, that it was a suicidal vengeance, the hero's task being to punish his usurping thoughts with death. This was why Hamlet's behaviour was that of a man faced with a paralysing dilemma. The function of the traditional plot Shakespeare was using, and therefore the underlying meaning which incidentally conflicted with some of the material in the playwright's great superstructure, was that of a purification ritual.[19]

The subject matter in a magical plot has a limited range and tends to be of a similar nature. There appears to be a repeated concern with primal situations: the characters usually turn out to be aspects of the hero in relation to aspects of maternal and paternal figures (who tend to appear as queens and kings, witches and wizards, or giants), and the interaction appears, from a superficial view, to be Oedipal. The desired state of mind brought about with the use of these primal characters is, meanwhile, frequently a sense of sovereignty; it may also be a sense of innocence or of having been cleansed, since aspiration within the context of the primal 'triangle' gives rise to fear of incest or the feeling of being a usurper. Why do we find this primal situation in the great majority of these plots?

The first reason, I would suggest, is that the magical plot employs an entirely primitive system of thought and therefore has no access — according to the evidence of the plots I have so far studied — to areas of experience beyond inner, solipsistic emotional experience, which is, itself, much confused with, and often directly concerned with, primal experience. I would therefore not expect to find a magical plot in stories concerned with, say, social conflicts, where, for example, the Mills and Boon heroine creates the kind of relationship she desires with a man, and Brer Rabbit triumphs over Brer Fox. Such stories may have a powerful effect, bringing about deep inner satisfaction, but a magical plot could not handle the details of the conflict, since these are concerned with transactions between people rather than with solipsistic inner feeling. In the case of the novel *Jane Eyre*, which is much concerned with social matters, a magical plot is used, but at the level of this plot — as opposed to the novelist's superstructure — the content is an inner conflict, one between the heroine's need for fatherly love and the threat which that need presents to her own power (there is also a fear of incest). The conflict is solved by a series of exorcisms in the last two moves with St John Rivers and the invalid Rochester: the heroine removes some of her fears through the use of St John, burns down the house haunted by her fears and lessens the power of Rochester. It might be argued that Jane Eyre's problem is male dominance — a social problem — but the problem at the level of the plot is the nature of the heroine's desire, that the desired lover is too like a parental figure; linked to this are her doubts and fears in relation to her own power.[20]

My second suggestion as to why the primal situation appears so often is that there is a need to resolve the problems created by the presence of this material in the mind. The magical plot is the most appropriate means of doing this, since it has appropriate devices for dealing with the feelings involved and it also provides effective concealment for this forbidden material.

The magical plot does not provide much clear evidence for the meaning of its primal, apparently Oedipal, material. It is difficult to tell whether it has directly to do with parents, expressing incestuous and parricidal or matricidal ideas, or whether it is the result of confusion, thoughts of parent figures being involved in magical themes of aspiration, sexual desire and love because this primitive level of thought sees everything in terms of such primal figures. Confusion is enough to create the fear and guilt apparent in some plots, and I have long believed that the confusion (or association) theory is the most important to consider. Hence, I see the apparent incest theme in *Jane Eyre* as being about a desire for fatherly love, with its attendant fear of incest, rather than a desire to marry the biological father.[21]

It is not possible to state categorically that devices in a magical plot are there for the purpose of disguise. A magical plot is, in any case, hidden from the rational mind. At rational levels of thought we see the plot from points of view different from that of the magical hero, and we do not detect the magical processes or easily understand the imagery and confused thinking of primitive fantasy. Moreover, devices which disguise the content can have more obvious functions. When the hero appears as two characters—the chief character (acknowledged hero) and another character enacting roles the hero disowns—disguise results, but the additional character makes possible the dramatic enactment of rituals. The multiplicity of characters, representing perhaps no more than three characters, also provides for the full acting out of the hero's feelings. None the less, the often taboo nature of the material, and the determination of the hero to appear exemplary, make it clear that disguise must be a function of the magical plot. I should add that, over and above its inscrutability and its disguises, the material in a magical plot has one further protection: the rational mind dislikes and fears the irrational, and it could be claimed that nothing protects magical material so well as the denial that it exists.

The magical plot is an ideal kind of plot for romance, but it is not the only kind of plot found in this genre, and it is not itself confined to this genre since it also appears in some folktales; moreover, it usually remains intact when used for more considerable, imaginative works. I think its appearance as the original product of the nineteenth-century author of *Jane Eyre*, in a form which might have been that of a medieval magical plot and yet which is like no other, demonstrates that the origin of magical plots must simply be the human mind, in the direct way that dreams originate in the mind. We may ask why the magical plot appears in certain periods. Magical plots themselves have no cultural origin, but there are times in the formation of a literature when they become popular. The occasions when they play a significant part in the formation of a body of literature — as in the case of the folktales and romances of medieval Western Europe and the nineteenth-century literature (to a lesser extent) of this part of the world — may or may not demand a discussion separate from those already in progress on the cultural circumstances giving rise to the romance, Victorian fantasy and so forth. Any separate discussion of the circumstances giving rise to the magical plot requires much pooling of expertise: it cannot begin before the distribution of these plots is known.

Before I go any further, I must give rather more attention to the matter of what happens when an author makes use of a magical plot. The effect of an author's development is most commonly the creation of an overlay, so that there are two works, so to speak, the plot, re-created so that it is in full magical operation, and the author's additional work. This additional work is dependent on the plot and takes the form of some development of character and other detail, some rationalising, and the introduction of themes, which infuse thought — on an entirely different level from the magical —

into the text. These two parts of the text usually operate in sufficient harmony, in spite of some strange effects; but they can have a discordant relationship, and the problem that a magical plot will operate beyond the control of an author's transforming art can lead to artistic failures in the case of even the most accomplished author.

A good example of this is the fate of Shakespeare's *All's Well that Ends Well*. It is recognised by critics that, in the 'All's Well' story, Shakespeare had somewhat intractable material for his purposes, and that this was because of its primitive character.[22] The particular problem is that the chief character forces a man into an unwelcome marriage with her by means of an indelicate stratagem (the bed-trick), and that the plot regards this act in a thoroughly positive light. Boccaccio re-creates the story to be one about a girl who, in the words of W. W. Lawrence, 'loves with a consuming passion a man above her in rank' and 'twice overcomes his natural opposition to marrying beneath him by signal proofs of her cleverness and devotion'.[23] Shakespeare's formula is that 'a noble girl loves a self-willed fellow incapable of realising her worth, though above her in station; she puts her life in jeopardy to win him, and he repulses her through false pride and stubborness'.[24] What has happened here, I believe, is that the 'All's Well' story is a 'heroine' magical plot, in which 'the heroine' (as opposed to 'the hero' in *King Horn*) wins her 'prince' by magical means, presenting herself, in her chief character, as clever and courageous (all excellent fun in a traditional story). The offending bed-trick is one of a series of magical devices for bringing about and sealing the marriage in 'the heroine's' mind — it consummates the marriage and brings about conception. As there is only a single point of view, the man concerned (Bertrand in Boccaccio, and Bertram in Shakespeare) is given no independent point of view. Both Boccaccio and Shakespeare have responded to their material by re-creating its magical purposes, and therefore accepting the heroine's presentation of herself, in her chief character (Gilette and Helena, respectively), as admirable. They have developed this character accordingly, and this creates a potential problem in a work involving moral themes, where the most satisfactory treatment of the plot must include some intervention in the heroine's progress, perhaps eclipsing the magical plot. Each author sets about the task of bestowing a point of view upon the desired husband. Boccaccio successfully makes discrepancy in social status Bertrand's motive for his reluctance to marry Gilette — a good motive for the fourteenth century, and one in tune with the feelings in the magical plot, where the heroine aspires to a 'prince' and will see him as finding her ineligible. Shakespeare, by contrast, makes Bertram's motive for refusing Helena part of his being an ignoble character, and this has a much less happy effect. Bertram's being made ignoble has to do with the playwright's themes of virtue, honour, nobility, love and forgiveness, but it conflicts with the feelings in the magical plot, where a noble husband is desired by the heroine. A 'quality of strain' and of 'harsh discord'[25] is found in the play for further reasons than this. The 'All's Well' story is not a profound magical story, as is the Hamlet story: it does not have the kind of feelings or conflicts upon which a dramatist can build a weighty play. Shakespeare has sought to build themes of nobility and love on a character who, at the magical level, does not have to struggle with deep conflicts, as does Hamlet, and who represents a heroine who can enjoy a sense of cleverness throughout, even though she feels the need for a number of rituals to secure her victory. Boccaccio's less ambitious use of the story is altogether more suitable.[26]

I do not think it would be useful to attempt a discussion here of how my work relates to structuralist and psychoanalytic approaches. How it may do so, and not do so, can only be shown effectively by practical demonstration, and this will be found in abundance in the studies to follow. Structuralist and psychoanalytic approaches are many and varied, and my own approach was originally worked out in direct response to the problems which confronted me in particular texts; I had no allegiance to any structuralist or psychoanalytic method. There were, however, two significant influences upon me: the formalism of Vladimir Propp, which guided me towards my formulation of a model, and my working knowledge of depth psychology, which, as I gradually learnt to use it appropriately, proved its value

chiefly in helping me to be patient with the confused nature
of the emerging content of the texts, and to accept its fre-
quent resistance to interpretation. Perhaps the most useful
maxim for anyone engaged in research is the comment of J.
S. Mill, that people who 'have been much taught, are apt to
be deficient in the sense of present fact; they do not see, in
the facts which they are called upon to deal with, what is
really there, but what they have been taught to expect'.[27] I
hope the studies in this book show some useful response to
this just and formidable observation.

It would be useful to draw attention here to the aspects of
my work which do seem close to that of other literary specialists. These resemblances are not as great as they might
seem, since they do not arise from a similarity of method;
but a discussion of them will help to clarify my own work.

Rosemary Jackson's argument that an 'uneasy assimila-
tion of Gothic in many Victorian novels suggests that within
the main, realistic text, there exists another non-realistic
one, camouflaged and concealed',[28] is one apparently close
to my theory of the magical plot and not irrelevant here,
because I have applied my theory to some Victorian texts.[29]
A comparison can be made between our analyses of the text
of *Jane Eyre*. Rosemary Jackson regards the realistic narrative as the main narrative, and she sees the realistic narrative attempting to 'repress and defuse the subversive thrust'
of the Fantastic narrative. I, by contrast, regard the magical
plot I discern as the main narrative, the realistic treatment
being dependent on it and not forming a complete narrative.
Rosemary Jackson sees *Jane Eyre* as being about an isolated
woman seeking emotional and sexual fulfilment, but unable
to create a 'whole' self within a hostile male order. Jane
Eyre cannot be reconciled with Bertha Mason, 'the demonic,
desiring, "other" side of herself', and her 'final union with a
severely maimed and blinded Rochester suggests that cultural survival is at the cost of extreme curtailment of desire'. I
agree, in the main, with these views of Jane Eyre, when I
consider the material in the light of the problems of the
individual living in society, but, in finding a magical plot in
this text, I find a plot which brings about 'the heroine's'
desires, through the use of a number of exorcisms. Magical

thought does not have recourse to reason and judgement, and the exorcisms hardly solve the problems as they are seen by the rational mind, but they solve them powerfully for a reader who enters the narrative as 'the heroine' of its magical plot.

Leo Bersani's examination of various narrative strategies to expel desire from the text should be mentioned here, especially as his study of the Victorian novel *Wuthering Heights* comes close to my own.[30] Leo Bersani notes that Emily Brontë is telling the same story twice, and that the narrative structure works towards the expulsion of the danger represented by Heathcliff. Bersani sees the material in terms of the problems of social integration, involving the restraining of desire, while I would suggest that this complex text contains a magical plot, which means that I see it as including, at one important level, a narrative concerned with desire, but not with social integration. This magical plot has two moves, corresponding with Bersani's division of the narrative, the first move being a journey into forbidden experiences — these made possible by magical devices which include the use of the narrators Lockwood and Nelly Dean[31] — and the second move being a replay of this journey, using Hareton in the Heathcliff role of the first move, with the aim of legitimising the Heathcliff character and exorcising the danger inherent in him. I see the magical plot's prime purpose as being to give free expression to 'the heroine's' desires as they appear in the first Catherine and in Heathcliff; the taming of the Heathcliff character in Hareton, and the re-establishment of the family, have magical roles as safeguards of that free expression in the first move. Such material can operate in harmony alongside the entirely distinct level of meaning demonstrated by Bersani.

My work resembles that of Stephen Prickett,[32] in that we both move towards the idea of a Fantastic language, a different mode of expression from the recognised literary modes: we both say that fantasy expresses itself primarily through images. However, in the case of the magical plot — as opposed to the Gothic and other styles of the Fantastic studied by Prickett — one cannot say that the plot is unimportant and quickly forgotten, as Prickett observes:[33] the plot is all-important, and, far from its being easily forgotten, it is a type of plot which has been faithfully preserved in oral tradition. I give less attention, in this present book than previously, to the pictorial nature of the magical plot, but it is always an important feature. There are occasions, as in the case of *Sir Gawain and the Green Knight*, when the ability to think about the plot in terms of the pictures it creates is essential.

The texts I discuss in this book have made as rewarding a study as any I have undertaken. The work began when I decided, three years ago, to make a study of Chrétien's *Perceval* so that I would be able to answer questions as to why I was not including it among my texts containing magical plots. I did not believe that my methods could be used in relation to this text, since it was unfinished and they required a complete plot. However, I found that, in Chrétien's rich text, the nine existing moves — as I found them to be — of the Perceval story proper (the plot up to the arrival of the Loathly Lady), provided sufficient evidence for my exploration of this earliest surviving Grail story and only pre-Christianised version we have. I was able to go further and explore the meaning of the Grail Castle with its bleeding lance and mysterious vessel, and I used my tentative interpretations in my examination of the hero's use of magic in the entire magical sequence. However, as my methods do not impose interpretation, anyone can take my model and make another attempt at interpretation. My model has also, I believe, thrown light on other problems in *Perceval*, supporting D. D. R. Owen's arguments that the work as we have it is two unfinished works joined together and that the scene with the hermit is an interpolation. Having studied Chrétien's magical plot, I found Wolfram von Eschenbach's *Parzival* a rewarding experience, as I traced how differently and yet how faithfully Wolfram had re-created the plot. The transmission of magical plots makes a particularly interesting study, but I have found few re-creations as fascinating in their alterations as Wolfram's version of the Perceval story. Chrétien's *Yvain*, with its complete plot and rich detail, and with the versions in English, German, Swedish and Welsh — both close to it and different — was also an exciting study.

There was so much evidence for me to work upon that I learned how I could refine my methods and present a much better argument for the magical plot. Other exciting texts included here, which helped me to take a step forward in my investigations, are the Latin Historia texts of the Apollonius of Tyre story. I studied the Apollonius plot a few years ago, using the play *Pericles* and its sources by Gower and Twine, but these texts did not provide me with evidence comparable with that since provided by the Latin texts. Nevertheless, I have included these texts in my study of the Historia: different versions of a magical plot provide illuminating variations, as also do different authorial treatments. Finally, the study of *Sir Gawain and the Green Knight* which appears in this book emphasises, in its great differences from my study of the romance in *Traditional Romance and Tale*, those methods which I have found from experience to be the most useful.

I have presented my studies in such a way that non-specialists can follow my arguments. Translations are provided with the quotations in medieval languages, wherever necessary, and I also provide summaries of the stories discussed. The subject of this book should interest a wider audience than literary specialists. Nevertheless, this present book, unlike my previous books, demands more specialist skills throughout for the material investigated, and the works chosen for the earlier chapters do not lead the reader gently into the subject. For this reason, and also to meet the needs of new specialist readers, I have paid special attention to the introductory material: following this Introduction is an introductory study, for which I have chosen a plot which illustrates the magical plot particularly clearly.

APOLLONIUS OF TYRE

An examination of the Apollonius of Tyre story, best known today as used for the plot of the play *Pericles, Prince of Tyre*, will make a helpful introduction to the studies in this book, since it reveals with exceptional clarity the characteristics of a magical story.

First, the questions raised by this story illustrate particularly well how often these questions are concerned with contradictions and inconsistencies in the behaviour of the characters. In these circumstances, it becomes appropriate to ask questions as to why the characters act as they do — and even more appropriate if the strangeness of the characters' behaviour shows a consistency. The questions raised by this story are also concerned with a fundamental incoherence in the text of each version studied here: the narrative (or dramatic text) not only fails to address all or most of the irrationalities and contradictions in the plot, but also lacks a consistent moral vision, and it sometimes introduces piecemeal rationalisations which make even more nonsense of the plot. Yet, while the text seems to be divided against itself, the narrative seems to have a tacit purpose.

Another reason why this story is useful for an introductory study is that it has often been used by able writers, while it has not been used by them as a vehicle for the expression of highly developed imaginative themes. A gifted author produces a powerful re-creation of a magical plot, rich in the detail necessary for a thorough investigation, while such an author's additional work results in a text confused by material which has no more than a superficial relationship to the magical plot. This additional work is useful to the seasoned investigator, as will occasionally be apparent even in this introductory study, because it gives rise to further contradictions in the text: these contradictions arise from the fact that, while an author will faithfully re-create a magical plot, his additional work is produced by other levels of the mind and shows no awareness of the magical purposes of the plot.

A further reason why the Apollonius of Tyre story makes good introductory material is that it was an outstandingly popular story in medieval Europe, and a typical feature of the magical story is that it has a remarkable grip on audiences. Albert H. Smyth refers to 'the endless stories of Apollonius in the Middle Ages'[1]. There are well over fifty surviving manuscripts of the Latin version widely distributed throughout Europe, and also eight versions of the story in English: Peter Goolden notes that it is the one story 'designed primarily for amusement and pleasure, that continued to be read and rehandled in Old, Middle, and Modern English'.[2] Albert H. Smith also points out another significant fact typical of the magical story: all the manuscripts differ widely in language and construction, but 'cling rather persistently to the type of the story'; 'The Apollonius Saga is remarkable for its *persistence* and its *stability*, that is for its duration and vitality, and for its retention of its original character and form'. 'It is remarkable that a saga so widespread should undergo so little change in the course of centuries', Professor Smyth continues, 'Occasionally an episode is broadened by the narrator, or local color is painted freely into the work; but the chief outlines of the story remain practically unchanged'.[3] It is all the more remarkable in view of the apparent absurdity of the story, and draws attention to the fact that the story cannot really be absurd: it must make some kind of important sense. A particularly intriguing study of the story is that of R. M. Dawkins, which reveals that an oral, village version collected on Kos early this century is still astonishingly close to the written versions.[4] It seems generally agreed that the origin of the Apollonius story is Greek.

This present study will concentrate primarily on the earliest versions of the Latin Historia, the texts designated R1 and R2 by Peter Goolden.[5] As these versions are as fine as any we have, it is scarcely necessary to turn elsewhere for evidence, but I shall also use the version of John Gower, in his *Confessio Amantis*,[6] and the play *Pericles, Prince of Tyre*,[7] because the authorial treatment they have received sometimes throws a fresh ray of light on a problem. I shall occasionally refer to the sixteenth-century version of Lawrence Twine,[8] which is based on the version in the *Gesta Romanorum*,[9] to which I shall also occasionally refer.

The outline of the plot, which I give below, necessarily excludes detail which will appear in my discussion. The page numbers given in this outline, and in the subsequent discussion, refer to the R1 text of the Historia, in Riese's edition cited in the notes. Whenever I refer to the R2 text of the Historia — which Riese has edited together with R1 in a parallel edition — this is stated. The page and line numbers given for other versions brought into the discussion relate to editions cited in the notes. There is no translation of R1 or 2, but a translation of the version in the *Gesta Romanorum* brings the reader close to these earliest surviving texts.

1. King Antiochus commits incest with his daughter and, in order to keep her for himself, he sets a riddle for her suitors, the answer to which is the existence of this incestuous relationship; suitors are to forfeit their heads if they cannot answer it. Many kings and princes come, despising death, because of the incredible beauty of the maiden, and those who discover the answer are put to death along with those who fail; all the heads are set up on the gate. (Historia I–III)

2. Apollonius, Prince of Tyre, arrives in Antioch as a suitor, and the king gives him the riddle: 'I am transported by wickedness; I feed on (enjoy) maternal flesh. I seek my brother, my mother's husband, my wife's daughter and I do not find.' Apollonius answers that Antiochus has not lied that he is transported by wickedness and has fed on maternal flesh: 'look upon your daughter'. The king denies his solution and allows Apollonius thirty days to solve the riddle, bidding him return to his own country. He then sends Taliarchus after him to kill him. (IV–VI)

3. Apollonius reaches home and decides that, as he has solved the riddle correctly already, he can now do nothing other than sail away to escape death. He does so with ships loaded with corn, gold, silver and garments. The city is grief-stricken. Taliarchus is glad to find him gone, but Antiochus proclaims a reward for whoever

captures or kills him. Apollonius reaches Tharsus, where a servant Hellenicus warns him that he is proscribed. Apollonius asks why, and the servant answers, 'Because you wished to be what the father is'. Hellenicus refuses to take up Apollonius' suggestion that he cut off his head and claim Antiochus' reward. Then Apollonius meets Stranguilio, who tells him about the poverty and famine in Tharsus. Apollonius relieves it in exchange for the people's keeping his arrival secret; he sells the corn to them but returns the purchase-money to the state. They erect a statue of him, with a superscription proclaiming that he saved the city. A few days later, Stranguilio and his wife Dionysiade persuade Apollonius to sail to Pentapolis and hide there, and he is conducted to his ship with great honour. (VI–XI)

4. Apollonius is shipwrecked and, alone of those on board, reaches Pentapolis. A fisherman assists him and gives him half his cloak, and he then impresses King Archistrates at a game with a ball in the gymnasium: the king declares him his equal ('"mihi comparandus est"', p. 25). Apollonius also baths him and the king says he has never bathed so agreeably. He is invited to the king's supper, but eats nothing and weeps. The king perceives that he is being reminded of his own lost wealth. Apollonius tells the king's beautiful daughter, Lucina, his story, and then she plays the lyre to take away his tears and delight the company, but he reveals that he can play it better. Lucina falls violently in love with him, and uses the ruse of giving him a house to detain him, and the further ruse of making him her teacher in order to be with him. Three suitors apply for her hand, and the king sends Apollonius to her with their names and the marriage settlements they offer, for her choice. She replies that she wishes to marry the shipwrecked man. One of the suitors lies that he has been shipwrecked, but the king shows Apollonius his daughter's letter, asking his advice, and Apollonius blushes upon reading that he is the one beloved. The king understands the situation and is glad: what his daughter desires is his own wish. The princess marries her teacher, and a child is conceived. Then a ship arrives from Tyre with a message to say that Antiochus and his daughter have been killed by lightning, and the kingdom has now fallen to Apollonius. He sets sail and his wife insists on accompanying him. (XI–XXV)

5. Lucina gives birth to a daughter in a storm and seems to be dead. Her body is put in a chest, with regal accoutrements, twenty sesterces and a leaden scroll asking the finder to bury the body; the chest is then cast into the sea. It arrives in Ephesus and is found by a physician, one of whose pupils, realising the lady is alive, revives her. She tells him she is the wife of a king and daughter of a king.

The physician adopts her as his daughter, and, at her request, he places her with the vestals in the Temple of Diana. Apollonius, meanwhile, arrives in Tharsus and leaves his daughter with her nurse, in the care of Stranguilio and Dionysiade, to be brought up with their daughter; she is to be called Tharsia, after their country. He leaves gold and silver for the purpose. Then he takes an oath that he will not cut his beard, hair or nails until his daughter is married. The couple are astonished at such a severe oath. They promise to care for the child, and Apollonius sails to Egypt. (XXV–XXVIII)

6. When Tharsia is fourteen, the nurse falls ill and tells her who she is and why she is there, including an account of her father's vow. The nurse then dies. Dionysiade hears people commend Tharsia and vilify her own daughter as ugly and a disgrace, and she reflects that Tharsia's father has never come to fetch his daughter and never written letters to them; she is sure he is dead and that she can therefore get rid of Tharsia. She bids Theophilus slay her while she is visiting the nurse's sepulcre. Theophilus gives Tharsia leave to pray before he kills her, and pirates seize her and take her away. Theophilus tells Dionysiade that he has obeyed her command, and Stranguilio sincerely mourns Tharsia, accusing his wife. A monument is erected to her, as the daughter ('"virgini"', p. 66) of their benefactor. The pirates take Tharsia to Mytilene and put her up for sale, and a bawd bids for her in competition with Athenagora, the prince of the city. Athenagora finally decides it would be cheaper to let the bawd buy her and put her in a brothel, and get there first himself to take her virginity at a cheaper price. When Athenagora arrives at the brothel, she falls at his feet and tells her story, and he is confused and penitent; he himself has a virgin daughter. He gives her forty gold pieces and tells her to behave similarly to other clients and it will ensure her freedom. Athenagora stays to see other clients come and leave in tears, having given her large sums of money. The bawd is furious, but Tharsia persuades the overseer of the women to let her earn money for them by playing the lyre in the forum instead. Athenagora watches over her virginity and nobility as if she were his own only daughter, and recommends her to the care of the overseer with many gifts. (XXIX–XXXVI)

7. Apollonius goes to Tharsus and is told of his daughter's death. He is grief-stricken ('tremebundus toto corpore', p. 77). Having read the inscription to 'Tharsiae virgini Apollonii', he sets sail and arrives in Mytilene, where the people are celebrating the festival of Neptune. Athenagora, who now loves Tharsia, sees the ship, goes aboard and learns from the sailors that their lord is dying of

sorrow; he has lost a wife and daughter. When he learns that this lord is Apollonius, he remembers that Tharsia has called her father by this name. He goes to Apollonius and sees a man lying in the dark, with dirty beard and shaggy, filthy head. Apollonius refuses his comfort, but Athenagora sends for Tharsia. When she arrives, he says that if she is able to bring the lord out into the light, he will give her ten pieces of gold and redeem her for thirty days from the bawd so that she can be free from having constantly to protect her virginity. Tharsia approaches Apollonius, bidding him be happy: no unchaste woman comes to console him, but an innocent virgin, who has preserved her virginity amid shipwreck and her chastity unviolated. She sings how she steps through filth and is privy to none herself. Apollonius sends her away with money, but Athenagora sends her back again to say that she seeks his welfare, not his money, and to bring him out into the light. Tharsia returns his money and takes hold of his mourning garment in an attempt to bring him out into the light. He pushes her so that she falls, and blood begins to flow from her nose. (In R2, Tharsia embraces Apollonius and speaks words of advice and comfort; he is angry and kicks her so that she falls, and blood begins to flow from her cheek.) Sitting there, she weeps and tells her story, not directly to Apollonius but addressing the power of the heavens. Apollonius recognises that she is his daughter and rejoices. He gives Tharsia in marriage to Athenagora. (In R2, Athenagora asks for her hand, saying that the maiden has endured through his good offices, and Apollonius gladly agrees, in view of Athenagora's great goodness.) He cuts his hair and the bawd is burned alive. Apollonius rewards the people for their kindness to him and his daughter, and they erect a statue with an inscription to Apollonius, the rebuilder of their city walls, and to Tharsia the most modest, who preserved her virginity. Tharsia and Athenagora are married. (XXXVII–XLVII)

8. Apollonius, his daughter and son-in-law all sail towards Tharsus, on their way home, but an angel comes in a dream to tell Apollonius to go to the Temple of Diana at Ephesus with his daughter and son-in-law, and relate all the events of his life from his youth. After this, he should take his revenge in Tharsus. Upon their arrival at the temple, Apollonius' wife comes forward as high priestess: none is as pleasing to Diana as she is. They fall at her feet, thinking she is Diana. Apollonius narrates his story and, when he finishes, his wife announces who she is (in R2, she first embraces him and is repulsed), and then she asks for her daughter. Apollonius recognises her and there is general rejoicing. They sail to Tyre, where Apollonius establishes Athenagora as king (in R2, they sail

first to Antioch, where Apollonius assumes the kingdom reserved
for him). Then they take an army to Tharsus and carry out their
revenge on Stranguilio and Dionysiade: they are stoned to death.
Theophilus is forgiven. Next, they go to Pentapolis and see Archistrates, who dies a year later, leaving half his kingdom to Apollonius
and half to his daughter. Apollonius rewards the fisherman and
Hellenicus. He and his wife have a son, whom he establishes in
Archistrates' kingdom. They live happily together for seventy-four
years. (In R2, Apollonius writes his story and has two volumes of it
made: one he places in the temple at Ephesus and the other in his
own library.) (XLVIII–LI)

I shall now list the main problems thrown up by this plot
and the various treatments of it by authors.

1. The most extraordinary features of this plot occur in its
second half. The material in the opening scenes presents
critics with no striking problems of the kind I have suggested. The behaviour of the characters may be somewhat
odd, but we do not expect characters in certain literary
genres to act in ways which would be effective in the world
outside art: it might be argued that they have better things
to do. Antiochus poses the riddle to suitors so that he can
keep his daughter to himself, though a far from difficult
riddle, to which the answer is the existence of this incestuous relationship, can make no sense as his chosen method
for doing this. Moreover, he kills those who find the answer,
along with those who do not, and sets their heads up on the
gate — a wise move, if we insist on introducing irrelevant
rationality — only then to change this policy unaccountably
in Apollonius' case, so that Apollonius escapes. We are aware
that Antiochus' curious folly is unlikely to have much to do
with the matter: the scenes need an ogre whom the hero
successfully confronts and escapes — a time-honoured
subject. It is when the contradictions in the characters'
behaviour, and in the narrative's treatment of it, continue
and show a consistency that we might suspect something is
going on which could be more fully defined than it has been.
This will be demonstrated as the study proceeds.

Where the treatment of a character's behaviour is con-
cerned, it is useful to look at the effects created in the play
Pericles by the introduction of rationalisations in relation to
Apollonius' flight from Antiochus. Pericles (Apollonius) gives

as his reason for his departure from Tyre the fact that Antiochus will invade Tyre with 'hostile forces' if he remains and that his subjects will suffer on his behalf — 'Which care of them, not pity of myself' motivates him (I.ii.24–33) — but this reason is not reconciled with his flight further from his refuge, Tarsus, when he hears that a single murderer, Thaliard, has been sent to Tyre in pursuit of him (II, Chorus, 23–7). He has also satisfied himself, before leaving Tyre, that Helicanus and his other subjects will 'mingle' their 'bloods together in the earth' if Antiochus should 'wrong' his 'liberties in' his 'absence' (I.ii.111–16), a precaution not reconciled with the reason given for his departure from Tyre. His absence is found by his subjects to be neglect ('kingdoms without a head, Like goodly buildings left without a roof, Soon fall to ruin', II.iv.35–7). The author is seeking to adapt one kind of art form into another, but the rationalisations are inconsistent, pointing up moral defects in the hero which evidently have no relevance in the plot, where the hero is a fugitive from an all-powerful enemy. This is a good example of what happens when an author attempts to rationalise such a plot, and it reveals more clearly the nature of the plot before us: it has the appearance of a nightmare in which even cowardice is not an issue.

2. My questions begin to become sharper when considering Apollonius' decision, upon taking flight, to weigh his ships down with a strangely specialised cargo (just a few items in large amounts). This decision can be seen to make at least some sense in retrospect, as Apollonius thus acquires a friendly city to assist him on more than one occasion: initially, it hides him, and, later in the plot, it gives much greater assistance of a strange kind, in (seemingly) unrelated circumstances. These details hint that the departure from Tyre has an unspoken purpose over and above flight from Antiochus, and this hint is supported by the unaccountable cowardice in the flight. *Pericles* superimposes a partial rationalisation which only serves to sharpen this impression: upon his arrival in Tarsus, Pericles explains that the famine there is known in Tyre and he has come to relieve it (I.iv.88–96); there is no mention of this mission in the scenes at Tyre.

3. The decisions taken by Apollonius' wife Lucina – to

marry Apollonius and then to remain in Ephesus — contradict each other sharply, and the second decision is, in any case, inexplicable. Far from addressing this problem, every text seems to be in collusion with the irrationality. Why does this enterprising, determined princess of the scenes at Pentapolis, who insists on her marriage and on accompanying her husband when he sets sail, not take ship from Ephesus and rejoin her husband in order to continue with the marriage? Her joy upon being reunited with her husband emphasises the problem. The text under discussion suggests that she is adopted by the physician when he knows her royal origin ('ut cognouit eam regio genere esse ortam, adhibitis amicis in filiam suam sibi adoptauit', p. 53), and we are not offered any explanation as to why he is not prompted instead to arrange for her journey home, especially as she reveals that she is the wife of a king (" 'uxor enim regis sum" ', p. 52). The adoption by a foreign social inferior, and the fourteen years in the Temple of Diana, require explanations and receive none in any text. Gower attempts an explanation – the queen thinks her husband and child are drowned (ll. 1246– 7) — but this does not explain her not returning to her father's kingdom, where she is heir. As she does not take the seemingly obvious course, can there be any reason why she decides instead to become the physician's daughter and a vestal in the Temple of Diana?

4. Apollonius' behaviour in relation to his daughter — remaining apart from her for fourteen years and then showing great grief upon hearing of her death — is equally contradictory, and neither extreme of behaviour makes much sense on its own. Why does he leave his daughter with the couple in Tharsus? She needs to be cared for and he is going to unknown and remote regions of Egypt ('ignotas et longinquas Aegypti regiones', p. 55), but with two important reasons why he should return to Tyre — his responsibility for the child and his duties as ruler — and no reasons given as to why he should travel to Egypt instead, the puzzle only deepens. In Gower, 'Appolinus' returns to Tyre, but this only makes more sense in one area at the expense of making more nonsense elsewhere: there can be no reason at all for leaving the child and her nurse in Tarsus when Appolinus is return-

ing home. The play *Pericles* has rationalisations for both areas, having Pericles return to Tyre because his 'twelve months are expired, and Tyrus stands In a litigious peace' (III.iii.1–3), and the baby unable to hold out as far as Tyre so that it has to be left at Tarsus (III.i. 77–9): these rationalisations do not address Pericles' leaving the child in Tarsus for fourteen years. If the text — indeed, all the texts — did not stress Apollonius' love for his daughter the problem would not be acute, but when Apollonius receives the news of her death, we are told of the physical effects of his grief ('tremebundus toto corpore expalluit', p. 77), and he goes to his ship, saying that he will throw himself into its hold; he longs to die at sea, having not been permitted to see light on land ('cupio enim in undis efflare spiritum, quem in terris non licuit lumen uidere', p. 79). In *Pericles*, and in Twine's version, endearments are introduced — 'a belovèd daughter' (V.i.28) and 'my deare daughter' (p. 460) — which bring out the contradictions more sharply. In none of these versions has there been any communication between father and daughter during the fourteen years: in the Historia, Tharsia's foster-mother believes Apollonius must be dead; and the fondest father of all is Yannaki, in the Kos village version, who tells his wife Angelica that he received letters from their daughter's guardian, giving him news of her. Apollonius' neglect of his daughter, and his grief for her, do not add up, and yet one senses a determination behind both of them, not least in the survival of such incongruities throughout the long tradition of this story.

5. Another strange detail which seems equally determined is Apollonius' oath that he will not cut his beard, hair or nails, until his baby daughter marries. Stranguilio and Dionysiade are astonished at the severity of the oath ('At illi stupentes, quod tam grauiter iurasset', p. 55), and R1 and R2 tell us how he looks when he returns to their house fourteen years later: before he sees them and speaks to them, he clears away his hair from his forehead and his shaggy beard from his mouth ('intrat Apollonius domum Stranguillionis, a fronte comam aperit, hispidam ab ore remouit barbam. Vt uidit eos lugubri ueste, et ait . . .', p. 76). In the ship, Athenagora sees his 'squalida barba, capite horrido et sordido' (p.

83). There is no reflection in the texts upon why Apollonius is so anxious to marry his daughter off from the time of her birth. It is interesting that the nurse adds a detailed description of this oath to her narrative for her charge ('"et sic uotum faciens, se neque capillos dempturum, neque ungues, donec te nuptui traderet"', p. 57).

6. Apollonius' violent repulsion of Tharsia when she seeks to comfort him is another strange but determined detail. It shocks Chaucer's Man of Law, who includes it, together with Antiochus' incest, among his 'unkynde [unnatural] abhomynacions'.[10]

7. Tharsia's marriage to Athenagora offers considerable problems. This is the man who was bidding for her in competition with the bawd, and decided to let the bawd pay the high price because he could still have her virginity by arriving at the brothel first. In taking pity on her in the brothel, he does no more than her subsequent clients. He is ruler of the city and could at least buy her freedom, but he leaves her to continue her struggle in the brothel: he even watches the subsequent clients go in and out, and, instead of sharing with her what he knows of the possible identity of Apollonius when he involves her in helping the stricken man, he tells her he will reward her success by redeeming her from the bawd for thirty days. This last is impossible to reconcile with the information that he now loves her ('qui Tharsiam ... diligebat', p. 80). I do not ask why Tharsia agrees to marry Athenagora, because it seems that her opinion is not asked. In the R1 text of the Historia, we are simply told that Apollonius gives Tharsia in marriage to Athenagora (p. 105), and in R2, we are told that Athenagora throws himself at Apollonius' feet and begs for her hand, pleading that he is prince of the city and that she endured through his good offices ('"mea ope permansit uirgo"', p. 100). However, it must be asked why there is no reflection in the texts on Athenagora's unworthiness: Apollonius says he cannot be opposed to Athenagora's suit in view of his great goodness and conscientiousness (R2, '"ego huic tantae bonitati et pietati possum esse contrarius?"', p. 100); in the *Gesta Romanorum*, he cannot be opposed in view of all Athenagora has done for his daughter ('Non possum tibi esse contrarius,

quia multa pro filia mea fecisti', p. 529) and in *Pericles*, because he has been 'noble towards her' (V.i.259–61). Even while we may be drawn to accept a change of heart in a character, we would expect one of more proven worth than Athenagora to win one of Tharsia's stature. Gower removes the problem by not having his Atenagoras involved in the brothel scene, while, in *Pericles*, the corresponding Lysimachus is a coarse frequenter of the brothel who is suddenly, quite unconvincingly, presented as testing Marina (Tharsia). There is no explanation of this testing and no apology for the distress Marina has been caused.

This story is full of manifest problems which have presented audiences, retellers of the tale and critics, alike, with little or no difficulty. If critics leave such material unquestioned, it means, on the face of it, their having a working assumption that audiences will enjoy and faithfully preserve a story in which the characters behave throughout in ways which we would normally regard as mad. It also means that we accept a narrative which shows an extraordinary degree of incoherence in character, action and moral vision while its narrator proceeds with zest, seeing no need to address these matters. If we feel no surprise at this apparent situation, this flies in the face of our awareness of the eternal human desire to have things coherent and explained, and to have evil distinct from good, the ignoble distinct from the honourable and heroic. These matters aside, I am going to float the notion that the story before us must make excellent sense, though not a sense which we can see because it relates to knowledge and ideas with which we are already familiar; that is a rationalising process. Here, I shall argue, we have to confront the craziness of the story directly, assuming that the sense the story makes will be a sense as crazy and surprising as the problems observed. We have to make a meticulous study of the detail in the narrative, prepared to find an unexpected internal logic.

Apollonius' departure from Tyre seems to have a hidden plan. A fugitive from death would not otherwise travel with a cargo, and such a cargo. The benefits to Apollonius of this cargo are that he has Tharsus in his debt and paying him

honour: he arrives there in need twice, the first time in flight
from Antiochus and the second time with a baby he clearly
does not wish to bring up. Proceeding with this line of
thought that there is a hidden plan, it can be seen that there
are two kings with a marriageable daughter in the story,
Antiochus and Archistrates (Simonides in *Pericles*), these
having precisely contrasting characters and attitudes to
Apollonius, while Apollonius presents himself in contrasting
ways to them. There are also two female characters, closely
related to the hero, left in distant countries for fourteen
years. It is clear from all Apollonius' courses of action relating to Tharsia that he has no affection for her, and yet his
feelings about her are clearly powerful: these have entirely
to do with getting her married, and this marriage takes
place with expedition as soon as they meet.

There are a number of details in the texts which suggest
an obsession with chastity and virginity in relation to female
relatives: the wife and daughter are separated from Apollonius in circumstances where they are emphasising that they
possess these qualities — the wife, in the Temple of Diana
the chaste (she is high priestess, none being so pleasing to
Diana as she is), and the daughter, succeeding in retaining
her virginity in the extreme situation of a brothel. After
these triumphs of the women, the family comes together
again. Turning to the beginning of the story, we see that
Apollonius' thoughts of marriage bring him to the discovery
of an incestuous relationship.

It is interesting that Apollonius is Antiochus' heir — a
matter unmentioned until after Antiochus' death and Apollonius' marriage (the detail does not appear in Gower and
Pericles). The conversation between Hellenicus and Apollonius now emerges as having a particular interest: Apollonius
asks Hellenicus the reason why Antiochus has proscribed
him, and Hellenicus replies, 'Because you wished to be what
the father is' (' "quia quod pater est, tu esse uoluisti" ', p. 14).
Do these words mean that he wished to be in his father's
place, or incestuous like his father? But both answers may
amount to the same incestuous conclusion. Apollonius' hidden plan may turn out to be a purification ritual. Something
of the kind has already been suggested by G. Wilson Knight,

who, commenting on *Pericles* specifically, sees the voyages of Pericles as an undergoing of purification and penitence.[11]

Evidently, the story before us has a concern with incest,[12] but this is a matter of little interest in itself: the aim of this investigation is to find out how one and all of the strange details in this story might hang together in a coherent scheme. I shall now apply the model of the magical plot, beginning by using the notion that there is only one point of view, that of 'the hero' (who may be seen as a storyteller creating, or a participant re-creating, the plot): he is performing a series of mental rituals, and is identified, in particular, with the chief character, Apollonius.

If this is a magical plot, it would appear that the hero's first step in the rituals, following the initial vision of incest, is to create a city (Tharsus) which will play essential roles in his scheme. The city performs a number of functions. It is a place where the hero's goodness and honour are emphasised at an early stage of his flight from incest, and, later, it is the place in his debt, where the hero can dispose of the daughter (identifying her with it by calling her Tharsia) and then arrange for her transfer to a brothel. If this is correct, Apollonius' ruthless use of this city, and of Stranguilio and Dionysiade, is a sharp indication of the status of characters and events in a magical plot, where the only point of view is the hero's.

The contrast between Apollonius' demeanour before Antiochus and his demeanour before Archistrates has already been observed by critics.[13] This character's authoritative boldness before Antiochus is as remarkable in the Latin *Historia* as in *Pericles*, and the king is usually portrayed as angry in response ('Indignatus', R2, p. 6). At Archistrates' court, Apollonius presents himself as destitute and yet such that the king regards him as an equal and entirely approves of him. He is totally passive in respect of his marriage. It must be important that this marriage appears to be the decision of the princess and her father: thus the hero would not seem to be wishing to be what the father is. However, as soon as he is married, he becomes what the father is: the news arrives immediately that Apollonius is heir to the now dead Antiochus.

The next courses of action are the separations from the wife and daughter. While the women prove that their chastity is unassailable, Apollonius takes himself off to the ends of the earth (unknown and far-removed regions of Egypt) and undergoes the penances of uncut hair and nails, and the voyage in the hold of his ship. This last penance is followed by a ritualised meeting with the daughter, which has several important steps. First, Tharsia assures Apollonius that no unchaste woman has come to console him, but an innocent virgin of indestructible chastity, who has preserved her virginity amid shipwreck ('"Non enim aliqua ad te consolandum ueni polluta, sed innocens uirgo, quae uirginitatem meam inter naufragium castitatis inuiolabiliter seruo"', p. 86). Each text cited in this discussion retains Tharsia's strange introduction to herself in some way. The Latin versions and that of Twine (p. 464) are almost identical, and, in Gower, the daughter's immediate words, upon being repulsed violently by Appolinus, are to say she is a maid (l. 1704). Here the emphasis may not be on the idea of 'virgin', but, in *Pericles*, the daughter's response, upon being pushed away, is, 'I am a maid, My lord, that ne'er before invited eyes, But have been gazed on like a comet' (V.i. 83–5). In the Historia, Tharsia then sings that she is surrounded by sin and yet is untouched by it herself (an odd choice of song since her task is to console Apollonius–'"ut consoleris dominum"', p. 85):

Per sordes gradior, sed sordis conscia non sum . . .
Lenoni nunc uendita sum sed numquam uiolaui pudorem.
(pp. 86–7)

The words are almost identical in the *Gesta Romanorum*, and Twine renders them as follows:

Amongst the harlots foule I walke,
    yet harlot none am I . . .
A bawd me bought, yet am I not
    defilde by fleshly crime. (p. 464)

The repulse is also a part of this ritual meeting, repeated in some way in every version. It receives particularly interesting treatment in Gower, where Appolinus strikes Thaise in anger when she approaches him in the dark of the ship's hold and touches him:

And in the derke forth she gothe,
Till she hym toucheth, and he wroth,
And after hir with his honde
He smote ... (ll. 1699–1702)

Both horror and ritual gesture seem to lie behind the violent
repulse. In the Latin texts, as in Gower, it takes place upon
there being physical contact (in R1, when Tharsia takes hold
of her father's garment, in order to bring him out into the
light, 'adprehendens ... uestem', p. 97; in R2, when she
embraces him, 'strictis manibus complexa', p. 97, and in the
Gesta Romanorum, when she embraces him, 'amplexebatur',
p. 528); in R2 and the *Gesta Romanorum*, Tharsia also speaks
words of comfort, but the immediate, violent repulse in R1
and Gower establishes that physical contact is the cause. As
a ritual gesture, the repulse declares that the hero would
never allow physical contact with the daughter. Tharsia's
narrative, giving the details of her history which proclaim
her identity, is the final step to the joyful recognition of the
relationship by father and daughter. The meaning of this
'recognition' will be determined by its context–which is the
establishment of the absence of incest in the relationship
and the giving of the daughter in marriage to Athenagora.

It is clear from the oath of the uncut hair that the hero's
recognition of the daughter must lead to her instant marriage, but why must her bridegroom be a whoremonger
defeated by her? His lechery and his defeat are both important: the bridegroom who seems so unsuitable to rational
eyes will be found to be entirely suitable at the magical
level. Athenagora is a sexually transgressing ruler with a
virgin daughter, details which are suggestive of his useful-
ness to the hero. He brings to his designs on the hero's
daughter both unscrupulousness and power, and yet she
dissuades him from carrying them out, and her triumph
over all her clients in the brothel proves that she would
always succeed in dissuading him. This will explain his not
rescuing her immediately from the brothel. The scenes in the
brothel do not only parallel the wife's becoming high priestess of Diana: they also parallel the meeting between father
and daughter, where, too, the impossibility of there being a
sexual relationship is established. Furthermore, while the
daughter is establishing this impossibility, the father per-

forms what can only be a ritual penance in the hold of his ship. His powerful feelings about the daughter have been identified as being horror that there might be a sexual relationship between them, and his anguish in the hold of the ship must relate to the events in the brothel, where a sexually transgressing ruler with a virgin daughter is dissuaded from his lust for another ruler's virgin daughter. Gower's not having his Atenagoras involved in the brothel scenes does not alter the role of these scenes fundamentally, although it affects their force: it is interesting that authors, in general, have adhered to Athenagora's involvement in the brothel scenes.

There is some interesting detail relating to Athenagora in the Latin texts. Athenagora tells Tharsia in the brothel that he has a virgin daughter for whom he fears the same misfortune as hers: ' "Habeo et ego filiam uirginem, ex qua similem possum casum metuere" ' (p. 70). How might the ruler's daughter ever come to be in her father's brothel? We are also told that Athenagora watches over Tharsia's virginity and nobility as if she were his own only daughter: 'Athenagora autem princeps memoratam Tharsiam integrae uirginitatis et generositatis ita iam custodiebat ac si unicam suam filiam' (p. 75). However, he does this by bribing the overseer in the brothel where he leaves her ('ita ut uillico multa donaret', p. 75). Lawrence Twine's treatment of his source from the *Gesta Romanorum* is telling here: 'Athanagoras ... had evermore a speciall regard in the preservation of her virginitie, none otherwise than if she had been his owne daughter, and rewarded the villaine very liberally for his diligent care over her' (p. 459). While these sentences can make no rational sense, their magical sense seems clear. The special regard for the preservation of Tharsia's virginity is that of the hero in the magical plot, and it is being magically dealt with through the use of Athenagora and Tharsia in the brothel. Since it is not for Tharsia's sake, as a child in need of care and protection, but for the hero's, as a father needing to exorcise his fear of incest, Athenagora's preservation of Tharsia's virginity within, rather than well away from, the worst environment possible for the preservation of virginity, makes excellent sense. Twine's treatment of Athenagora's claim on presenting his suit is also telling: 'through my meanes she hath continued a virgin, and by my procurement she is nowe come unto the knowledge of thee her father' (p. 468; in the *Gesta Romanorum*, '"meo auxilio virgo permansit et me duce te patrem agnovit"', p. 529). By giving 'virgo' the sense of virginity and also emphasis in the final position, and by similarly emphasising 'thee her father', Twine brings out the magical sense that — far from giving rational assistance to the girl and her father — Athenagora has been an agent in rituals preserving a virginity and bringing about a 'recognition' by the hero of the daughter. The Latin words could make no sense in meaning that Athenagora has assisted the girl, since he has not and she has not needed his help (being magically invested with total power to succeed), and the absence in the texts of any comment on the untruthfulness of Athenagora's claim suggests that it has no active sense at a rational level.

When the daughter is married, Apollonius travels with her and her husband to the Temple of Diana. Lucina has proved herself supreme in chastity, as has her daughter, being high priestess among the chaste vestals in the temple of the chaste goddess,[14] none being so pleasing to Diana as she is ('nulla tam grata esset Dianae nisi ipsa', p. 106); and, in Twine's version of his Latin source, 'for the great love which she bare unto chastitie all men reverenced her, and there was no virgin in al the number in like estimation unto her' (pp. 471–2; *Gesta Romanorum*, p. 530). She steps forward, upon their arrival, and they fall at her feet, thinking she is Diana: 'ipsam esse putarent deam Dianam' (p. 106). Apollonius recounts his history before her, addressing her as '"magna Diana"' (p. 108), and, at the end of the narration, Lucina announces that she is his wife ('"ego sum coniunx tua"', p. 109) and throws herself into his arms, identifying him as Apollonius, her teacher who had received her from her father Architstrates. The marriage is resumed. This parallels the sequence between Apollonius and Tharsia, where she tells her story, he announces that she is his daughter ('"tu es filia mea Tharsia"', p. 99) and her marriage follows. In each case, the narration appears to have the function of opening the door to the naming of the relationship, which

should be seen in relation to the fourteen years during which
the wife and daughter have been, respectively, the adopted
daughter of the physician and the foster-daughter of the
Tharsus couple, named after their city. That marriage follows in each case raises questions to which I shall return as
to the meaning of the recognition, and the relationship of the
two marriages. In the R2 text and the *Gesta Romanorum*
(and therefore in Twine), Lucina throws herself into Apollonius' arms before she announces who she is, and is repulsed
by him; then she makes the announcement and the narrative
proceeds as in R1. This addition of an embrace followed by a
repulse, parallel to those of Tharsia but placed *after* the
narration of the history, rather than *before* as in the case of
Tharsia, has no part in the magical plot, because each narration comes only when the exorcisms are complete and the
repulse is an exorcism. Interpolations such as this second
embrace and repulse do not alter the progression of a magical plot; they only delay it. In this case, the interpolation
gives 'I am your wife' an additional sense to the magical one,
since it acts as an explanation at the rational level as to why
a chaste vestal appears to be embracing a man.

It will be important that the daughter and her husband
are present at Ephesus. At this point, I must mention a
strange confusion in *Pericles*:

> That you aptly will suppose
> What pageantry, what feats, what shows,
> What minstrelsy, and pretty din
> The regent made in Mytilene
> To greet the king. So he thrived
> That he is promised to be wived
> To fair Marina, but in no wise
> Till he had done his sacrifice
> As Dian bade ... (V.ii.5–13)

It is Pericles, not Lysimachus, whom Dian bids to do 'his
sacrifice' (V.i.239–48). Why does the writer of this speech
not take the trouble to distinguish clearly between these two
characters here? We have to consider the possibility that
there is no clear distinction between them,[15] and this would
mean that Lysimachus (and the Athenagora character in all
the versions) must also be involved in the rituals at Ephesus.

At Ephesus, the chastity of the wife is established and the hero is able to resume the marriage, but the true meaning of this is that it is the chastity of the husband (the hero) which has been established — the husband of the wife and, it seems, the husband of the daughter. In a magical plot, the hero frequently appears as two or more characters. As can be seen here, this gives greater scope for the enactment of rituals — Athenagora seeks to take the maidenhead of the daughter while Apollonius performs a penance in the darkness of the ship's hold — and it also gives scope for disguise. Athenagora is the unacknowledged hero, and Apollonius the acknowledged hero.

Just as there is no clear distinction between the two husbands found chaste at Ephesus, there is also apparent confusion of daughters with mothers. The answer to the riddle 'I feed on (enjoy) maternal flesh' ('"maternam carnem uescor"', p. 6) is 'You have not lied: look on your daughter' ('"nec et hoc mentitus es: filiam tuam intuere"', p. 7). Gower has 'I ete, and have it not forlore My moders flesshe' (ll. 414–15) and *Pericles* has 'I feed On mother's flesh which did me breed' (I.i.65–6). Antiochus is presented, however, as committing incest with his daughter, not his mother, but, when we take up the point of view of the magical hero and see the incest as the hero's fear of his own involvement in incest, the riddle's statement that the perpetrator is involved with his mother, rather than with his daughter, immediately makes more sense: the hero is heir to Antiochus and therefore the royal couple at Antioch have the appearance of parents to him. Other details contribute to the impression that the hero is afraid that his marrying will mean taking his mother from his father. In the Historia, Antiochus proscribes him because he wished to be what the father was (which indicates that the idea of acquiring a kingdom is present in the idea of marriage); and Antiochus' warning to Pericles, in the play, which is supposed to be about the risks of pollution or the death penalty, comes over as being about taboo:

Before thee stands this fair Hesperides,
With golden fruit, but dangerous to be touched,
For deathlike dragons here affright thee hard. (I.i.28–30)

The disguises are many. That Apollonius is heir to Antiochus is concealed during his suit in Antioch. Antiochus is accused of the incest and his partner appears as an eligible partner for the hero, not one who is taboo — hence her being a daughter. Meanwhile, the correct point of view is hidden, so that, at rational levels, we see the story from the wrong points of view. Not all these disguises are intended as such and it is hard to tell which are, but each has the effect of concealment.

Both the kings, Antiochus and Archistrates, have a single daughter in a queenless court. The hero cannot obtain the first in marriage owing to his fear of incest, and he marries the second within a number of conditions which seek to remove the fear of incest — the use of a new king and princess at a distance, the arrangement of the marriage by the princess and king while the hero is entirely passive, and the whole-hearted approval of the king. However, upon the hero's becoming husband of the princess, and king in Antiochus' place — and also upon the princess' becoming a mother (of Tharsia) — fresh exorcisms begin. It should be noted, too, that the exorcisms begin again when the hero becomes father of a daughter.

There is evidence in the texts of a struggle to retain a vision of the desired bride as a young girl. The teacher–pupil relationship of Apollonius and Lucina is given much emphasis in the Pentapolis scenes (he is called 'magister') and again, later, in the temple, when Lucina announces that she is his wife: he is her teacher, who instructed her with a skilled hand; he is the man who received her from her father, Archistrates ('"tu es magister, qui docta manu me docuisti, tu es qui me a patre meo Archistrate accepisti"', p. 109). It is likely that the function of this teacher–pupil relationship is to distance the lurking idea of a mother in Lucina. In Ephesus, Lucina is made the daughter of the physician, but, at that particular stage of the plot, that detail will be an announcement that she is no longer the hero's wife.

While the wife is established as a daughter, to exorcise the idea that she is a mother, there is also the hero's daughter, Tharsia, in the narrative: why are there these two female characters involved in the exorcism of the fear of incest? We also have to contend with the enigma of the marriage to Athenagora — still more enigmatic now that Athenagora has emerged as an unacknowledged representative of the hero. But, rather than proceed straight to interpretation, and wonder whether this plot is about incestuous desire secretly indulged in amid the safeguards of magical rituals, this investigation must adhere strictly to what the texts tell us. Lucina and Tharsia play parallel roles in the purification rituals, so their roles may parallel each other in further ways. They are both king's daughters — Lucina, at least in part, converted into one from a mother figure, and Tharsia firmly a daughter, but the hero's own daughter, so threatening incest from another angle. These two characters echo different aspects of the Antioch situation. The hero's use of Lucina at Pentapolis has failed and, in the Ephesus–Mytilene exorcisms, we have the double power of two king's daughters, a mother (now mother of Tharsia) and a daughter. Using the dangerous Tharsia material — king's daughter and also daughter — the hero plays out his fear and 'proves' it unfounded. The joy and recognition of Apollonius in his meeting with Tharsia must relate to the success of the exorcisms, and 'You are my daughter' ('"tu es filia mea"') must mean that the ritual separation (when she was made the Tharsus couple's daughter) is successfully concluded. In Tharsia's marriage, we find a marriage between the king's daughter and the impure ruler whose relationship with her is vindicated, and, since the following move (at Ephesus) must be a consequent step, this marriage will play a role in bringing about the resumption of the marriage between the acknowledged hero and Lucina. Tharsia's marriage seals the exorcisms: it declares finally that there is no incestuous relationship between the king's daughter and the king (we find Apollonius released from his penance of uncut hair upon the marriage) and it also seals the rightness of the marriage between the king's daughter and the impure ruler (we are told that Athenagora's goodness makes it impossible to oppose the marriage: '"ego huic tantae bonitati et pietati possum esse contrarius?"'). The ambiguous function of this marriage is the purification of the marriage with Lucina.

The plot seems to have seven moves; that is, there are seven
steps in the rituals, each step being a re-enactment of the
hero's feelings, organised in the direction of bringing about a
solution to his conflicts. In this particular plot, the conflict
seems to be between desire which is affected in some way by
thoughts of incest — chiefly by associations suggesting it —
and the fear (or guilt) which this gives rise to. The fear is
dealt with (effectively, since the story was so popular) by
magical means: the exorcisms enacted in move after move. I
shall attempt to trace how the moves are linked: this will
necessarily result in considerable simplification of a plot
which is multiple, tortuous and self-contradictory in meaning, but it will indicate the kind of form to be expected in a
magical plot.

After the initial vision of incest (the first move at Antioch),
the hero transfers himself to Tharsus (the second move),
where he has his goodness affirmed, and then he transfers
himself to Pentapolis (the third move, and a second Antioch
situation), where conditions are set up which allay the fear
of incest, thus enabling his marriage to take place. But this
cannot be the end of the story, because his new status, and
that of his wife, renew the fear; the approval of the king, and
his own passivity, at Pentapolis have not been strong enough
exorcisms. The fourth move — the storm at sea and dispos-
als of wife and daughter, ending with the hero's departure to
the ends of the earth — is concerned with the purifying
statements that the hero is no longer engaged in these relationships. In the fifth move, the hero tackles his fear of incest
using the daughter character, and declares her unassailable:
he assails her (in the brothel scenes) while, at the same time,
he enacts a penance (in the ship's hold) which lends power
to the defeat of his fear and to the victory of his desire for
proof of his innocence. The meeting between the hero and
the daughter character forms a new move, the sixth, since
the acknowledged hero — as opposed to the unacknowledged hero, Athenagora — is now involved in the rituals
declaring the daughter unassailable — and, specifically, this
time, declaring the absence of incest. These rituals culmin-
ate in Tharsia's marriage, which finally exorcises the

thought that there is incest between the king and the king's daughter, and also exorcises the thought that the (impure) ruler may not marry the king's daughter. The exorcisms complete, the hero now passes on to his seventh move. At Ephesus, the king's daughter appears supreme in chastity — which is the crowning proclamation of the purity of her husband — as a result of both the Tharsia and Lucina exorcisms — and the marriage can be resumed. With this final solution to the desires and fears at Antioch, the story may end. The punitive journey to Tharsus does not have a significant role in the magical plot, since the Tharsus couple have only been agents in the hero's arrangements.

Each move is full of magical devices not so far discussed, not least the oath of the uncut hair and nails, and the statues with their inscriptions proclaiming the goodness of the hero and the virginity of the daughter. The Historia texts are alive to the magical power of words. They organise them into inscriptions, into announcements (such as Tharsia's initial announcement of her chastity at her meeting with Apollonius), and into Tharsia's song to her father. They also use the repetition of single words with an important role, words such as virgin, teacher ('magister') and Diana. There are, furthermore, many acts invested with special magical power, particularly the penances of the uncut hair and nails, and sojourn in the dark hold of the ship, the adoption of the wife by the physician and naming of the daughter after Tharsus, and the father's violent repulse of the daughter. It should finally be added here that the riddles in the Historia texts are interpolations and no more than intrusions on the plot.

The versions in Gower and *Pericles* do not provide such full and excellent detail for the study of this magical plot as do the Historia texts, but they illuminate the plot in a variety of ways. A striking detail in *Pericles* which should not go unmentioned is the description of the Apollonius story in the opening chorus:

> It hath been sung at festivals,
> On ember-eves and holidays,
> And lords and ladies in their lives
> Have read it for restoratives. (I, Chorus, 5–8)

We are told that the story contributes to fun, but is also involved at times of vigil before fasting and prayer (Ember eves) and is read for its healing power ('for restoratives'). The play's epilogue has equally interesting lines:

> In Antiochus and his daughter you have heard
> Of monstrous lust the due and just reward;
> In Pericles, his queen, and daughter seen,
> Although assailed with fortune fierce and keen,
> Virtue preserved from fell destruction's blast,
> Led on by heaven, and crowned with joy at last. (Epilogue, 1–6)

'Virtue preserved' sums up the magical business of the plot (this is the case whatever the nature of the feelings in the plot, since the reference is to the hero's state of mind), and 'Have read it for restoratives' calls attention to its healing role among audiences.

It is interesting, in retrospect, to look at Philip Edwards' comment on the plot of *Pericles*. It 'is about people who suffer unaccountable misfortunes and gain equally un-accountable good fortune ... In the end, the simplicity of the relationships in *Pericles*, the unlikelihood of the events, the lack of cause-and-effect in the plot, make the play a presentation of images which, while individually they ex-pand into wide and general meanings, yet as a whole sequ-ence withdraw from asserting how things run in this world. We are offered ideas or propositions about love and suffering and chastity, and the relation of them to a divine will, but we are not offered a clue to any meaning lying in the pro-gression of events'.[16] This is a fine description of a magical plot, viewed in the light of how it appears to be different from the 'rational' plots we generally expect and find, rather than in the light of how it functions as an irrational one.

I believe that the model of the magical plot — by offering a systematic approach which addresses such irrationalities on their own terms — has offered clues to 'meaning lying in the progression of events'. It has shown that the events are accountable and that, far from there being a lack of cause-and-effect, the plot is strikingly organised in this respect. At the same time, it has shown that the relationships in the plot are simple in one remarkable respect only — that magical thought has no concern with the realities of character and relationship: they are complicated in other respects, since magical thought creates characters and relationships out of confused and tortuous desires and fears. The plot is indeed a sequence of images unconcerned with how things are in the world external to the mind. This has evidently not affected the story's popularity: for humankind, the mind is as important a place as the world beyond it.

PART ONE

CHAPTER ONE

YWAIN

Chrétien's Yvain and his counterparts

Chrétien's *Yvain*[1] was a popular romance. Three close translations of it have survived: the English *Ywain and Gawain*,[2] the German *Iwein*[3] and the Swedish *Herr Ivan*.[4] There is also a Welsh version, known as *Owein* or *The Lady of the Fountain*,[5] which may or may not be dependent on Chrétien's version.

As the versions are so close to each other, the brief plot outline which I give below is useful for all of them. The purpose of the outline is to provide an overall view of the plot; the detail will be given as the need for it arises in my discussion. Chrétien's version will be my chief text, since it is certainly the source of most of the others and may be the source of all, and also because its detail has proved the most interesting for my study. However, material in the other versions has played a major role in my investigation.

The Ywain material has received ample scholarly attention. In particular, I must mention at this point Tony Hunt's bibliographical essay,[6] in which he discusses the many versions, including some not dealt with here, and another article by Tony Hunt,[7] in which he poses the very questions which I must tackle in my investigation. The French, German and Welsh versions have all been translated into English.

My outline of the plot ends at the point where scholars believe Chrétien's source ended and where he added material. My findings support theirs in this respect, and there is no need to include an analysis of the final episodes in this particular investigation.

1. While Arthur is asleep, the queen joins a group of knights outside his chamber door to hear Calogrenant tell the tale of his fountain adventure. He tells how he set out in search of a testing adventure, and, after a night with a hospitable host, met a giant herdsman, who directed him to a fountain where he performed a rain-making ritual and raised a terrifying storm. After the storm, a knight came galloping up to accuse him of making war on him. They fought and Calogrenant was defeated. The fountain knight took his horse, and he returned ashamed, but, on his way, he was welcomed by the host with undiminished kindness. At the end of the tale, Ywain (Yvain, Iwein, Ivan, Owein) says he wishes to undertake the adventure to avenge Calogrenant's shame; Kay jeers his disbelief that he would dare to do so and the queen rebukes Kay. When Arthur wakes, the queen retells Calogrenant's tale to him and he plans to undertake the fountain adventure himself.

2. Ywain secretly sets off immediately on this adventure and defeats the fountain knight. He pursues the mortally wounded knight back to his castle gate, where the descending portcullis shaves off his spurs and kills his horse, and he is trapped. The fountain lady's companion, Lunete, saves him from retribution by making him invisible with a ring. He falls in love with the grief-stricken lady of the fountain. Lunete persuades the lady (Laudine) to marry Ywain, arguing that she urgently needs a defender of her land as Arthur is on his way to the fountain. Thus Ywain becomes the fountain knight, and, upon Arthur's performing the ritual at the fountain, he fights Kay, who has asked for the battle, and defeats him. Then he returns Kay's horse to the king and makes himself known. Arthur and his company are entertained at the fountain castle.

3. When Arthur decides to return home, Gawain persuades Ywain to go with them, and the lady of the fountain gives permission, provided Ywain returns no later than a year from that date. Ywain forgets to return and a maiden arrives to denounce him and tell him he has lost his lady. He becomes a madman in the forest until he is cured by the lady of Noroison and her damsel, who use an ointment made by Morgan le Fay; the lady needs Ywain's help against her enemy Count Alier. When the count comes to plunder, Ywain defeats him, and the count gives pledges that he will always live on peaceful terms with the lady and make good the losses he has caused her. The lady wishes Ywain to remain and be lord of her possessions, but Ywain departs.

4. Retracing his path through a wood, Ywain hears a cry and finds a lion in the grip of a dragon. He rescues it and it places itself

at his service. Arriving at the fountain, he discovers that Lunete is
imprisoned in the chapel on a treason charge for advising her
mistress to receive Ywain. Ywain tells her that he will help, and he
spends the night with relatives of Gawain, who are suffering from
the plundering attacks of the giant Harpin of the Mountain; Harpin
is demanding that they surrender their daughter to him. Ywain
defeats Harpin with the help of his lion, and then he rescues
Lunete, again with the help of his lion, by defeating the steward
who has accused her, and his two brothers. The Welsh version ends
here with Owein's return to the lady of the fountain, while, in the
other versions, Ywain speaks to the lady of the fountain, giving her
his name as the Knight of the Lion, and then moves on to further
adventures. Ywain and the lady are finally reunited by a renewal of
the schemes of Lunete.

The central questions concerning the problems of the plot,
as it is used by Chrétien, have already been posed by Tony
Hunt and it remains for me to restate them here.

1. What 'is the moral value of Yvain's undertaking and his
conduct of the adventure?' Calogrenant is innocent of the
fountain knight's charge of making war ('"vos me meüssiez
guerre"', v. 496), while Arthur sends a messenger (if, indeed,
la Dameisele Sauvage, v. 1620, is his messenger). Yvain's
undertaking of the adventure is in full knowledge of the
fountain knight's grievance, and, having dealt him a mortal
blow, he pursues him to take him dead or alive ('mort ou
vif', v. 893) in order to secure some visible tokens of his
victory.[8]

2. 'Nothing could be more ambiguous than the apparent
marriage of convenience which takes place between Yvain
and Laudine.' Laudine changes from hate of her husband's
slayer to love and later back to hate again. Her previous
husband is forgotten entirely upon the marriage: we are told
that the people love and esteem the living knight more than
they ever did the one who is dead (vv. 2165, 2168–9). 'Is
Laudine's craven court (none of her barons would defend the
fountain) a reliable touchstone for judging the hero's chivalric status?'[9]

3. With reference to Yvain's adventures following his loss
of Laudine, how 'does Yvain come to embrace such a new
conception of chivalric prowess?' In these adventures we

find a display of 'compassionate, discriminating prowess placed in the service of the oppressed.'[10]

4. 'It is anything but clear how the adventures relate to the rewinning of Laudine.' It 'is difficult to divine the hero's intentions and even more difficult to see anything more than a technical link between the chivalric adventures and the rewinning of Laudine.'[11]

These questions suggest the presence of the kind of problems which arise when an author uses a magical plot. They point to contradictions between the author's moral treatment and Yvain's behaviour, and to puzzles as to why the characters act as they do; moreover, the latter part of the material is presented as relating to the rest of it while the nature of the relationship is quite obscure. Tony Hunt traces Chrétien's ironic treatment of both the love theme and the moral ambiguity surrounding Yvain's actions, and scholars have explored the themes which have made a coherent whole of *Yvain*, but, where a magical plot has been used, problems of a particular character always remain.

In order to present my discussion as clearly as possible, I shall first of all trace briefly how the plot before us might be magical, setting about this task by addressing Tony Hunt's questions. Some of the difficult detail, especially that relating to the initial scene at Arthur's court, including Calogrenant's tale, will be omitted at this stage. My next step will be to give attention to some of the omitted problems. Throughout this part of the discussion I shall limit myself to Chrétien's text. After this, I shall examine parts of the English, German, Swedish and Welsh texts, where they may throw fresh light on the plot they are using; some details, given little or no attention before, will be dealt with at this stage. Finally, I shall survey the plot as a whole, and some material still unexamined will be attended to there.

I

Yvain's first, openly declared, reason for undertaking the fountain adventure is to avenge Calogrenant's shame: '"se je puis et il me loist, J'irai vostre honte vangier"' (vv. 588–9).

Kay makes fun of this. When the king decides to undertake the adventure himself, Yvain is put out, believing that Kay or Gawain may be given the battle, and he resolves to go alone, ahead of Arthur's expedition. He is over-anxious ('trop ... cusançoneus', v. 700) to find the narrow wooded path Calogrenant took and impatient to see the herdsman ('Li veoirs li demore et tarde Del vilain', vv. 710–11).[12] As Stephen Knight emphasises, there is an urgent secrecy about Yvain's departure.[13] The repetition, as Yvain mounts his horse, of his intention to avenge, if he can, his cousin's shame ('Qui vangera, s'il puet, la honte Son cosin', vv. 748–9) appears by now to have little to do with it, but it is reiterated once more when Yvain pursues the mortally-wounded fountain knight: he is afraid he will have wasted his effort if he does not take the knight dead or alive, for he still recalls Kay's taunts; he has not yet carried out the pledge which he has given to his cousin (Calogrenant) and he will not be believed unless he returns with visible tokens:

Qu'il crient sa painne avoir perdue,
Se mort ou vif ne le detient;
Que des ranposnes li sovient,
Que mes sire Kes li ot dites.
N'iert pas de la promesse quites,
Que son cosin avoit promise,
Ne creüz n'iert an nule guise,
S'ansaingnes veraies n'an porte. (vv. 892–9)

There was, in fact, no pledge to do more than avenge Calogrenant's shame, which would require no more than the fountain knight's defeat in the same way that he defeated Calogrenant: the fountain knight neither killed Calogrenant nor wounded him severely, and he left him free, only taking his horse. Meanwhile, to pursue a defeated opponent in order to take him dead or alive — denying him mercy and approaching him from behind — for the purpose of acquiring 'ansaingnes veraies' of victory to show Kay and the court, is itself a shameful act, breaking the rules of warfare set out in canon law and a variety of legal texts.[14]

But the problems are deeper than this moral problem. Yvain's encounter with the fountain knight is a totally different kind of encounter from Calogrenant's:

Ains dui chevalier si angrés
Ne furent de lor mort haster. (vv. 838–9)

Never were there two knights so intent upon each other's death.
(Comfort, p. 191)

Why should either knight be 'angrés' (furious) to this extent?
Yvain, for his part, only has to defeat the fountain knight,
not kill him. He claims later, to Laudine, that the fountain
knight attacked him, with intent to kill or capture him, and
he had to defend himself: '"Quant vostre sire m'assailli,
Quel tort oi je de moi deffandre? Qui autrui viaut ocirre ou
prandre, Se cil l'ocit, qui se deffant, Dites, se de rien i
mesprant?"' (vv. 2000–4). But Yvain's mood, both before
and after the battle, makes it difficult to be convinced that
self-defence is his motive. Meanwhile, there is no reason
known to the fountain knight why he should treat Yvain
differently from Calogrenant, and yet he does so from the
outset, not as a result of discerning a different kind of opponent. He does not explain his anger to Yvain as he did to
Calogrenant. Immediately he gallops up to the fountain we
have the following lines:

Et maintenant qu'il s'antrevirent,
S'antrevindrent et sanblant firent,
Qu'il s'antrehaïssent de mort. (vv. 815–17)

As soon as they espied each other they rushed together and displayed the mortal hate they bore. (Comfort, p. 190)

In his protest to Calogrenant, the fountain knight accused
him of making war on him — '"vos me meüssiez guerre"' —
and described the action and the harm done in terms of war.
He complained that Calogrenant had caused him shame and
harm '"Sanz desfiance"', that is, without issuing a formal
challenge, and that if there was any quarrel between them,
the knight should first have challenged him or at least
sought justice before making war on him: if he could, he
would see to it that the damage done to his woods would
redound on Calogrenant's head; within his woods and castle,
Calogrenant had made such an attack on him that men,
arms and fortifications would have been of no use —

'Vassaus! mout m'avez fet
Sanz desfiance honte et let.

Desfiër me deüssiez vos,
S'il eüst querele antre nos,
Ou au mains droiture requerre,
Ains que vos me meüssiez guerre.
Mes se je puis, sire vassaus!
Sor vos retornera li maus
Del domage, qui est paranz;
Anviron moi est li garanz
De mon bois, qui est abatuz ...
Qu'an mon bois et an mon chastel
M'avez feite tel anvaïe,
Que mestier ne m'eüst aïe
De jant ne d'armes ne de mur.' (vv. 491–501; 508–11)

In the following battle, the fountain knight returned the shame (Calogrenant felt '"honte"', vv. 527, 542, 560), but he did not return the physical damage. The hospitable host and his daughter told Calogrenant, on his return journey, that, as far as they knew, no one had ever before escaped without being killed or kept prisoner ('"fust morz ou retenuz"', v. 576), so why, after his protest, did the fountain knight leave Calogrenant free and able to walk home? Perhaps we are intended to understand that Calogrenant made the fountain knight less angry than did his predecessors and Yvain, this leaving the knight able both to explain himself and be merciful. Yvain has certainly come to the fountain hard upon hearing about Calogrenant's adventure and in full knowledge of the fountain knight's grievance, but seven years have elapsed since Calogrenant's adventure ('"pres a de set anz"', v. 175) and the text does not indicate that the fountain knight has distinguished Calogrenant's innocence or Yvain's lack of it. The storm raised by Yvain is no greater than that raised by Calogrenant. Calogrenant only sprinkled water on the stone ('"De l'eve au bacin arosé"', v. 438) and the violence of the storm made him fear he had poured too much ('"Mes trop an i versai, ce dot; Que lors vi le ciel si derot"', vv. 439–440), while Yvain pours the basin full of water upon the stone ('Versa sor le perron de plain De l'eve le bacin tot plain', vv. 803–4), only to raise a storm which is no more than usual: 'Et maintenant vanta et plut Et fist tel tans, con feire dut', vv. 805–6. The birds sing joyfully after both storms. In any case, when Arthur arrives at the foun-

tain, he pours the basin full of water on the stone ('Versa de
l'eve plain bacin', v. 2219) in order to see the rain, not storm
('por veoir la pluie', v. 2218), and rain duly pours at once ('Et
plut tantost mout fondelmant', v. 2221); this time there is no
mention of a terrifying, damaging storm.

We hear, in fact, four different accounts of the consequ-
ences of pouring water on the stone at the fountain — the
one imparted by the giant herdsman and hospitable host to
Calogrenant, Calogrenant's own experience, and those relating to Yvain and to Arthur. The storm itself varies, from the
terrifying manifestation of thunderbolts ('"foudres"',
v. 447), snow, rain and hail ('"noif et pluie et gresle"', v.
444), wind and splintered trees ('"des arbres, qui de-
peçoient"', v. 448) of the earlier accounts of the giant herdsman (vv. 401–7), Calogrenant and Yvain, to Arthur's experience, which seems to be no more than rain-making. The
fountain knights differ in each account: the host's knight is
invincible and merciless, Calogrenant's explains his anger
and is merciful, Yvain's is merciless without explanation
and defeated, while Yvain, in the role, is intent on inflicting
a little shame ('un po de honte', v. 2240) on Kay. The giant
herdsman's description of the storm closely resembles the
hospitable host's description of the fountain knight: he says
that Calogrenant will see such thunderbolts, winds and
splintered trees, rain, thunder and lightning, that, if he can
get away without great trouble and distress, he will be more
fortunate than any knight has ever been.

> 'Car tu verras si foudroiier,
> Vanter et arbres peçoiier,
> Plovoir, toner et espartir,
> Que, se tu t'an puez departir
> Sanz grant enui et sanz pesance,
> Tu seras de meillor cheance
> Que chevaliers, qui i fust onques.'

The host and his daughter are clearly referring to the fountain knight in their words that, as far as they know, no one
has ever escaped from the place Calogrenant has come from,
without being killed or kept prisoner ('"qu'onques mes hon
N'iere eschapez ... De la, don j'estoie venuz, Que n'i fust
morz ou retenuz"', vv. 572–3; 575–6), but the herdsman is

referring to the manifestations of the storm in saying that no
knight ever escaped without ' "grant enui" ' — great grief,
harm or vexation — and ' "pesance" ', distress. Calogrenant
describes his great alarm in the storm (' "mout fui
esmaiiez" ', v. 449) and his fear of death from the thunderbolts (' "çant foiz cuidai estre morz Des foudres" ', vv. 446–
7), but the parallel suggests a meaning beyond this, for it
brings into sharper relationship the role of the storm and the
role of the battle. This matter will be explored later: for the
present, it is enough to note that the fountain adventure is of
an intriguingly inconstant character, altering, it seems,
according to the requirements of the narrator at different
stages of the plot. We have, evidently, a rain-making ritual
in accordance with that described by Wace as taking place
at the Fountain of Bérenton and which also took place elsewhere in the Middle Ages,[15] here being used to express an
act of aggression in someone else's territory; the variation in
the resulting manifestations will probably relate to variation
in the context, but no further progress can be made in this
direction until much more is known about these contexts.

The fountain knight's protest to Calogrenant appears to be
an over-reaction. Calogrenant had caused a considerable
amount of damage and only for the reason that he was in
search of an adventure which would test his prowess and his
courage (' "Avantures por esprover Ma proesce et mon har-
demant" ', vv. 362–3); he had also known, from the herdsman's description, that the storm would damage trees. But
he can hardly be accused of making war. We might compare
this seeming over-reaction with the treatment of Arthur's
fountain adventure. Arthur — while he knows the fountain
knight's grievance, the queen having retold Calogrenant's
story to him word for word ('tot mot a mot', v. 659) — plans
to undertake the adventure in order to see the storm and the
marvel ('Qu'il iroit veoir la fontainne … Et la tanpeste et la
mervoille', vv. 665, 7); he will spend a night there ('Et s'i
prandra la nuit son giste', v. 670) and all who wish may go
with him. The Lady of the Fountain learns of this from the
Dameisele Sauvage, but the text does not indicate that this
character is the king's messenger: we learn only that she has
sent a message in letters (' "Vos an avez eü message De la

Dameisele Sauvage, Qui letres vos an anvea"',vv. 1619–21).
Later, the Lady of the Fountain's seneschal speaks to the
fountain lords saying that war is upon them ('"guerre nos
sort"', v. 2081), for the king is preparing to come to lay
waste their lands ('"Por venir noz terres gaster"', v. 2084).
Whether or not the Dameisele Sauvage is the king's messenger, she has either converted the king's picnic into a devastating war or the storm-making ritual has a meaning much
more violent than is apparent. The storms do not last long
('"li tans gueires ne dura"', v. 452), and the subsequent song
of the birds, to say nothing of the entertainment the lady is
able to give the king and his company, in spite of these
storms, belies the extent of the devastation they are supposed to cause. In the midst of all the inconsistencies in the
text, the ideas of war conflicting with the evident motives of
Calogrenant and Arthur, it is clear that Yvain's expedition is
war indeed: the violence on both sides is astonishingly greater. Neither of the reasons given for Yvain's pursuit of the
mortally wounded fountain knight — his desire to avenge
Calogrenant's shame and his desire for visible tokens of
victory to show Kay and the court — explain the violence of
this pursuit. The pursuit is likened to the action of a gerfalcon hunting a crane, swooping upon it and yet missing it
when on the point of seizure: the knight flees with Yvain
pursuing him so close that he can almost seize him in his
arms and yet cannot quite come up with him, though he is
so close that he can hear him groan with the agony he feels
—

> Si con girfauz grue randone,
> Qui de loing muet, et tant l'aproche,
> Tenir la cuide, mes n'i toche:
> Einsi fuit cil, et cil le chace
> Si pres, a po qu'il ne l'anbrace,
> Et si ne le par puet ataindre,
> Si est si pres, que il l'ot plaindre
> De la destresce que il sant ... (vv. 882–9)

Tony Hunt points out that 'What is unexpected is the fierce-
ness and impetuosity of Yvain's pursuit — a gerfalcon pursuing the crane (such nature imagery reinforces the impression of violence)'. Hunt continues, 'As if Caligula's "strike him

so that he feels death upon him" were ringing in his ears, Yvain grabs at his opponent from behind, clearly hearing his groans of agony.'[16] Chrétien has a moral and ironic approach to his material, but it is becoming clear that — as is always the case when a magical plot is being used — there are gaps left between the plot's secret and relentless purposes and the author's development and other treatment of this material. Yvain's anxiety to undertake the adventure alone, his subversive behaviour in giving his king the slip, and the violence that ensues when the fountain knight arrives at the fountain, have clearly to do with something insufficiently explained in the narrative and yet which is a concerted and consistent action throughout: by means of the strange events recounted, Yvain gets himself inside the castle and into the position of the fountain knight.

I shall leave this matter for the moment and turn to Tony Hunt's questions concerning the marriage to the Lady of the Fountain. Tony Hunt observes that the lady (known as 'la dame de Landuc' in all but two of the manuscripts, and as Laudine in only one, probably due to a misreading of 'la dame'[17]) remains mysterious; Chrétien's comment that all her arguments giving military necessity as her reasons for her hasty marriage are merely *pro forma*, and that she loves Yvain and would have married him anyway, dispels little of the ambivalence of this episode.[18] Hunt asks how seriously Chrétien takes the love of Yvain and Laudine, and suggests that Chrétien has systematically dismantled a courtly theme — that of the love of a lady inspiring the knight to displays of chivalric prowess which in turn intensify the lady's love.[19]

The lady's motive of military necessity for her marriage does not only rest on an inexplicable defence problem within her dominion: it makes no sense at all in the light of what we know of Arthur's intentions. Moreover, within the evidence of the text, the only serious attack on the fountain dominion is the astonishing, unexplained one made by the killer of its lord. Meanwhile, there is little evidence that the lady loves Yvain[20] and, instead, emphatic evidence that she loved Esclados, the fountain knight: her grief and that of her people is beyond description ('les criz Et le duel, qui ja n'iert descriz; Que nus ne le porroit descrivre', vv. 1173–5) and

Esclados was a man with whom no one could compare
('"Qu'el monde son paroil n'avoit, Ne Des ne hon ne l'i
savoit, N'il n'an i a mes nul de tes"', vv. 1237–9). And yet
we are asked to accept that this knight is forgotten entirely
upon the marriage taking place almost immediately after his
death ('li merz est toz obliëz', v. 2165) and that the people
already love and esteem Yvain, his killer, more than they
ever did Esclados ('les janz aimment plus et prisent Le vif,
qu' onques le mort ne firent', vv. 2168–9). Chrétien's treatment is undoubtedly ironic here,[21] but, nevertheless, this
material has every appearance of being magical. In a magical plot, the problem of the lady's motives would dissolve
because she would have no independent point of view; the
only point of view would be that of the hero. The inconsistencies would emerge as having arisen either from our examining the material from the wrong point of view or from
the treatment of the author, Chrétien, who has evidently
developed the material considerably and attempted rationalisations.

Further clarification of the marriage can only arise from
further examination of its context, so I shall move on to
Tony Hunt's questions concerning the adventures following
the loss of Laudine. Yvain seems to have changed character
remarkably, being now entirely in the compassionate service
of the oppressed, and it is difficult to see what his intentions
are. How do the adventures relate to the rewinning of
Laudine?

In the case of the first adventure, with the lady of
Noroison, it is clear that there is a significant contrast with
the fountain adventure. In the fountain adventure, Yvain
kills a man and takes his place as husband and lord. In the
Noroison adventure, Yvain brings to an end Count Alier's
thieving attacks on a widow's land (the count and his men
'mistrent feus et pristrent proies', vv. 3143–5), and obtains
pledges from him that he will live on peaceful terms with
her and make good her losses, and he then himself turns
down the lady's offer that he should become her husband
and lord of all her possessions. The lines given to Count
Alier's pledges have a special interest:

Et par foi et par seiremant
Et par ploiges l'an fist seüre.
Ploiges li done et si li jure,
Que toz jorz mes pes li tandra
Et ses pertes restoerra ... (vv. 3306–10)

By (his) word and by oath and by pledges he secures it to her; he gives pledges and thus he swears to her that he will for ever keep peace with her and restore her losses.

There is an emphasis here in the echoing syntax and the piling on of ritual bindings to secure this peace and reparation. The function of the Noroison adventure cannot yet be judged, but it has the appearance of being a magical move concerned with the removal of guilt associated with the fountain adventure. If this is the case, the function of the move would probably be the transformation of the thief invading a lady's dominion into one sworn never to do it again, and, also, the restoration of the dominion to its previous state (he will rebuild her houses, v. 3312). This would be followed by the hero's declared renunciation of the lady and her possessions. The hero's defeat of Alier would also declare him the champion of sovereign ladies against such theft.

Leaving the lady of Noroison much chagrined ('leissa mout la dame iriee', v. 3325), Yvain retraces his path ('se mist a la voie arriere', v. 3324) and rides thoughtfully through a deep wood, where he acquires his lion in a notable scene. Tony Hunt shows that there is a significant dualism in this lion's nature — ferocity and compassion — and that these are unambiguously placed in the service of its master; the lion's role is to reinforce the power of Yvain's own responses and aid the execution of his decisions; it is not autonomous.[22] With the lion, Yvain arrives at the fountain, where he finds Lunete accused of treason. The lion assists him in the battle with her accusers which clears her of the charge. This adventure contrasts with the Noroison adventure in a way which suggests that it is a fresh magical move. Yvain leaves the lady of Noroison to return to the fountain, the scene of his own action, rather than Count Alier's, in order to prove innocent of treason ('"traïson"', v. 3604,

3645; '"traître"', v. 3619) Lunete, the agent of his rescue
from punishment and of the bringing about of his marriage.
If this adventure is a fresh move in a magical plot, its
purpose is probably to attempt a deeper exorcism of the
hero's guilt than that attempted in the previous move;
the acquisition of the lion is probably to do with the greater
difficulty of this exorcism. This can only be speculation for
the present, attending upon close examinations of the charge
of treason, the role of the lion and much other essential
detail elsewhere in the plot.

It remains at this point to do a preliminary investigation
of the adventure with Harpin of the Mountain, which is
placed between Yvain's discovery of the imprisoned Lunete
and his rescue of her. Scholars generally regard this episode
as an example of Chrétien's interlace method of narrative,
where the narrator starts on one adventure, interrupts it
approximately in the middle by relating the whole of a
second, and then returns to complete the first.[23] At the start
of my investigation as to whether Chrétien had used a
magical plot, I was prepared to find either that the Harpin
episode was an integral part of such a plot used by Chrétien,
or that, while Chrétien had indeed added it, it was nevertheless integral at the magical level, or, alternatively, that the
Harpin episode was an intrusion in a magical plot Chrétien
had used.

Yvain's host tells him that he has suffered much from a
giant — Harpin — who insists that he give him his daughter,
who surpasses in beauty all the maidens in the world.
Moreover, not a day passes without his taking all of the
host's possessions which he can lay his hands on ('"N'est
nus jorz, que del mien ne praingne Tot, quanquë il an puet
ataindre"', vv. 3858–9). He has killed two of his sons and
will kill the other four, unless the host finds someone to
deliver his sons or unless he consents to surrender his
daughter to him. When Harpin has the daughter in his possession, he will hand her over to the foulest fellows in his
house for their pleasure; he would scorn to take her for
himself:

'... et dit, quant il l'avra,
As plus vils garçons, qu'il savra

An sa meison, et as plus orz
La liverra por lor deporz;
Qu'il ne la deigneroit mes prandre.' (vv. 3871–5)

A few lines later, the host says, '"Neither in town nor in fortress has the giant left us anything, except what we have here. If you had noticed, you must have seen this evening that he has not left us so much as an egg, except these walls which are new; for he has razed the entire town. When he had plundered all he wished, he set fire to what remained"' (Comfort, pp. 230–1):

'N'an chastel ne an forteresce
Ne nos a leissié li jaianz
Fors tant, con nos avons ceanz.
Vos meïsmes bien le veïstes
Anuit, se garde vos preïstes,
Qu'il n'a leissié vaillant un oef
Fors de cez murs, qui tot sont nuef,
Ainz a trestot le borc plené.
Quant ce, qu'il vost, an ot mené,
Si mist el remenant le feu.' (vv. 3888–97)

The giant may not come early enough the next day before Yvain has to leave to rescue Lunete, and his host offers him all he would wish to take of his lands or possessions if only he will wait a little longer:

Lors li ofre a doner del suen
Li sire, s'il an viaut avoir,
Ou soit de terre ou soit d'avoir,
Mes que ancore un po atande. (vv. 4054–7)

Yvain replies, '"Des m'an deffande, Que je ja nule rien an aie!"' (vv. 4058–9); '"God forbid that ever I should take anything of yours!"' (Comfort, p. 233). If the Harpin episode were an integral part of a magical plot, it would seem to represent the invader of the fountain dominion in the grossest terms. These gross terms may appear too much for the context: would the hero's removal of this monstrous snatcher be appropriate after Count Alier's ritual and just before the vindication of the hero's seizure of the fountain dominion (through the rescue of Lunete)? I shall return to this question when more evidence has come to light.

It is with the rescue of Lunete that the Welsh version, *Owein*, comes to an end (apart from a disjoined episode) and it seems highly satisfactory that it does so. There is much agreement that the tale from which Chrétien developed his *Yvain* ended where the Welsh version ends,[24] and I have to add my own agreement to this. The magical plot I detect undoubtedly ends here. A need for further moves is not there, and it is clear to me, as it is to many scholars, that in the adventures which follow, we have a markedly different kind of writing. Arthur C. L. Brown has drawn attention to the almost total absence of traditional material in them[25] and even Loomis is in agreement.[26] There is much skilful linking of Chrétien's added adventures to the adventures taken from his source: for example, the two monsters in the Castle of Very Evil Adventure echo the words of the seneschal whom Yvain fights to rescue Lunete (vv. 4449–67; 5536–63), and Lunete uses a ruse once again to unite Yvain and Laudine at the end of the romance. It is likely that Chrétien has used an oral tale, rather than a written source, for the plot under scrutiny,[27] and it is evident that he has transformed it considerably, this superstructure of writing uniting the tale and the additions through the development of themes such as that of the ironic subversion of courtly values[28] and that of Yvain's victories over a series of vices, reminiscent of the battle between the virtues and vices in the *Psychomachia*.[29]

II

In this section, I shall examine the role of Calogrenant's tale, giving particular attention to the giant herdsman and the storm-making ritual; I shall also examine the portcullis incident and the lion. Further areas needing detailed examination will remain, areas which are best discussed when I have brought the other versions into the study and their detail can be compared with Chrétien's.

The sequence of events in the fountain adventure is as follows. It begins with a journey through thick forest, full of briars and thorns. At last, open country is reached and the knight (first Calogrenant and then Yvain) sees a tower, where he is given hospitality by a vavasor who has a beautiful daughter whose company he does not want to leave. As he departs the next day, his host begs him to return on his way home. (Calogrenant does so, receiving an equally kind and respectful welcome.) Then the knight comes to a clearing, where he sees wild bulls engaged in terrifying battles, and, nearby, a giant herdsman, surly, grotesquely ugly and dressed in skins. The herdsman tells him he tends and controls the wild beasts so that they never leave the neighbourhood. He directs him to the fountain and describes the ritual he must perform there to bring about the adventure he desires: he must take water in the basin he will see there and spill it on the massive stone by the spring; this will raise a great storm. The knight follows his instructions and the storm proves terrifying, but it is soon over and beautiful birdsong begins. While the knight is enjoying this joyful singing, he hears a sound as of ten knights approaching him, and this commotion turns out to be the single fountain knight.

The giant herdsman is a familiar character in Celtic tradition. Two Celtic stories in particular may help us here. We find the herdsman in *Culhwch and Olwen*, playing an identical role. He is met on the way to the adventure and this adventure has the purpose of seizing the chief giant's daughter and killing the giant. Culhwch, Arthur and the rest of the party have a difficult journey to a fort, and it is there that they meet the giant herdsman. This herdsman, Custennin, has never lost a sheep or lamb, and no company has ever passed him without his doing it harm; his breath would burn every dead tree and bush that was on the plain to the ground. However, no such fate afflicts Arthur's company: the herdsman is instrumental in bringing about the next stage of their adventure, and he and his wife give them generous hospitality; Culhwch is nephew to his wife. The chief giant's daughter, Olwen, is sent for to meet Culhwch at the herdsman's house, and the herdsman's son helps Culhwch to win her and kill her father.[30] The Irish *In Gilla decair*, preserved in three eighteenth-century manuscripts, is also of particular interest for us here, because the story includes analogues of both the herdsman and the fountain events. The adventure is initiated by a trick of the eponymous Slothful Gillie, misshapen, huge and grumpy. This character arrives and is welcomed by Finn, but he has brought a gaunt horse with him, which brutally attacks the Fianna's horses. One of the Fianna, Conan, halters it and Finn tells him to gallop the horse to death. The horse will not stir when Conan mounts it and Finn says a number of men should mount it. The Gillie leaves and the horse follows him with fourteen men on its back and a fifteenth holding on to its tail. Finn follows and thus the adventure begins. After a sea journey, Diarmaid, one of Finn's party, undergoes the fountain adventure. *In Gilla decair* ends with the stealing of the Greek king's daughter, who becomes Finn's wife.[31]

The Welsh version of the Ywain story, *Owein*, gives its corresponding character, the Keeper of the Forest, the distinct description of a Fáchan, the Celtic one-legged, one-eyed and often one-handed figure.[32] Arthur C. L. Brown explores the herdsman in his study of the Ywain story,[33] but he has the notion of there being fixed archetypal origins for the character in Celtic story, while my only interest in examining the various appearances of a character of this kind in tradition is that they might give us clues as to why it appears in the plot before us. What interests me in the Welsh version is that the hospitable host gives the visiting knight directions to find the Keeper of the Forest, this bringing him into sharper relationship with the Keeper, who, in turn, gives directions to the fountain adventure.[34] Moreover, the Welsh version includes the Keeper of the Forest in its description of the return journey of the Calogrenant character (Cynon),[35] and the Keeper's mockery contrasts with the continued kindness and respect of the host (who is yet more welcoming than previously and replaces Cynon's horse). In Chrétien and the other versions, the host makes no mention of the herdsman, and the two characters are not brought into any obvious relationship.

Calogrenant's tale seems to be a formula, made up of visions and rituals, these being invested with a special magical power to propel the hero to the acquisition of a dominion. This magic formula's ingredients are well known in tradition, as magical aids tend to be. In his over-anxious ('trop ... cusançoneus') reflections before his secret departure (vv. 695–722), Yvain lists the details of the tale, item by item — the narrow wooded path; the plain with the castle; the pleasure and delight ('le solaz et le deport') with the host's fair daughter; the host who takes pains to dispense honour; the bulls; the great 'vilain' (this word includes the idea of his being morally base), and then the items at the fountain and the storm he will raise. He will keep his purpose secret because it will lead him to great shame or great honour ('Grant honte ou grant enor'). It must be important that the behaviour of the hospitable host and daughter is unchanged after Calogrenant's defeat. Calogrenant found the host the same ('"tot autel"'), just as glad and courteous ('"Aussi lié et aussi cortois"') as previously ('"einçois"', vv. 562–4), and it is in the particular context of the role played by the host and his daughter that we should understand the picture they give of the fountain adventure as one from which no one has previously escaped without being killed or kept a prisoner: this role appears to be one of approval, support and reassurance. It must also be significant that Yvain is directed to the place where he will behave more like a beast than a knight, with violence and brute force, and with an enormity he later tries to exorcise, by a character who presents such qualities as virtues. The herdsman is master of his beasts through sheer physical strength. When he can get hold of one, he presses it down so much by its two horns with his hard, strong hands that the others tremble with fear and gather around him as if to cry for mercy:

'... quant j'an puis une tenir,
Si la destraing par les deus corz
As poinz, que j'ai et durs et forz,
Que les autres de peor tranblent
Et tot anviron moi s'assanblent
Aussi con por merci criër ...' (vv. 346–51)

Anyone else would be killed by these beasts (vv. 352–4). This herdsman's chief characteristics are his monstrousness and hideous animal features (which are described in detail, vv. 295–304), and his dominant association with fighting wild beasts. There is also a sense of his having control over these beasts and his restricting them to that particular place ('"cest porpris"',v. 342). Chrétien frequently uses imagery of

hunting animals and birds (for example, of falcons hunting
teal, v. 3195, and lions among deer, v. 3203, in the description of the battle against Count Alier), but it is probably
relevant here to recall the image of the gerfalcon pursuing a
crane in the description of Yvain's pursuit of the fountain
knight.
  Altogether, there seem to be significant patterns of violence and reassurance in Calogrenant's tale. The host and
the herdsman give parallel information that no one has
escaped from the fountain adventure without serious trouble, the host referring to the fountain knight and the herdsman to the storm. It may be that two sequences of events
within the adventure parallel each other: the devastating
battle, surrounded by the approval and reassurance of the
host, and the devastating storm, surrounded by the beauty
of the fountain scene, especially the singing of the birds after
the storm. Calogrenant's tale includes reassurance among
its magical ingredients for the bringing about of violent
ends.
  Arthur C. L. Brown assembles much material interesting
for the problem of the fountain ritual.[36] The Other World
landscape described in Irish stories, such as the *Serglige Con
Culaind*,[37] the *Imram Brain* (Voyage of Bran),[38] the *Immram
Curaig Maíle Dúin*,[39] and the *Immram Snédgusa ocus Maic
Riagla*,[40] suffices to indicate that Yvain's fountain, and its
magnificent tree and birdsong — though not the storm-
making feature — are traditional Celtic Other World material. Above all, there is the extraordinary analogue to be
found in *In Gilla decair*,[41] where these Other World details
reappear, the scene having been reached by means of a
journey through a dense, tangled woodland. In addition to
the vast tree with interlacing boughs, there is a great mass of
stone by the well. The activity at the well, however, is to
drink from it, using an ornamented drinking-horn found on
the stone. Diarmaid, the single adventurer here, stoops to
drink and hears a loud and rumbling noise approaching
him: he realises that there is a spell that no one should drink
from the well, but he does so, nevertheless. A *gruagach*
appears (that is, a hairy, uncouth person, who could be a
goblin, ogre, wizard or fearsome warrior), and, without

greeting Diarmaid, he upbraids him for roaming his forest
and drinking his water. They fight all day until the *gruagach*
dives into the well; Diarmaid then kills a stag and spends
the night there. These events are repeated three times and,
on the third evening, Diarmaid tries to catch hold of the
gruagach as he dives into the well, and, in the effort, dives in
with him. At the bottom of the well is open, beautiful country and a splendid city: the *gruagach* makes for this city with
Diarmaid in pursuit, and the fortress gates are shut behind
him. Diarmaid, left outside, has to fight the whole host of
defenders; he defeats them and then another *gruagach* heals
his wounds. The succeeding details have little similarity
with the Ywain plot, but, in both stories, the fountain adventure enacts the invasion of a domain and conflict with its
lord. In the Ywain plot, this is more violent than in *In Gilla
decair*: Diarmaid has merely trespassed and he does not kill
the *gruagach*, while Calogrenant is accused of causing the
lord shame and of destroying his woods; Yvain later kills
this lord and takes his place. The difference in the activity at
the well seems essential: in considering the presence of the
storm-making alternative to drinking from the well, we have
to include a consideration of its introduction of violence and
the correspondence of this violence with the greater violence
of the context. We also have to consider the more strikingly
sexual nature of the imagery of the Ywain fountain adventure, the storm-making coming as a culmination.

To turn now to the portcullis incident, it is easy enough to
see why the idea of the amputating portcullis might be a
favourite motif. It is made fun of in *The Travels and Surprising Adventures of Baron Munchausen*,[42] and an incident in *La
Mule Sanz Frain*, where the door of the revolving castle
removes part of the mule's tail as Gawain rides in, is also
burlesque.[43]

The gateway to the fountain castle is given a precise description as a piece of engineering (vv. 907–31; 1099–1103).
Normally, it is wide enough for many people to pass through
together, but it can be set as a trap. When it is set, it has
such a narrow central way in that two men or two horses
could not enter abreast without great difficulty. This trap is
constructed like a trap set for a rat intent on mischief:

> Car ele estoit autressi feite,
> Con l'arbaleste, qui agueite
> Le rat, quant il vient au forfet ... (vv. 913–15)

'Concealed above [a rat trap] is the blade which shoots out and strikes home the moment it is released by anything touching the trigger mechanism, however gently' (Hunt, p. 391):

> Et l'espee est an son aguet
> Dessus, qui tret et fiert et prant;
> Qu'ele eschape lués et desçant,
> Que riens nule adoise a la clef,
> Ja n'i tochera si soef. (vv. 916–20)

Similarly, in the fountain gateway, a portcullis can be triggered to fall, cutting to pieces ('detranchiez toz', v. 927) whoever is beneath. Yvain triggers this portcullis and its descent cuts off his spurs flush with his heels ('... anbedeus les esperons Li trancha au res des talons', vv. 951–2) and severs the hind quarters of his horse. Yvain is spared being split in two by the fact that he is leaning forward, holding the fountain knight's saddlebow as they hurtle into the gateway. There is a second portcullis, just like the first, which falls behind the fleeing fountain knight, trapping Yvain in the gateway. Trapped and alone, Yvain is worried about nothing so much as not knowing what has become of the fountain knight:

> Mes de rien si grant duel n'avoit
> Con de ce, que il ne savoit,
> Quel part cil an estoit alez. (vv. 967–9)

But, almost immediately, Lunete arrives.

A rat intent on mischief is a quite different kind of entrant into the castle from a knight who enters by mistake in his eagerness to obtain visible tokens of victory. Stephen Knight comments that the action of the portcullis is an image of the male fear of castration upon entering the vagina,[44] and certainly the trap suggests an appropriate punishment for the wrongful entrant into the lady-cum-castle. Magical reasons for Yvain's entrance peep through Chrétien's extensive development of this part of his romance. It is striking that, while there is a meticulous

description of how the trap works, we are left with the
problem that the setting of a trap for Yvain would mean
that the castle was in expectation of his capture — or his
death or exclusion outside — and yet no one is on the scene
to deal immediately with him, not even before the castle
becomes disorganised by grief. We are also faced with the
oddness of Lunete's arrival on the scene before that of the
punitive retainers: as confidante and companion to Laudine
('sa mestre et sa garde', v. 1593), she could hardly be away
from her mistress's side at such a time, however negligent
she was. How could she be neglecting her duty to the principal mourner, when the grief of the household prevents
those who should be on duty at the gateway from being
there? In fact, we learn that a kindness in the past from
Yvain (vv. 1009–15) weighs more with Lunete — prompting
her to help him — than the tragedy which has just struck
her own people. It must be significant that Chrétien has
overlooked the important matter of what the occupants of
the castle would be likely to be doing upon the arrival of its
stricken lord and his killer.

Finally, the lion needs more attention. This lion has been
thoroughly investigated by scholars and clearly has important roles in Chrétien's themes; meanwhile, it is likely that it
also has a role in the emerging magical plot, that of
empowering the bringing about of a solution in the final
move. Chrétien clearly has a fondness for this character and
his treatment of it is both humorous and ironic, but it is
unlikely that he has introduced it to the plot. Whatever its
origin here, the motif of the thankful lion is common
enough,[45] the lion of Androcles perhaps being the best
known, and the rescue of a lion from a dragon or serpent
also appears elsewhere, notably in *Guy of Warwick*.[46]

An examination of the lion's attributes will clarify the
nature of its magical power, even where the attributes have
chivalric, scholastic or Christian sources. An author often
develops his plot at the magical level, remaining faithful to
it as he does so. Scholars have tended to see qualities such as
fidelity, courage, nobility, humility, and force or strength, as
values represented by the lion; they have also seen in it a
figure of Grace or Christ.[47] Tony Hunt argues that ferocity

and compassion are the outstanding qualities of the lion,
these qualities being placed at the service of its master. Its
'natural hunting instinct, its pursuit of *bestes sauvages*, its
drinking of warm blood (*Yv*. 3416–55) are a reminder of its
natural ferocity', and 'its conduct at the fountain' (becoming
so grief-stricken that it plans suicide, on believing that its
master — overcome upon returning to the fountain — has
died) 'symbolizes a rare degree of *compassio*'. Hunt argues
that the lion always acts in support of decisions already
taken, and reflects and gives effect to the determination and
compassion of its master. He observes that 'the lion's service
to its master accommodates both aggression and submis-
sion, strength and humility', and he draws our attention to
the importance of a traditional trait of the lion, that it
spares the defeated ('Parcere prostratis scit nobilis ira
leonis').[48]

The circumstances in which Yvain finds the lion must be
important. A dragon is holding it by the tail, burning its
hindquarters with flames of fire. Yvain wonders which of the
two he should help. Then he decides to help the lion because
the dragon is wicked and venomous while the lion is a
noble-hearted beast. He has to cut off a piece of the lion's
tail to get at the dragon's head, as it is holding the tail in its
teeth, but the lion, once rescued, does not attack him — it
does him homage and accompanies him, wishing to serve
and protect him. The adjectives in the passage condemn the
dragon three times as 'felon', wicked or treacherous (vv.
3357, 3361, 3377), and describe the lion as 'jantil et franche',
noble-hearted (v. 3375), even before Yvain has undertaken
the rescue. After the rescue, the lion acts nobly and generously ('Con fist que frans et de bon' eire', v. 3393). Chrétien
presents the lion as in a ridiculous predicament, while, at
the same time, the hero delivers goodness from evil and
arms himself with its qualities. These virtues are named at
the moment that the lion offers itself to him: it behaves
nobly and generously; then it bows and kneels down, its face
moist with tears of humility ('tote sa face moilloit De lermes
par humilité', vv. 3400–1). At the magical level, it will probably be particularly important that this new magical agent
has been freed from evil (sexual evil?) and that this has been

done by the hero. The hero becomes Knight of the Lion, master of the lion and all it represents, and uses this new name — perhaps with the force of magic words — instead of his own, on two occasions: after he has slain Harpin and after he has slain the accusers of Lunete. Both these occasions are in parts of the plot which may be additions, and yet it is still likely that the name 'Chevalier au Lion' has a magical function in the magical plot.

III

The English, German, Swedish and Welsh versions all throw further light on aspects of the Ywain plot. The Swedish version has proved the least useful for this investigation, since it does not offer illuminating variations, as does the Welsh version, and nor does it, unlike the other versions, show an energetic engagement in the magical plot at the verbal level. This last comment will be illustrated in the course of this discussion.

The Middle English version *Ywain and Gawain* does not throw much more light on the plot, since it is a close translation of Chrétien and one favouring the flow of the narrative rather than those illuminating elaborations and developments found in Chrétien and other writers, which point up absurdity and often supply revealing verbal detail. There are occasional places, however, where the Middle English treatment helps my investigation, and the chief of these concerns the denunciation of Ywain by the maiden for forgetting to return to his lady, an important and as yet unexamined part of the plot.

In Chrétien's version, Yvain is denounced in courtly love terms:

'Bien a sa jangle aparceüe,
Qui se feisoit verais amerre,
S'estoit fel, soduianz et lerre.
Ma dame a cist lerre soduite,
Qui n'estoit de nul mal recuite,
Ne ne cuidoit pas a nul fuer,
Qu'il li deüst anbler son cuer.
Cil n'anblent pas les cuers, qui aimment,

Si a tes, qui larrons les claimment,
Qui an amor vont faunoiant
Et si n'an sevent tant ne quant.
Li amis prant le cuer s'amie
Einsi, qu'il ne li anble mie,
Ainz le garde, que ne li anblent
Larron, qui prodome ressanblent.
Et cil sont larron ipocrite
Et traïtor, qui metent luite
As cuers anbler, dont aus ne chaut;
Mes li amis, quel part qu'il aut,
Le tient chier et si le raporte.' (vv. 2722–41)

'She has seen through the guile of the man who cast himself in the
role of perfect lover, who was all the time treacherous, deceitful
and dishonest. This thief hoodwinked my lady, who did not suspect
any trickery and who never imagined that he would later steal
away her heart. Those who love do not steal hearts, but there are
some who call them thieves and who themselves cheat in love
without knowing anything about it. The true lover takes his lady's
heart in such a way that he does not steal it, but rather takes care
of it, so that it is not stolen by thieves made to resemble honest
men. Those who scheme to steal hearts about which they do not
care are dishonest rogues and hypocrites. The true lover, wherever
he goes, holds dear the heart and returns it safely.' (Hunt, p. 394)

The words conveying the accusation, ' "fel, soduianz et lerre" ', mean, fundamentally, wicked ('felon'), deceitful and a
thief. The words 'lerre', 'larron' and 'anbler' (steal) are much
repeated, and the idea of thieving, played upon here in
courtly love terms by Chrétien, is an essential idea in the
magical plot. I would also prefer to translate ' "de nul mal
recuite" ' as meaning that the lady did not suspect evil or
harm. The use of the word 'trickery' for ' "mal" ', like the use
of 'dishonest' for ' "lerre" ', seems too interpretative within
the context of Chrétien's courtly love treatment, and I need
to probe to see whether Chrétien is transmuting into courtly
love terms material in the plot he is using which is quite
different in meaning. Chrétien may have invented all this
material for his courtly play on the idea of the thief who has
stolen his lady's heart without caring for it, but it is more
likely that he has transmuted the magical theme of the hero
who has stolen the fountain knight's wife and position.

It is also important to examine the accusation that Yvain is a traitor, unambiguously stated in v. 2738 above but obscured again in the translation. The charge of treason has already arisen in this investigation: it appears in the accusation against Lunete, vindicated by Yvain. The Middle English text directs our attention firmly to the accusation of treachery against Ywain:

'He es ateyned for trayture,
A fals and lither losenjoure;
He has bytrayed my lady,
Bot sho es war with his gilry.
Sho hopid noght, þe soth to say,
Þat he wald so have stollen oway;
He made to hir ful mekyl boste
And said of al he lufed hir moste.
Al was treson and trechery,
And þat he sal ful dere haby.' (ll. 1601–10)

With the courtly love treatment removed, we find treachery referred to four times in a context which does not transmute it to the crime of stealing a lady's heart; Ywain is also a wicked ('"lither"'), deceiving rascal ('"losenjoure"', '"his gilry"'). There is no mention of theft, the idea of stealing appearing here only in '"stollen oway"'.

The Middle English poet's treatment of Syr Alers' (Count Alier's) pledges expresses again the sense of there being ritual bindings to secure the peace and reparation:

On a buke þe erl sware
Forto restore bath les and mare,
And big ogayn bath toure and toune,
Þat by him war casten doune,
And evermare to be hir frende.
Umage made he to þat hende;
To þis forward he borows fand,
Þe best lordes of al þat land. (ll. 1947–54)

The earl swears on a book, he makes a formal acknowledgement of allegiance (through an act of homage) and he finds the best lords in the land to stand surety to his promise.

Hartmann von Aue has made a great many superficial alterations in his German version of Chrétien's romance, which I shall only mention here where they are directly relevant to

my investigation. A major motive behind Hartmann's alterations is his greater interest in relations than in situations:[49]
this has had a particular effect on his treatment of Laudine
and Lunete, leading to his attempting to lift their characters
and behaviour further than does Chrétien out of the exigen-
cies of the plot. What this can mean for my study is illustrated by Hartmann's version of the denunciation of the
hero, which takes me no further in my investigation of the
hero's crimes because it is too developed in terms of the
point of view of the women characters — Laudine's vulner-
able position and Lunete's concern for her. However, Hartmann's treatment is helpful in illuminating the important
scene with Arthur at the fountain, which has not yet been
examined.

Having defeated Keii at the fountain, Iwein leads Keii's
horse to Arthur and says,

> ... 'diz ors hân ich genomen:
> herre, heizet etewen komen
> von iuwerme gesinde,
> der sichs underwinde.
> ich enger niht iuwer habe,
> ichn gewinnes iu anders abe.'
> des gnâdet er im verre.
> er sprach 'wer sît ir, herre?' (ll. 2603–10)

'I have taken this horse ... Have it handed over to someone of your
household who will take care of it. I do not desire anything of yours
unless I gain it from you in a different fashion.' The King thanked
him warmly. He said, 'Who are you, sir?'

> 'ich bin ez Îwein.' 'nû durch got.'
> 'herre, ich bin ez sunder spot.'
> nû saget er im mære
> wie er worden wære
> herre dâ ze lande. (ll. 2611–15)

'I am Iwein.' 'Good God!' 'Sire, I am surely he.' Then he told him
how he had become lord of the country. (Fisher, p. 207)

These lines are very closely paralleled in the French, English
and Swedish versions, including the apparently trivial act of
returning the defeated Keii's horse to the king, but, of these
versions, only the Swedish places such emphasis on the

dominion: in Chrétien, there is reference only to the honour won (v. 2284) and, in *Ywain and Gawain*, to Ywain's good fortune (l. 1354). Hartmann also devotes much space and emphasis to how all rejoice at Iwein's advancement and Keii's disgrace (ll. 2616–52). Moreover, it is characteristic of his version that Laudine and the fountain dominion are referred to in combination: Iwein has won ' "ein vrouwen und ein rîchez lant" ' (l. 3528, a lady and a rich land), ' "eine künegîn unde ein lant" ' (l. 2880, a queen and a land), 'vrouwen unde lant' (l. 2420) and ' "ir lîp unde ir lant" ' (l. 3158, herself and her land). This lady and land 'package' is familiar enough to students of the sovereignty theme, and Hartmann's treatment makes quite clear the presence of this theme again: that the business of the plot is the seizure of a kingdom. The Swedish version also makes this clear: in its description of the marriage we are told, 'han ær een hertogh vældogh nu / ower Landewans land ok swa the fru' (ll. 1653–4), 'he is a powerful duke now over Laudunet's land and also the lady' (Laudunet is Laudine's father in Chrétien).[50] The scene with Arthur at the fountain has the appearance of a ritual, in which Iwein first returns in a ritual gesture an object representing the king's property (Keii's horse), with an accompanying statement that he would not take anything belonging to the king. This will be a very important statement, as Iwein is about to declare his identity and that he is the lord of a dominion. His position is then acclaimed and affirmed by Arthur and the court, and the dissenting voice, embodied in Keii, is derided. It is interesting to look at the corresponding lines in the other versions.

In Chrétien we have:

'Sire! feites prandre
Cest cheval; que je mesferoie,
Se rien del vostre retenoie.'
'Et qui estes vos?' fet li rois ...
Lors s'est mes sire Yvains nomez,
S'an fu Kes de honte assomez
Et maz et morz et desconfiz,
Qu'il dist, qu'il s'an estoit foïz.
Et li autre mout lié an sont,

Qui de s'enor grant joie font.
Nes li rois grant joie an mena ... (vv. 2272–5; 2279–85)

'Sire,' says he, 'now take this steed, for I should do wrong to keep
back anything of yours.' 'And who are you?' the King replies ...
Then my lord Yvain told him who he was, and Kay was overcome
with shame, mortified, humbled, and discomforted, for having said
that he had run away. But the others were greatly pleased, and
made much of the honour he had won. Even the king was greatly
gratified ...' (Comfort, pp. 209–10)

In *Ywain and Gawain* we have:

'Sir Kyng, I gif to þe þis stede,
For he may help þe in þi nede;
And to me war it grete trispas
Forto withald þat ȝowres was.'
'What man ertow?' quod þe kyng ...
'Lord,' he sayd, 'I am Ywayne.'
Þan was þe king ferly fayne;
A sari man þan was Sir Kay ... (ll. 1337–41; 1345–47)

The king, here, is 'wonderfully content' ('ferly fayne') and the
lines continue, beyond those quoted, much as Chrétien's do,
but the 'welefare' (l. 1354, good fortune) of Ywain is the
reason for the court's joy, while it is his 'enor' (honour) in
Chrétien; in Hartmann, it is his land and his spring and all
his honour: 'sînes landes und des brunnen / und aller sîner
êren' (ll. 2648–9). The Swedish version echoes the others in
the following lines:

'Iak vil thetta ørs ey hædhan føra,
iak ær ey thæs skyldogh at gøra;
ænga the hafuor iak hafua vil
ther konung Artws kompanum hørir til;
nu lætin thetta ørs væl bewara;
iak vil min vægh nw hædhan fara.'
Konung Artws swarar honum tha:
'Hwar æst thu ther hær talar swa? ...'
Tha swaradhe honum thæn ædhle man:
'Herra, iak heter Iwan' ....
han var vntfangin ther medh æra. (ll. 1781–8; 1793–4; 1798)

'I do not wish to take this horse away, I am not guilty of doing that;
I desire none of the possessions belonging to the companion of King
Arthur; now let this horse be well cared for; I will be on my way.'

King Arthur answers him then: 'Who are you speaking these
words? ...' Then the noble man answered him: 'Sir, I am Ivan' ...
He was entertained there with honour.

The language is now pedestrian rather than resonant, but,
once again, the material is strikingly close — more so than is
usual elsewhere among the versions. The lines beyond those
quoted deal mildly with the disgrace of Kay, and then Ivan
responds as follows to the king's request that he tell his
story:

'Thet vil iak, herra, giærna gøra,
lyster idher ther a at høra.
Iak hafuer vunnith thetta land,
sidhan iak foor bort, medh minna hand,
ok the sama frugha ær nu miin
som førra atte herra Wadein.' (ll. 1809–14)

'That I will willingly do, sir, listen and hear me. I have won this
land with my own hand since I went away, and the same lady is
now mine as was formerly married to lord Wadein.' (Wadein is the
fountain knight in this version.)

This version, like the German, deals explicitly with material
which Chrétien has treated with a more graceful reticence,
but it is the German version, in particular, which — with its
combined explicitness and powerful control of language —
most clearly points to the ritual nature of the material. The
impression is reinforced by a comparison of the four versions, which reveals an unusual adherence to small detail
and to its order. The ritual that has emerged shows the
importance of Arthur in the plot, and may throw fresh light
on the recurring motifs of theft and treachery.
    There is apparently similar material in the Harpin epi-
sode, and, again, all three dependent versions adhere to it
closely. In their anxiety that Ywain should delay his departure in order to help them, the women of the family are
about to prostrate themselves before him, and, later, the
host offers his lands or possessions. On both occasions,
Ywain refuses: in the words of Chrétien's Yvain, he says, on
the first occasion, ' "Des m'an deffande, Qu'orguiauz an moi
tant ne s'estande, Que a mon pié venir les les!" ' (vv. 3983–
5); ' "May God defend me from ever giving place to such

pride as to let them fall at my feet!" ' (Comfort, p. 232), and, on the second occasion, he says, ' "Des m'an deffande, Que je ja nule rien an aie!" ' (vv. 4058–9); ' "God forbid that ever I should take anything of yours!" ' (Comfort, p. 233).[51] There again seems to be a ritual declaration that Yvain will not take what belongs to the lord, and present, also, is the request for Yvain's identity. This time his answer is that he is the Knight of the Lion (' "li Chevaliers au Lion" ', v. 4291). Only the Swedish version follows Chrétien strictly in the request for the knight's identity (Ivan's reply is that he is ' "Leons riddare" ', l. 3551).[52] It is useful to consider this material at this point, taking another step in the consideration of the status of the Harpin adventure. If it is Chrétien's addition, it might appear well integrated into the plot, and yet the emerging evidence as to the concerns of the rest of the plot casts doubt on the relevance to it of the issue of giving way to pride, and, more important, it casts doubt on the relevance of Yvain's concern at this stage of the plot with the removal of the monstrous snatcher and accompanying declaration that he does not desire the property of a lord. The hero has performed his ritual before Arthur, and would not gain greater effect from using a new, surrogate, character for any repetition of this; nor could he be concerned to do so two moves later. Two moves later, moreover, he has clearly moved from the surrogate situation with Count Alier and the lady of Noroison to the situation of his own action, which is a logical order in a magical plot. The Harpin episode is inset in the hero's exorcism of his sense of his treachery in the seizure of the fountain dominion: this direct confrontation with the crime and the perpetrator is the only course left to the hero, who has already used a statement that he has no desire to take the property of a lord and, furthermore, an action (the defeat of Count Alier) to declare that he is the champion of sovereign ladies against such thieves. The Harpin adventure is clearly quite out of place here. Of course, it might be argued that the use of Lunete as the traitor is no more a direct confrontation with the hero's guilt than the use of the Alier and Harpin thieves, but the hero is dealing magically with thoughts, not rationally with actions in a rational fiction, and some disguised arrangements are more useful at a particular stage of an exorcism than others. Lunete relates directly to the hero's own crime.

To turn now to the Welsh version, this is the one version markedly different from Chrétien's. There are good arguments on both sides as to whether the Welsh material precedes Chrétien's material[53] or whether its source was Chrétien's version, the differences being due to its adaptation for a Welsh audience by a writer skilled in the tradition of Welsh story-telling.[54] My own study will be limited by my not being able to spot clues in the Welsh author's choice of language, but the work in translation still offers insights into the nature of the plot before us. While I shall be limiting my discussion of this version to detail still helpful at this stage of my investigation, there is nevertheless much to discuss.

One of the puzzles not yet fully examined is Arthur's visit to the fountain. This visit is highly ambiguous. Arthur knows the fountain knight's grievance and yet he plans a pleasure trip to see the storm and marvels at the fountain. Even if the Dameisele Sauvage is his messenger (which must remain in doubt), his behaviour would seem to be as reprehensible as that of Yvain. The Dameisele Sauvage seems, in any case, to have misrepresented the king's plans, for the people of the fountain dominion believe that he is going to lay their country waste. When he arrives, he appears to be engaged in no more than rain-making, and the succeeding event is jousting between Yvain and Kay. Chrétien has overlooked the problems here. In the Welsh version, however, Arthur has never planned to undertake the adventure: Owein has been away for three years and the king misses him so much that he must find him or die (Jones & Jones, p. 170). Meanwhile, in Chrétien's plot, it is clear from Yvain's ritual of Kay's horse that Arthur's arrival at the fountain is important, in the same way that the vindication of Lunete at the fountain is important: the fountain expresses the dominion which is the object of the hero's thoughts, thoughts hedged about with a sense of treachery. Some pretext has to be found for getting the king there, and the Welsh version uses the well-known one that the king loves his lost knight and seeks him. Such a pretext has itself an important function in the plot, since the love of the king is necessary to the hero. Owein's absence for three years in this version, rather than a few days, provides a reason for the king's anxiety but creates problems elsewhere in the plot, to which I shall return. The pretext in Chrétien's plot has the virtue of providing a further pretext, one for Laudine's hasty marriage; perhaps, too, the pretext of the king's desiring the adventure provides a cover for the hero's own action. Arthur's visit to the fountain is emerging as highly logical at the magical level. The hero needs Arthur at the fountain, and he also needs the marriage to the Lady of the Fountain: the king's pleasure trip serves one of these purposes (by providing a friendly context for the king's recognition and affirmation of the hero's sovereignty) and the misinformation that the king intends war serves the other (it secures the marriage, and in such a way that it leads to, and justifies, the hero's appearance as fountain knight before the king).

The ritual of Kay's horse does not appear in the Welsh version. This version has a different emphasis, the king arriving in love and playing a different kind of crucial role, in which he ends the contest of equals (the fight between Owein and Gwalchmai) by affirming their own recognition that they are friends, not foes, and that neither is the winner: '"Give me your swords ... and then neither of you has vanquished the other"' (pp. 172–3). It is possible that this battle between Owein and Gwalchmai has been taken from that between Yvain and Gawain in Chrétien's added tale of the daughters of the Seigneur de la Noire Espine (vv. 5991–6383),[55] but what is important here is that it plays a role in the reconciliation which is so strong a feature in this version. Owein's declaration that he is Owein and lord of the fountain is made in conjunction with the offering of the victory to Gwalchmai, the giving of the swords to the king, who declares no one the winner, and the embraces: 'And Owein threw his arms around the emperor Arthur's neck, and they embraced. And with that his host came pressing and hurrying towards them to try and see Owein and embrace him, and very nearly were there dead men in that press' (p. 173). The contemptuous treatment of Cei is absent. Differences which appear great can prove small where variant treatments of a magical plot are concerned. The

differences here probably have much to do with the traditional Welsh treatment of Arthur and Cei. Both versions of
the meeting between the hero and the king at the fountain
are concerned with the declaration that there is no conflict
between them, combined with the recognition of the hero's
sovereignty by the king.

To turn now to the matter of Owein's absence for three
years, rather than a few days as in Chrétien, this provides a
good reason for Arthur's journey to the fountain, and a good
reason, too, for Owein's leave of absence from the fountain
dominion. The Welsh version appears rational where Chrétien's appears irrational, but the difference in the period of
time makes other aspects of the characters' behaviour
appear stranger. Owein's sending no messenger to his king
during his three years as fountain knight makes no sense at
all, especially in view of the affection between them portrayed in the text. Moreover, the denunciation of Owein
emerges as even more irrational. As fountain knight for three
years, he had used his battles at the fountain to bring ran-
som money into his dominion (pp. 169–70). His leave was to
be for three months, but he has stayed away three years.
Since Chrétien's Laudine sends a messenger soon after Yvain
exceeds the limit of his leave, we can expect the Welsh
countess — wife of three years and well served by her knight
— to send hers even more promptly. Instead, she does nothing for three years, and Owein, on his part, does not keep
in touch with the wife and dominion which had meant so
much to him. Then comes the denunciation. Owein is denounced as '"dwyllwr aghywir bradwr"' (ll. 569–70),[56]
meaning literally 'deceiver faithless traitor'; this accusation
is followed by a deadly insult, '"yr meuyl ar dy varyf"' (to
bring shame on thy beard).[57] At least, at this stage, Owein
might be expected to summon up some of his remarkable
determination and contemplate seeing his wife to sort the
matter out; he returns to her eventually, so why does he not
think of attempting to return to her now? He could find
some explanation for his extraordinary amnesia, and the
wife who had sent no inquiry in three years, and had been
too angry to find any other explanation than treachery,
might listen. The Welsh version, with its different periods of

time, makes questions raised by Chrétien's text yet more
pressing. The same magical plot will creak in different
places when used and developed by different authors.

Owein's response to the denunciation is to remember his
adventure and be sad; the next day, he makes for 'the
bounds of the world and desolate mountains' (pp. 173–4).
The Welsh version takes the form of a 'chwedl', that is, a
sophisticated literary development of the popular tale, many
characteristics of which it has retained,[58] and sometimes
this very fact helps to clarify features of the plot somewhat
obscured by the treatment of the authors of the other versions. A particularly good example is the Welsh version of
the madness in the woods. It does not include any elaborations as to how Owein lived there: we are told in a few lines
that he wandered there 'till his clothes perished, and till his
body was nigh perished, and till long hair grew all over his
body; and he would keep company with wild beasts and feed
with them till they were used to him' (p. 174). When he grew
so weak that he could not keep up with the wild beasts, he
came down from the mountains and 'made for a park, the
fairest in the world, and a widowed countess owned the
park'. This traditional treatment reveals the episode for
what it must be within the context of the magical plot
emerging: a ritual period in the wilderness.

In the Welsh version, the lady corresponding to the lady of
Noroison appears as a widow who was left with two earldoms, but now there is nothing left to her name except one
house ' "which the young earl who is her neighbour has not
taken, because she would not go to him as wife" ' (p. 175).
The Llanstephan MS. 58 version is clearer here: ' "a young
earl, a neighbour of hers, is taking them from her because
she would not marry him" '.[59] It makes excellent sense in the
magical plot that the Count Alier character should be a
suitor. The defeated earl returns to the countess the two
earldoms in return for his life, and in return for his liberty
he gives up 'the half of his own dominions, and the whole of
her silver and gold and her jewels, and sureties to that end'.
It seems, from what must be a corrupt text, that the countess
then offers Owein no more than a welcome, 'him and the
whole of his dominions' (p. 176), which Owein refuses. As

Owein has no dominions, this is a surprise. The Llanstephan
MS. 58 reading is, 'And the countess offered all those lands,
namely the two earldoms that the earl had taken from her,
to Owein, and Owein would not take them . . .'[60] Once again,
the Llanstephan writer may have clarified what the earlier
version intended (perhaps the scribe missed something out,
the dominions being not Owein's but those given up by the
earl). In any case, the Llanstephan MS.58 reading is the one
in accordance with Chrétien's text and with the magical
plot.

The Welsh treatment of the accusation against Lunete (pp.
177–8) is revealing. It has nothing to do with the countess,
and nor has it directly to do with 'Luned': Owein is accused
of being a traitor by two chamberlains, and Luned is in the
role of agent. The chamberlains call Owein a false traitor in
Luned's presence, and she responds that the two of them
could not contend against him alone. She is to die unless he
comes to defend her. The accusation — ' "dwyllwr
bradwr" '[61] — echoes the maiden's denunciation at Arthur's
court. This treatment makes quite clear the role of the battle
for Lunete in the plot — that it is to free the hero of the
charge of treason, not Lunete. It also presents the charge of
treason without any reference to the Lady of the Fountain,
giving us a chance to separate it from Owein's failure to
return. In the other versions, there is a total confusion of the
charge with Ywain's having exceeded the limit of his leave.

Owein's adventure corresponding to the Harpin adventure
(pp. 178–80) fits less well than in the other versions. The
giant does not seize any land and the daughter is to be killed
rather than appropriated by the giant. Owein, moreover, is
not offered any of the host's possessions. The most likely
explanation for the presence of such material here is that the
Welsh writer was indeed following Chrétien. The material
obviously plays no role in the magical plot, and I have never
come across an example of an intrusion like this in the final
move of a traditional magical plot. The Harpin episode
could have been added by Chrétien, who has added much to
the end of this plot, and who has, with many skilled touches,
integrated the episode — although not at the magical level.
It is much less likely that the Welsh writer added the epi-

sode to his *chwedl*: his version is about to end, with the end
of the magical plot, and an intrusion in the middle of the
climax is more of an intrusion than it is in Chrétien's leng-
thened plot. It is also easiest to accept that Chrétien added
the episode, in view of the inspiration he shows in his treatment of it, and that the Welsh writer followed him, his own
skilled responses to traditional material leading to his revealing in his treatment the lack of any relationship between the
episode and its magical context.

IV

It is now time to review the plot as a whole. I would see the
magical plot of Ywain as having four moves: the scene at
Arthur's court; Ywain's fountain adventure; the events between leaving the fountain dominion and leaving the lady of
Noroison, and, finally, the vindication of Lunete.

D. G. Mowatt has pointed out that there are parallels
between Guinevere, Laudine and the lady of Noroison.[62] I do
not myself see these parallels as being that they all run a
queen-centred, queen-dominated, barren and virtually king-
less court, and share strong views on how knights, Ywain in
particular, should behave, but these details have their relevance. An examination of Guinevere's role may help us to
understand the role of these queen-figures. In Chrétien's version, the first detail in the narrative is that the king leaves
the company for his own chamber, to the company's great
astonishment because he has never done this before on such
a feast-day; some are greatly displeased ('mout greva') and
make a great fuss about it ('mout grant parole an firent', vv.
44–5). The king also remains a long time in his chamber, for
the queen detains him, and he remains so long at her side
that he forgets himself and falls asleep:

> ... la reïne le detint,
> Si demora tant delez li,
> Qu'il s'oblia et andormi. (vv. 50–2)

Calogrenant, Yvain, Kay and three other knights are outside
the chamber door and Calogrenant begins his tale. The
queen joins them so stealthily that she suddenly appears

among them ('Se fu leissiee antre aus cheoir', v. 66), and
Calogrenant's seeing her, and rising first, rouses the scorn of
Kay: Kay says the queen must now assume that Calogrenant surpasses them all in courtesy and prowess (vv. 77–9).
The queen rebukes Kay and commands Calogrenant to tell
his tale to her. In this first move, in which Calogrenant's tale
is recounted, the queen is distinctly present and the king
distinctly absent, while it is in their court, and outside their
chamber door where they have been distinctly together, that
the magic formula for the fountain adventure is first re-
hearsed. The Welsh version gives us very little of this detail,
but Arthur retires to sleep and Gwenhwyfar remains present
for the tale. What the queen hears of the fountain adventure
is the adventurer's defeat at the hands of the fountain knight.
This first move seems to express a vision of the hero's desires
and how they might be achieved; and the hero also secures a
sense of the support of the king and queen. The king and
queen play roles similar to those of the host and daughter in
Calogrenant's tale, except that they primarily support the
adventure while the host and daughter support the knight
undertaking it. The queen rebukes Kay for mocking Yvain's
desire to undertake the adventure, and perhaps her words
about his babbling tongue are significant — that if it were
hers she would accuse it of treason ('"je l'apeleroie De
traïson, s'ele estoit moie"', vv. 625–6); the treason seems to
be firmly placed well away from the hero, and in the camp
of the unsupportive scorn. Then the king appears and, upon
hearing Calogrenant's tale from the queen, he sees it as an
adventure which must be undertaken; he will undertake it
himself for fun.

Then Yvain steals away from the court and seizes the
fountain dominion. His adventure forms a new move, and its
mood is quite distinct from the mood of the first move, as
tends to be the case with new moves. This move continues
up to the point of Yvain's departure from the Lady of the
Fountain, the explanation for this departure being found in
the denunciation, which must relate to the hero's feelings
about his action in the second move. The reason given in
Chrétien's narrative for Yvain's departure is Gawain's persuasion, which has no role in the magical plot beyond pro-

viding an excuse, but it may well be more than a rationalisation, having a role in Chrétien's themes. Tony Hunt, who
discusses such a role for Gawain's persuasion,[63] is particularly concerned with its specious nature. I would add that
Gawain's arguments suggesting that Yvain will degenerate
through inaction if he does not leave with him for the
tournaments, and that he will be suspected of jealousy if he
remains with his wife, have the flaw that they ignore Yvain's
marital role as defender of the fountain dominion. In the
Welsh version (which does not need special reasons for
Owein's departure with Arthur) the role of fountain knight is
a busy one, Owein having enriched the dominion with ran-
som money. The specious nature of Gawain's arguments
must largely be due to the difficulty of rationalising such a
departure as Yvain's, almost immediately upon his marriage
and assumption of the duties of defender of the dominion.

The new, third, move once again shows a change of mood.
The hero who confidently has his sovereignty affirmed by the
king in his second move, when he makes a ritual declaration
that he would never take anything belonging to the king, is
now a traitor and a thief. The charges in the denunciation
are connected with the lady, but they have nothing to do
with his failure to return: the content of the third and fourth
moves makes it plain that they are the reason for his departure in the first place. That the hero's guilt goes beyond the
fountain couple is suggested by a number of curious details:
the arrangements made to bring King Arthur to the fountain
and the content of the ritual performed before him; the
striking primal scene[64] presentation of the king and his
queen in the initial move, and Yvain's giving his king the
slip with such urgent secrecy and such a poor excuse for it
(we are told that he knows the king would give Kay or
Gawain the fountain battle rather than him, but there is no
reason why he should not make his request immediately for
the chance to avenge his cousin's shame, a desire the queen
has already heard him express). An understanding of the
structure of a magical plot is also a help in understanding
the hero's guilt: the moves are cycles of thought on the same
theme, the same characters reappearing in different guises
in each move. The hero feels that his thoughts are treacher-

ous and thieving because he sees sovereignty (whatever that may mean) as belonging to only one man — the king (whatever his being king may express).

The final two moves are steps in the hero's attempt to exorcise the theft and the treachery. First, he undergoes a ritual penance in the wilderness. Then he is restored through the use of a magic ointment; it is prepared by Morgan le Fay in Chrétien (not in *Owein*) and prescribed by the lady of Noroison — two queen-figures — and is lavishly used. Thus powerfully healed, the hero, using Count Alier, transforms the thief for ever, and also reverses the theft, the thief being sworn to restore the lady's damaged dominion to its previous state. In this action, the hero declares himself the champion of sovereign ladies against such theft, and the power of this move is increased by his final renunciation of the lady's offer of herself and her dominion. The beginning of a new, fourth, move can be identified by the hero's leaving the substitute scene of the Noroison dominion for the scene of his own action, the fountain dominion. Upon leaving the lady of Noroison he retraces his path ('se mist a la voie arriere', v. 3324) and eventually arrives at the fountain. On the way, he acquires his lion. Only in Chrétien's version of the rescue of the lion do we find an elaborate treatment of the dragon and lion as representatives of wickedness and various specific virtues: in the other versions, the strong mythical associations of dragons with evil and destructiveness, and of lions with courage, nobility and power, express all that is required for the magical plot. The hero frees the lion qualities from the grip of wickedness and makes them his devoted servants: they even become his identity, his name now being The Knight of the Lion. The lion is a powerful magical agent for the exorcism of the hero's sense of his wickedness. In this move, treachery is the particular crime to be removed, and the hero exorcises it through the use of Lunete, the agent of his rescue from punishment for the killing of the fountain knight, and the agent also of his marriage. The vindication of Lunete directly removes the hero's sense of his treachery in his seizing sovereignty. Undoubtedly, this final exorcism should bring about the hero's return to the Lady of the Fountain.

PART TWO

CHAPTER TWO

CHRÉTIEN'S PERCEVAL

The *Perceval* or *Conte du Graal* of Chrétien de Troyes[1] is the only text we have which can give us evidence as to the nature of the Grail story before it was Christianised. This evidence is imperfect as the work was left unfinished by Chrétien, and there is also Christian material in one episode towards the end of it. For reasons which will become apparent during the course of my discussion, I shall concentrate on Chrétien's narration of the Perceval story, up till just before the arrival of the Loathly Lady at Arthur's court. In further chapters, I shall discuss other versions of the Grail and Perceval stories for the light they can throw on the problems before us, and these chapters will be dependent on a reading of the present chapter on Chrétien's Grail story.

For the convenience of readers, I am presenting brief parallel outlines of the four plots to be investigated. In the case of Chrétien's *Perceval*, and the two famous versions based upon it, Wolfram von Eschenbach's *Parzival*[2] and the Welsh *Peredur*,[3] only the Perceval story proper, so far as Chrétien related it in the first half of his *Conte du Graal*, is given. In the case of the Middle English tail-rhyme romance *Sir Perceval of Galles*[4] — which lacks the Grail Castle — the complete story can be given in the same space. Where the versions are described as the same in brief outline, they are, of course, often different in detail, and, in my subsequent analyses, I find some of these differences significant. The line numbers, and the page numbers for translations, which are given in the outlines and also during my subsequent studies, refer to the texts cited in the notes. The line numbers given in the outline of Chrétien's *Perceval* refer to the T text of this romance, one of the fifteen surviving texts. I also refer to the A text during my discussion, and, whenever I do so, this is stated.

Chrétien's Perceval	Wolfram's Parzival
Perceval's father is dead, and his mother and he live apart from the world. The mother keeps him ignorant of deeds of arms to save his life, but he meets knights and set out for Arthur's court. The mother gives him advice and, after his departure, dies of grief. (vv. 69–634; pp. 2–7)	As in Chrétien, for all important detail. (ll. 116, 5–129, 17; pp. 70–6)
Perceval takes kisses, ring and food from a woman alone in a tent. She has been awakened from sleep by his arrival. Her jealous Proud Knight says she will be punished until he has taken his revenge. He wants Perceval's head. (vv. 635–833; pp. 8–10)	As in Chrétien, except that Parzival sees the woman asleep before she wakes and he is more violent. (ll. 129, 18–138, 1; pp. 76–80) In this version, the hero has his first meeting with Sigune at this point. She is mourning her lover, killed by the tent lady's husband. (ll. 138, 2–142, 2; pp. 80–2)
At Arthur's court, the Red Knight, who is contesting Arthur's land, has snatched the king's cup and spilt its contents over the queen. Perceval demands knighthood and the Red Knight's arms from the king and is mocked by Kay. A girl laughs, this being a prophecy that Perceval will be the finest knight. Kay strikes her and her fellow-prophet, the fool. Perceval kills the Red Knight and, taking his arms, leaves, sending the cup back to the king and a message back to the girl that he will avenge her. The king admires Perceval and is anxious for his safety. (v. 834–1304; pp. 10–15)	As in Chrétien, the chief difference in detail being that the Red Knight is a kinsman of the king and of Parzival, and a knight of some courtesy and friendliness towards Parzival. The court mourns him and the narrator says that Parzival will come to regret his deed. (ll. 145, 7–161, 8; pp. 83–91)

Welsh Peredur	English Sir Perceval
As in Chrétien, for all important detail. (pp. 183–5)	As in Chrétien for all important detail, except that the mother's advice appears as one tiny point, while she also gives Perceval a ring as a sign of recognition. She is no more than sad at her son's decision. (ll. 1–432)
As in Chrétien, except that the woman is not in bed but seated in a golden chair. She herself gives him the food, ring and kiss, and Peredur kneels for the kiss. (pp. 185–6)	Perceval takes food, a kiss and ring from a sleeping woman in a hall and leaves his mother's ring instead, on the woman's finger. (ll. 433–80)
As in Chrétien, the chief differences in detail being that Peredur does not see the king, and that a he and she-dwarf take the places of the laughing girl and the fool as prophets. The knight of the goblet does not wear red armour. (pp. 186–9)	At Arthur's court, Perceval's appearance reminds the king of his dead brother-in-law (Perceval's father), and he straightway loves the boorish youth. The Red Knight incidents are similar to those in Chrétien, except that Arthur arms Perceval. No special prophecy is spoken. After killing the Red Knight and taking his armour, Perceval scorns to return to court to be knighted, claiming that he is as great a lord as Arthur. (ll. 481–824)
	In this version, Perceval kills the witch mother of the Red Knight, who mistakes him for her son and says she can heal him. (ll. 825–68)

100   PART TWO

Chrétien's Perceval	Wolfram's Parzival
Perceval has one night of instruction in the knightly arts from an old man, Gorneman, who knights him and advises him. He does not stay longer because he is anxious to see his mother. (vv. 1305–698; pp. 15–19)	As in Chrétien, the chief differences being that Parzival stays a fortnight and Gurnemanz sees Parzival as a replacement for his three dead sons; he offers him his daughter. (ll. 161, 9–179, 12; pp. 91–99)
Travelling to find his mother, Perceval arrives at Beaurepaire, a castle besieged by its lady's suitor, Clamadeus. She is niece to Gorneman. She visits him in the night and tells him her plight: they must surrender tomorrow. Perceval finally defeats the suitor and sends him to Arthur, where he tells the king Perceval is the most valiant knight he has ever seen. Perceval takes leave of Blancheflor to find his mother, promising to return. (vv. 1699–2975; pp. 19–32)	As in Chrétien, the chief difference being that Parzival and the lady, Condwiramurs, marry. (IV; chapter 4)
Travelling to find his mother, Perceval cannot cross a river and spends the night at the Grail Castle. There he finds a wounded king who gives him a sword. Then a bleeding lance is borne through the hall, followed by a girl bearing a grail. Perceval receives warm hospitality from the king, but in the morning the castle has vanished. (vv. 2976–3421; pp. 32–7)	As in Chrétien, except that the Grail is a jacinth stone borne by a queen, and the lance is dripping with blood, not bleeding; lamentation accompanies its entrance. There is a great company of people and a great presence of women. The sword is presented last of all. (ll. 224, 1–249, 10; pp. 120–132)

Welsh Peredur	**English Sir Perceval**
Peredur spends a night at the court of a lame fisherman uncle who tests his prowess and advises him. The test is a fight with sticks and shields which proves Peredur will one day yield to none with a sword. (pp. 189–91)	An old knight entertains Perceval because he has killed his greatest enemy, the Red Knight. He does not instruct him, and Perceval leaves in the middle of the meal to rescue the Lady Lufamour of Maydenlande, who is besieged by a sultan lover. (ll. 869–1060)
In this version, the Grail Castle, followed by the meeting with the mourning female relative, comes next.	In this version, a scene at Arthur's court comes next. The king is distressed and anxious on Perceval's behalf and then he learns that Perceval is in Maydenlande. He goes there with three of his knights. (ll. 1061–124)
Then Peredur rescues the besieged lady, as in Chrétien, but there is no question of marriage to her. He establishes and settles her in her dominion. (pp. 194–7)	In Maydenlande, Perceval fights his way to the lady like a superman, and she thinks him worthy to govern and that he might win her in the field. Arthur witnesses Perceval's slaying of the sultan and his marriage to Lufamour. After a year, Perceval leaves to see his mother, feeling anxious about her. (ll. 1125–808)
Peredur spends a night at the court of a handsome uncle who tests his prowess by having him smite a column with a sword three times and then mend both column and sword. He fails to mend them the third time, but the uncle prophesies he will yield to none when his full strength is reached. Then a huge spear, with three streams of blood along it, is brought in, and a salver with a man's head	

Chrétien's Perceval	Wolfram's Parzival

Perceval meets his cousin, mourning over her lover, beheaded by the tent girl's knight. She is dismayed that he did not ask why the lance bled or who was served from the grail, for these questions would have healed the king (whom she calls the Fisher King) and restored his rule. She warns him that the sword he has been given will break. She also tells him his mother has died of grief on his account, and it is his sin against her which has caused his failure at the Grail Castle. (vv. 3422–690; pp. 37–40)

Parzival meets his cousin, Sigune, for the second time; she is now mourning for her lover embalmed in her arms. The conversation is much as in Chrétien, the chief difference being that Parzival should have asked one question only, inquiring about the king's suffering. Another difference is that it is not Sigune, but the hermit, later, who tells Parzival about his mother's death. (ll. 249, 11–255, 30; pp. 132–5)

Perceval meets the tent girl again. She is being punished by her jealous lover, while he seeks Perceval for his revenge. Perceval defeats him, exonerates the girl, and sends them to tell Arthur all that has happened. Arthur says Perceval's service to him since the defeat of the Red Knight has been so good that he is setting out in search of him at once. (vv. 3691–4143; pp. 40–5)

As in Chrétien, the chief difference being that Parzival swears the lady's innocence on holy relics in the hermit's cell. The ring is also returned to the knight, who puts it back on the lady's finger. (ll. 256, 1–279, 30; pp. 135–46)

Outside Arthur's camp, Perceval sees three drops of blood on the snow — those of a goose

As in Chrétien, the chief difference being that the knights have Arthur's permission to

Welsh Peredur	English Sir Perceval

on it, surrounded by blood.
There is lamentation. Peredur
takes his leave the next
morning. (pp. 191–2)

Peredur's foster-sister,
mourning over her dead
husband, tells him he is the
cause of his mother's death. She
also tells him the dwarfs are
those 'of thy father and thy
mother'. He overthrows the
killer of the husband and orders
him to marry the foster-sister,
before sending him to Arthur.
Arthur decides to search for
Peredur. (pp. 192–4)

Peredur meets the tent lady,
who is not having two nights
together in the same place until
her husband has his revenge on
Peredur. Peredur rescues her
from her plight by defeating the
knight and having him make it
known that she has been found
innocent. (p. 198)

In this version, the hero goes off,
at this point, with one of the
witches of Caer Loyw to be
trained in knighthood. (pp. 198–
9)

As in Chrétien, except that the
disturbances of Peredur's
musings are cruder. Twenty-

Perceval meets the woman from
whom he stole a kiss and a ring,
tied to a tree because her lover,
the Black Knight, judges her
faithless. Her ring prevents
death or hurt for the wearer. He
defeats the Black Knight and
exonerates her, but he cannot
exchange rings because the
Black Knight has given his
mother's ring to the lord of the
land, a giant brother of the
sultan. (ll. 1809–2004)

Perceval slays the giant and the
ring flies out of the treasure
chest. The porter explains that

Chrétien's Perceval	Wolfram's Parzival
wounded by a falcon and since flown off. This reminds him of his beloved's face, and he muses for a long time. In this state of mind he is assailed by knights seeking to bring him to Arthur. The second assailant, Kay, is wounded. Gawain seeks out Perceval courteously, jeered at by Kay, and Perceval learns from him that he has wounded Kay. He declares that he has therefore avenged the girl who laughed, and this is when Gawain realises that he is the knight the king is seeking. Perceval is acclaimed, and the king says the prophecies are fulfilled. (vv. 4144–602; pp. 45–50)	fight the musing Parzival as an impudent interloper. Much space is given to Parzival's musings over his love and to a description of the court's admiration of the hero. (ll. 280, 1–312, 1; pp. 147–162)

This text presents fewer obvious problems of the kind I have been investigating, but the following questions, which may seem, on the face of it, inappropriate, point to there being inconsistencies and unexpected, inexplicable details, of the kind found in *Yvain*.

1. There is some conflict between Chrétien's treatment of the scene where the mother gives her parting advice and his treatment of the scene with the woman in the tent. The mother gives advice about her son's relations with women, the latter part of which is oddly particular from a woman about to die of grief, but it is otherwise consistent with her role in the plot. She says to him, ' "... if you should desire the love of any, take care that you don't annoy her by doing anything to displease her. And a maid who kisses gives much; so if she consents to kiss you, I forbid you to take more: for love of me, leave with the kiss" ' (p. 7). She goes

Welsh Peredur	English Sir Perceval
four knights follow the initial knight, before Cei does, and each strikes Peredur when he does not answer his questions. (pp. 199–202)	the giant was in love with Perceval's mother and offered her the ring; she assumed her son was dead and went mad with grief. Perceval leaves off his armour and walks in goat-skins to find her. He finds her by a well and she recognises him. When she is recovered he takes her to his bride. (ll. 2005–288)

on, ' "But if she has a ring on her finger or a purse at her waist, and for love or through your pleas she should give it to you, then in my eyes it would be fine and good that you should take her ring; yes, I give you leave to take the ring and purse" ' (p. 7):

'Mais s'ele a anel en son doi
Ne a sa corroie almosniere,
Se par amor ou par proiere
Le vos done, bon m'ert et bel
Que vos em portez son anel.
De l'anel prendre vos doinz gié
Et de l'aumosniere congié.' (vv. 550–6)

Perceval's interpretation of this advice is attributed by Chrétien to boyish crudity and confusion: his mother tells him he should visit churches to pray and, in his ignorance,

he enters a beautiful tent to pray to God for food. While
there, he forces himself on a woman and steals her ring. It is
too much to accept that this behaviour arises from a misunderstanding, in the way Chrétien suggests. While we are
told earlier in this scene that Perceval hears very little of
what his mother is saying to him about the fate of his father
and brothers, he does pay attention to some of his mother's
advice on behaviour. He asks questions ('"... what is a
church? ... what is a minster?"') when she advises him to
pray, a few lines below the above quoted lines, and he also
obeys the instruction she gives immediately following her
counsel on taking a ring or purse, that he should ask the
name of anyone he shares company with; he obeys this to
the letter when he meets Gorneman, proudly adding that it
was his mother who advised him. It is therefore inexplicable
that he says to the girl in the tent that he will not go away,
'"No, by my life! I'm going to kiss you! ... I don't care who
it upsets, for my mother told me to!"' (p. 8).

— 'Ains vos baiserai, par mon chief,
   Fait li vallés, cui qu'il soit grief,
   Que ma mere le m'ensaigna.' (vv. 693–5)

The girl refuses to kiss him but he forces her: he lays her
down full-length beneath him, while she struggles with all
her might, and kisses her seven times (in the T text; twenty
times in the A text, v. 707). Afterwards he takes her ring by
force, even though she weeps and says she will be sorely
treated for it. She has already told him she has a lover.
It is impossible that the boy can have misunderstood his
mother to this extent. And why does he steal the ring? No
explanation is offered, apart from his misunderstanding of
his mother.
    In his introduction to his translation of Chrétien's Perceval,
Nigel Bryant points out that 'In the early episodes of the
romance Chrétien skilfully exploits the comic potential of
[Perceval's] ignorance; but there is at the same time something deliberately unsettling in Chrétien's depiction of the
innocent leaving his mother collapsed in a heap outside her
house, almost assaulting a girl to take her ring, and killing a
knight to get his arms. It becomes hard to distinguish between the innocent and the primitive.'[5]

2. The scene at Arthur's court, where the king is sitting silent at the head of the table, in grief and anger, while his knights are all laughing and joking, needs a full explanation and development. The shameless behaviour of the knights does not square with the treatment of them elsewhere in the text. The king and queen have just been insulted: the Red Knight has snatched the king's cup so recklessly that he has poured the whole cupful of wine over the queen. The queen has become suicidal with anger ('"ele s'ocist"', v. 965). The Red Knight is, moreover, King Arthur's greatest enemy ('"li pire anemis que j'aie"', v. 945) who has now contested his land ('"M'a chi ma terre contredite"', v. 947). The entire scene is, of course, extraordinary: the Red Knight is not presented as supernatural (he is killed by Perceval), so how can he, single-handed, be such a threat to a king, and why is the king so cowed by him? But the questions which point to inconsistency and inexplicable behaviour are the most useful questions here: the strange inaction of Arthur's knights may have its explanation at a level beyond the reach of Chrétien's chivalric treatment.

3. Why does Perceval postpone avenging the laughing girl? Helen Adolf also asks this question: '... it does not make much sense that Perceval, having won the Red Knight's armor and considering himself a knight, does not come back immediately to chastise' Kay.[6] (She suggests that this is because Chrétien joined together two independent branches of the Great Fool story — the Red Knight tale and the Laughing Damsel tale, the latter story determining that Perceval must become a knight and prove his valour before he might come home and punish Kay.) Perceval has Clamadeus (the vanquished suitor at Beaurepaire) promise to tell the laughing girl that he, Perceval, longs to avenge her if God gives him strength (' ... il le vengera son woel ... Se Diex force l'en velt doner', vv. 2697, 99). However, God has given him the strength to defeat Clamadeus and the invincible Red Knight. Later, Perceval commands the Proud Knight of the Heath (l'Orguelleus de la Lande, the tent girl's lover) to tell the girl he, Perceval, will never, on any account, enter any court King Arthur holds until he has avenged her ('"... Que ja n'enterrai por nul plait En cort que li rois Artus ait, Tant que je l'arai si vengiee ..."', vv. 3977–9).

The best way of meeting Kay is to go to court, where he will
have no difficulty in avenging the girl. His eventual revenge
is somewhat inconsequential, being incognito on the part of
both knights and also being in response to further misbe-
haviour on the part of Kay — this time directly against
Perceval himself, rather than against the girl who is now
declared avenged ('"Dont ai je bien, ce quit, loëe La pucele
que il feri"', vv. 4476–7).

4. Why should King Arthur be quite so 'worked up' about
Perceval? He grieves, fears for his safety, longs for news and
takes his court on a journey searching for him (pp. 15, 31,
45; vv. 1301–2, 2823–6, 4136–9). Perceval's killing the Red
Knight is the given reason, but the danger of the Red Knight
is a matter also insufficiently explained. Perceval has, in any
case, killed the Red Knight in order himself to become a red
knight (vv. 996–99; 1134–5): he does not care a jot ('. . . ne
prise une chive . . .', v. 968) about the king's suffering. His
being handsome and fair ('bel et . . . gent', v. 978) is a scarcely convincing explanation for the attraction to a visitor so
lacking in the social graces. Chrétien's humorous treatment
seeks to bestow a youthful appeal upon Perceval, but a
temperate response on Arthur's part still seems to be the
response from the king which would be in accordance with
other detail in the text: we would expect the gentle king to
be glad of the lad's services and content to see no more of
him than would be necessary if he became one of his
knights.

5. Perceval and his cousin discuss his stay at the Grail
Castle at length, while the cousin sits holding her newly
beheaded lover in her arms. Chrétien's treatment of her
seems curiously divided. He devotes thirty lines to her grief
(vv. 3430–60) and she is still absorbed in it when Perceval
arrives and asks her who killed the knight lying in her lap.
She answers,

> — 'Biax sire, uns chevaliers l'ocist,
> . . . hui cest matin.
> Mais molt me merveil de grant fin . . .' (vv. 3464–6)

'"Good sir . . . a knight killed him, this very morning. But
there's something that quite amazes me"' (p. 37) — and she

immediately turns the subject to the fresh appearance of
Perceval and his horse, who seem to have had a comfortable
and restful night; the subject of conversation then remains
Perceval's Grail Castle adventure, the newly beheaded lover's fate and loss postponed until line 3628.

6. Helen Adolf rightly points out that 'it is quite incredible that when [Perceval] finally returns to court in his red
armor, he is not recognised by anybody though all have been
searching for him'.[7] In the English tail-rhyme *Sir Perceval*,
Sir Gawain realises that the knight in red will either be
Perceval who slew the Red Knight or another who has slain
Perceval (ll. 1433–60).

Chrétien has used a plot containing some extraordinary
situations. In the case of the Fisher King, we are presented
with a king who suffers over a long period from both loss of
health and loss of land and does no more about it than wait
for one particular character to help on his own initiative.
The questions which might be asked here do not point so
sharply to inconsistencies and inexplicable behaviour on the
part of the characters, as do my questions 1 to 6; they do
not, therefore, draw attention to the possibility that Chrétien
has used a plot taking a quite different course from his own
concerns in using the material (a course which he would
have re-created but not acquired control of as a conscious
artist). Chrétien has undoubtedly used the Fisher King as
magical material for his theme of Perceval's education in
knighthood. There are, however, small problems of an interesting kind, which I shall glance at here.

The suffering of the Fisher King seems a problem, though
a minor one, as material for Chrétien's chivalric themes: the
king can be restored to health and rule by two apparently
easy questions which have not been asked by any character,
and yet, at the same time, we are to understand that Perceval is in training to become a member of a chivalrous society.
Chrétien's themes seem to come into conflict with another
scheme, within which it makes sense that the king's suffering should be the concern of Perceval alone. If there were not
a concerted scheme of this kind, in which Chrétien was
involved, he would perhaps have addressed this matter in

some way, however unsatisfactorily; as it is, he does not address it at all. The problem is not obtrusive, but gaps in the author's moral treatment can be an indication of the presence of a magical plot, since a magical plot has the power to divert the author's attention away from moral themes — which could not, in any case, alter it profoundly. A magical plot contains no vision, moral or otherwise, which involves all the characters as subjects: only the hero or heroine is a subject (appearing in the plot as the chief character, and perhaps a few others), and all the characters are figments of his or her thought.

Chrétien's treatment of the Grail episode gives it a dream-like atmosphere. David C. Fowler argues that Chrétien intends the castle to be an apparition: he has both the Fisher King and Perceval's cousin suggest that Perceval's journey has been much longer than he thinks it has, and it is some time before Perceval is able to see the castle; at first he can see nothing but sky and earth (vv. 3035–49).[8] However, I would point out that Perceval's cousin speaks of the Fisher King's residence as more solid than an apparition. She says of the crippled sportsman, ' "That's why he likes to live in this house just here; for in all the world he could never find a retreat so suited to his needs, and he's had a house built befitting a rich king" ' (p. 38):

'Et por che li plaist converser
En cest repaire ci alués,
Qu'en tot le mont a oés son oés
Ne puet trover meillor repaire,
Et si a fait teus maisons faire
Come il covient a riche roi.' (vv. 3528–33)

There seems to be an inconsistency in the treatment here, of a type I often come across where an author has used and developed a magical plot. Chrétien seems to jump from one kind of rationalisation to another, contradictory, kind. His treatment of the castle as an apparition may be a response to the mystery in the adventure, this mystery arising entirely from the magical nature of the material and its inscrutability to the rational mind, while his different treatment in the following scene with the cousin may be due to a desire for explanations and some development of the king's situation, prompted by the tantalising absence of such elucidation in the magical material. There is another interesting contrast between, on the one hand, Chrétien's characterisation in his treatment of Perceval's gaucherie in the castle (the king's apology for not being able to rise to greet him is met with Perceval's '"... may God give me joy and health, it doesn't upset me at all"', p. 34; '"... qu'il ne me grieve point, Se Diex joie et santé me doint"', vv. 3111–12) and, on the other hand, Chrétien's dreamlike king who says nothing about his knowing Perceval, even while he distinguishes him as the one for whom the precious sword has been destined. This could well be part of the author's design for a magical castle where Perceval is to be tested, but in the light of what seems to be emerging about the nature of the plot, it can be suspected that such effects are the result of partial transformation of magical material, the author's development of character being in part rather than comprehensive.

It seems likely from the questions raised by the text that here we have a magical plot, one left by Chrétien in full magical operation. A plot can only be magical if it has a complete sequence of moves (interrupted or not by the author's additional work). Here, in the case of the plot of an unfinished work, it will be much more difficult to ascertain whether the author is re-creating a magical structure. However, the questions raised by this plot, and Chrétien's treatment in relation to the problems, suggest that this is a magical plot, one not eclipsed by Chrétien's transforming work but given an overlay, this overlay including chivalric material, superficial rationalisations, some development of character and some sensuous treatment of detail. I shall now investigate the plot, with the use of my model, to see if this is the case.

If the plot is magical, the hero's first adventure (with the tent girl) will relate closely to the situation in the initial move, where the hero has placed himself alone in a remote home with the mother, the father dead. The explanation for the conflict in Chrétien's treatment of the two scenes will have to do with his re-creation of the magical relationship, and his simultaneous rationalising treatment. The most like-

ly explanation for the mother's advising Perceval as she does
would be that there is a connection between the hero's desires in the initial move and those in the move with the tent
girl: he would therefore have the mother speak of them and
— most important — give them sanction. The absence of the
mother's point of view — except where the author has super-
ficially introduced it with some touches of maternal wisdom
— would explain the incongruous character of some of her
advice, incongruous as the preoccupation of someone about
to die of grief. In his treatment, the author would be prompted by his material to provide motives accessible to our
rational minds for both the mother's advice and the son's
behaviour, developing the mother's role as adviser to her son
and seeking to explain the son's behaviour as due to a misunderstanding. Such rationalising development would be
superficial only, leaving the magical material intact, and the
juxtaposition of the irrational and rationalisations produces
even stranger effects than the irrational alone produces.

If the plot is magical, the strange events connected with
the Red Knight and King Arthur make good sense. The
absence of the point of view of Arthur and his knights, and
presence only of the hero's, explain all the extraordinary
events at the court, whatever they may mean precisely. A
similarity between the Red Knight and Perceval can be seen.
Both barge into Arthur's court with the utmost rudeness to
make their demands: the Red Knight 'snatched the king's
cup so recklessly that he poured the whole cupful of wine
over the queen' (p. 11) —

> Et si folement l'en leva
> Que sor la roïne versa
> Tot le vin dont ele estoit plaine. (vv. 959–61)

— and Perceval, on horseback, 'pulled his mount so near the
king, like the rude soul that he was, that — I tell no lie — he
sent the king's hat flying from his head to the table' (p. 11):

> Mais si pres del roi l'ot mené,
> A guise d'ome mal sené,
> Que devant lui, sanz nule fable,
> Li abati desor la table
> Del chief un chapel de bonet. (vv. 933–7)

The demand made by Perceval — to be made a knight — is
not the behaviour of a thief, whereas the Red Knight's demand for the king's land and his seizing of the cup are, but it
is important, here, to recall that Perceval has stolen kisses
and a ring off someone else's woman, so he too is a thief
when he arrives at Arthur's court. Perceval and the Red
Knight are in the same business. Arthur tells Perceval that
the Red Knight is '"mad enough to claim that he'll have [all
Arthur's land] unconditionally, whether [Arthur] likes it or
not"' (p. 11):

'... M'a chi ma terre contredite;
Et tant est fols que tote quite
Dist qu'il l'avra, ou weille ou non.' (vv. 947–9)

Perceval similarly lays claim to the kisses and the ring,
whether the tent girl likes it or not: '... but she fought in
vain, for whether she liked it or not the boy kissed her seven
times in a row' (p. 8):

Mais desfense mestier n'i ot,
Que li valleś en un randon
Le baisa, volsist ele ou non,
Set fois ... (vv. 706–9)

Chrétien treats Perceval as a charmingly artless bumpkin.
Perceval greets the tent girl with, '"I give you greeting, girl,
as my mother taught me to do. She told me I should greet
girls whenever I met them"' (p. 8):

'... Pucele, je vos salu,
Si com ma mere le m'aprist.
Ma mere m'ensaigna et dist
Que les puceles saluaisse
En quel que liu que jes trovaisse.' (vv. 682–6)

At Arthur's court, he says, '"Make me a knight, lord king ...
for I want to go"' (p. 11); '"Faites moi chevalier ... Sire
rois, car aler m'en weil"' (vv. 972–3). This treatment gives
additional pleasure to the narrative, but, at a magical level,
a hero's presenting himself as simple and rustic can be a
device for both the expression and disguise of his feelings: as
a fool and bumpkin he can act out aggressions without being
condemned or suspected. Chrétien's treatment could be a

faithful development of material in a magical plot, where
the hero seeks to present himself as a lovable, untaught
youth whose behaviour can be excused and understood on
these grounds.

If this is a magical plot, it is important that only the Red
Knight steals from King Arthur: Perceval rescues Arthur
from the thief. Why should one thief rescue Arthur from
another? The answer might lie in what he gets out of doing
so, but an examination of the scene reveals that the hero is
up to a number of things at once at Arthur's court. He seems
to be engaged in becoming the Red Knight, the thief of the
king's property. At the same time, he is engaged in making
himself a knight and a greater one than any of the Round
Table, none of whom can defeat the Red Knight. Furthermore, in killing the king's enemy he arranges to receive
the king's love as well as his admiration. If this is a magical
plot, in removing the thief of the king's property the hero
will remove the idea that there is a thief about the place and
establish himself as the remover of the thief rather than a
thief. He does not steal at Arthur's court, although he makes
himself the Red Knight. ' "Good lord king," said the boy,
" ... I shan't be a knight for long without being a red knight.
Grant me the arms of the one who took your cup of gold
... " ' (p. 12):

'... Fait li vallés, biax sire rois,
Ne serai chevaliers des mois,
Se chevaliers vermeus ne sui.
Donez moi les armes celui
Qui vostre colpe d'or em porte ...' (vv. 995–1000)

When he dons the Red Knight's arms, he sends the cup of
gold back to the king.

What is the significance of the theft of the cup? Helen
Adolf argues that there is plenty of evidence to show that the
rape of a cup is synonymous with the rape of a maiden.[9] She
draws attention to significant lines in the *Elucidation* (a
prologue of 484 verses prefixed to one extant manuscript —
Mons, known as the P text — and others now lost):

[King Amangons] Des puceles une esforcha,
Sor son pois le despucela

Et la coupe d'or li toli,
Si l'emporta ensamble od li
Puis s'en fist tot adiés servir ...

[King Amangons] did violence to one of the maidens,
Against her will he violated her
And took away from her the gold cup
And carried it off with him,
Then he caused himself to be served out of it ...

Helen Adolf concludes that 'the Red Knight in the *Conte del Graal*, *Syr Percyvel* and *Parzival* was no better than King Amangons in the *Elucidation*, for it is he who must have abducted the Queen'. She agrees with Arthur C. L. Brown, who states that originally the Red Knight carried off the queen,[10] and she gives as supportive evidence the absence of the queen when Perceval first enters the hall, and her excessive anger at the spilt wine. Glenys Goetinck says that liquid — wine, water or ale — is a symbol of sovereignty, and to steal the cup of wine would be the equivalent of stealing the kingdom. A kingdom was also conceived of as a woman, or it was personified by the queen, and liquid was often an important factor in the ritual surrounding the union between king and goddess. This may explain the spilling of the wine on Guinevere. Dr Goetinck also points out that Guinevere was often the subject of abduction stories.[11] (It should perhaps be noted that Arthur's queen is not actually called 'Guinevere' in *Perceval*.)

Another important event occurs at Arthur's court: the laughing girl and the fool prophesy that Perceval will be the finest knight ever known and finer than all those to come. For this, Kay strikes them. Why does Perceval not return to court to collect the knighthood promised by the king and avenge the laughing girl immediately, rather than say he will avenge her, if he can, before he dies? If this is a magical plot, the reason will be that the hero feels no need to do either. He will not desire Arthur's knighthood, since he will want the Red Knighthood, a rather different knighthood which he will use for his subsequent adventures. He also will not really be interested in avenging the laughing girl: his real concern, hidden behind this chivalrous vengeance, will

be the vindication of the prophecy that he will be the finest
knight. The girl will be no more than an agent for proclaiming him the finest knight, and, equally, Kay will be no more
than an agent for expressing the disagreement with this
which the hero is to prove wrong. The hero will already have
proved the laughing girl right, and Kay wrong, by defeating
the Red Knight, who has defeated Kay and all the other
knights of the Round Table: thus a vindication using the
chastisement of Kay will be superfluous.

If this is a magical plot, far from feeling the need for
vengeance, the hero will have business to get on with as the
Red Knight, a Red Knight enjoying the love and admiration
of the king; this will be a Red Knight who has proclaimed
that he is not threatening the king. He will have removed the
threat by returning the king's cup. If we have a magical plot
here, there will no longer be any difficulty in understanding
the king's extraordinary love for Perceval: it will have been
arranged by the hero himself.

The model of the magical plot seems useful enough for this
discussion to continue as if it were certain that we have a
magical plot before us. In the hero's next move, Gorneman
performs the service Arthur would have performed had
Perceval returned to court: he gives Perceval instruction,
admires him, loves him and knights him. Affirmation of the
hero seems to be the fundamental, magical function of
Gorneman. He does not train the hero so much as test him:
Perceval has only a few hours with him and in that time it
all comes naturally to him — 'Car il li venoit de nature' (T
text, v. 1480; A text, v. 1476) — and Gorneman 'said to
himself that if the boy had spent his whole life working and
engaged in arms this would still have seemed a fine display'
(p. 17):

> Et si disoit en son corage
> Que s'il se fust tot son eage
> D'armes penez et entremis,
> S'en fust il assez bien apris. (vv. 1487–90)

Gorneman also gives advice to Perceval. He repeats the
mother's advice about aiding those in distress and going to
church, and he also advises him to spare opponents who beg

for mercy and to beware of talking too much. These last two pieces of advice, like the two former, are related to Chrétien's imaginative overlay: sparing opponents is chivalrous but it also gives a rational explanation as to why Perceval always sends his defeated opponents to Arthur; meanwhile, the advice about talking too much is likely to prove a rationalisation in preparation for Perceval's not asking the questions in the Grail Castle.

Perceval sets out to find his mother, feeling anxious about her, and arrives at Beaurepaire castle, the home of Gorneman's niece. The situation of this young woman (which Gorneman does not mention) is that she is in charge of a castle and its knights, and they have been killed or made captive in the struggle to prevent her being married to a suitor who has besieged her castle for an entire winter and summer. The pattern of the action in this adventure with a woman is similar to that in the move at Arthur's court: the hero engages in the double action of winning the woman and her dominion while, at the same time, proving himself a remover of snatchers rather than one himself. Meanwhile, the snatcher is sent to King Arthur to tell him he has been overcome by the hero, and the king's love for the hero is reaffirmed as part of the ritual enabling the adventure at Beaurepaire. More important than winning the woman herself, the hero wins sovereignty in this move: he is 'the one who had fought [Clamadeus] for the land and for the beautiful girl ...' (p. 32; '... cil qui avoit desraisnie Vers lui la terre et la pucele ... bele', vv. 2910–12); 'The land would now have been his, entirely and undisputed, had his heart not been elsewhere' ('si fust soie toute quite La terre, se il li pleüst Que son corage aillors n'eüst', vv. 2914–16). Perceval's heart is with his mother ('de sa mere au cuer li tient', v. 2918) and he leaves without marrying Blancheflor, saying that this is because he wishes to see his mother; he promises to return. This Beaurepaire move is considerably developed and transformed by Chrétien: in particular, the relationship between the lovers is given courtly treatment.

Next, the hero transfers himself to the Grail Castle. At least, this is what I am going to assume for the purpose of this present exercise. It does seem that the Grail Castle will

prove to be an integral move in the magical plot which is
emerging, because it does, in important ways, fit into the
pattern of the moves. There is a distinct relationship with
the move at Arthur's court: in both cases, the king is wounded yet very kind to Perceval, and Perceval is, it seems, in-
sensitive to his suffering. Moreover, just as Arthur's court
follows upon the adventure with the tent girl, so the Grail
Castle follows the adventure with Blancheflor.

Perceval leaves Blancheflor, thinking of his mother, and
arrives at the Grail Castle. Here he finds an old and wounded king, who not only shows him great hospitality but also
distinguishes him by bestowing upon him a precious and
significant sword. Not only is the wounded king reminiscent
of Arthur but also of Perceval's father. Perceval's father was
'"par mi les janbes navrez"' (v. 434, A text) or '"parmi la
jambe navrez"' (v. 436, T text), and the Fisher King is
wounded '"par mi les hanches amedos"' (v. 3499, A text) or
'"Parmi les quisses ambesdeus"' (v. 3513, T text). There is a
suggestion that the wound is sexual (castration?), and Wolfram has his hermit tell Parzival that the king is wounded
through the testicles ('"durch die heidruose sîn"', l. 479,
12). Arthur's wound is not physical, but it is immediately
connected with the Red Knight's snatching of his cup. This
wounded, suffering king is central to the move at the Grail
Castle.

The first event in the castle is the presentation of the
sword. I will give the entire detail here, for the discussion
immediately to follow and for the fuller discussion to come
later in this chapter.

Que que il parloient ensi,
Un[s] vallés entre par la por[t]e
De la maison et si aporte
Une espee a son col pendue,
Si l'a al riche home rendue.
Et il l'a bien demie traite,
Si vit bien ou ele fu faite,
Car en l'espee estoit escrit.
Et avec che encore i vit
Qu'ele estoit de si bon achier
Que ja ne porroit depechier,

Fors que par un tot seul peril
Que nus ne savoit fors que cil
Qui l'avoit forgie et tempree.
Li vallés qui l'ot aportee
Dist: 'Sire, la sore pucele,
Vostre niece qui tant est bele,
Vos a envoié cest present;
Ainc ne veïstes mais plus gent
De lonc ne de le que ele a.
Vos le donrez cui vos plaira,
Mais ma dame seroit molt lie
Se ele estoit bien emploïe
La ou ele sera donee.
Onques cil qui forga l'espee
N'en fist que trois, et si morra
Que jamais plus n'en forgera
Espee nule enprés cesti.'
Tantost li sire en ravesti
Celui qui laiens ert estranges
De cele espee par les ranges,
Qui valoient un grant tresor.
Li pons de l'espee estoit d'or,
Del meillor d'Arrabe ou de Grisce,
Li fuerres d'orfrois de Venisce.
Si richement appareillie
L'a li sire au vallet baillie,
Et dist: 'Biax frere, ceste espee
Vos fu voëe et destinee,
Et je weil molt que vos l'aiez;
Mais çainniez le, si le traiez.'
Cil l'en merchie, si le chaint
Einsi que pas ne s'en estraint,
Puis l'a traite del fuerre nue;
Et quant il l'ot un poi veüe,
Si le remist el fuerre arriere.
Et sachiez que de grant maniere
Li sist au flanc et miex el poing,
Et sambla bien que al besoing
S'en deüst aidier come ber. (vv. 3130–79)

While they were talking thus, a boy came in through the door; he
was carrying a sword hung round his neck, and presented it to the
nobleman. He drew it half out of its scabbard, and saw clearly
where it was made, for it was written on the sword. And he also

learned from the writing that it was of such fine steel that there
was only one way it could ever be broken, which no-one knew
except the one who had forged and tempered it. The boy who had
brought it to him said:

'Sir, the beautiful fair-haired girl, your niece, has sent you this
present; you never saw a finer sword as long and as broad as this.
You may give it to whoever you like, but my lady would be most
happy if it were put to good use where it's bestowed. The one who
forged the sword has only ever made three, and he's about to die, so
this is the last he'll ever make.'

And straight away the lord girded his guest with the sword by its
straps, which themselves were worth a fortune. The sword's pom-
mel was made of the finest gold of Arabia or Greece, and the
scabbard was of golden thread from Venice. With all its rich de-
coration, the lord presented it to the boy and said:

'Good brother, this sword was intended and destined for you, and
I very much want you to have it; come, gird it on and draw it.'

The boy thanked him, and girded it on so that it was not restricting, and then drew it, naked, from the scabbard; and after gazing at
it for a while, he slid it back into the sheath. And truly, it lay
splendidly at his side, and even better in his hand, and it seemed
indeed that in time of need he would wield it like a man of valour.
(pp. 34–5)

Later, Perceval's cousin says to him:

> 'Mais ou fu cele espee prise
> Qui vos pent a[u] senestre flanc,
> Qui unques d'ome ne traist sanc
> N'onques ne fu a besoig traite?
> Je sai bien ou ele fu faite
> Et si sai bien qui le forja.
> Gardez ne vos i fïez ja,
> Qu'ele vos traïra sanz faille
> Quant vos venrez en grant bataille,
> K'ele vos volera en pieces.' (vv. 3654–63)

'But where did you get that sword that hangs at your left side,
which has never spilled a man's blood and has never had occasion
to be drawn? I know very well where it was made and I know very
well who forged it. Beware! Don't ever put your trust in it. It'll
betray you, I promise you, when you find yourself in a great battle,
for it'll fly into pieces.' (p. 40)

Helen Adolf makes some important points about this sword.
'A sword . . . may be a symbol of its bearer . . . Therefore . . .

the Grail sword, which had never been used and is destined
to break once in battle, stands for the youthful hero to whom
it is given and who will once experience failure.'[12] However,
she says, there is some discrepancy about the gift of this
sword which has never spilt a man's blood ('"Qui unques
d'ome ne traist sanc"', v. 3656) to Perceval, who has spilt
many men's blood.[13] She also points out that the sword
drops completely out of the story.[14] It is important to note
that '"The one who forged the sword has only ever made
three, and he's about to die, so this is the last he'll ever
make"' (p. 34). The Fisher King's niece has sent him the
sword to bestow on whomever he likes, provided it is put to
good use. The king tells Perceval it '"was intended and
destined"' for him (p. 34). It is clear that the presentation of
the sword expresses the king's recognition of Perceval: he
knows who he is and he regards him worthy of this unique
weapon. It is possible that there is a recognition of sonship
by the king and also by the mysterious niece; the three
swords of Triboet (or Trebuchet) the smith echo the three
sons of Perceval's father, of whom Perceval is the third. Why
is the sword unused in battle and — to point out another
discrepancy – how can the sword bestowed on Perceval by
the kindly Fisher King, with such ceremony, be untrustworthy?

The next event in the Grail Castle is the appearance of the
bleeding lance.

> Que qu'il parloient d'un et d'el,
> Uns vallés d'un[e] chambre vint,
> Qui une blanche lance tint
> Empoignie par le mileu,
> Si passa par entre le feu
> Et cels qui el lit se seoient.
> Et tot cil de laiens veoient
> Le lance blanche et le fer blanc,
> S'issoit une goute de sanc
> Del fer de la lance en somet,
> Et jusqu'a a la main au vallet
> Coloit cele goute vermeille.
> Li vallés voit cele merveille
> Qui la nuit ert laiens venus,
> Si s'est de demander tenus
> Coment ceste chose avenoit ... (vv. 3190–205)

While they were talking of one thing and another, a boy came from
a chamber clutching a white lance by the middle of the shaft, and
passed between the fire and the two who were sitting on the bed.
Everyone in the hall saw the white lance with its white head; and a
drop of blood issued from the tip of the lance's head, and right
down to the boy's hand this red drop ran. The lord's guest gazed at
this marvel that had appeared there that night, but restrained
himself from asking how it came to be ... (p. 35)

Helen Adolf points out that a bleeding lance stands for a
wounded man,[15] and she adds that ' ... a bleeding lance,
which is carried around, reminds those who are present of
the bleeding warrior'.[16] David C. Fowler identifies the lance
with Perceval's father or the Fisher King and sees it as
having bled since Cain slew Abel.[17] L. T. Topsfield says the
lance contains within itself the suggestion of destruction and
of spiritual revelation and enlightenment.[18] Norris J. Lacy
sees an analogy between the bleeding lance and the weapon
that has injured the Fisher King.[19] There is no Christian
explanation of the lance in Chrétien: it is the First Continuator of the *Conte du Graal* who gives it the Christian
explanation that it is the lance of Longinus, a relic of the
Passion. D. D. R. Owen thinks the lance secondary to the
grail, as the very title of the romance suggests,[20] and Helen
Adolf remarks that ' ... it has always been difficult to
account for the presence of both lance and vessel at the Grail
Castle'.[21] R. S. Loomis finds that while the Grail Bearer
passing through the hall plays a useful, rational part, the
youth with the bleeding lance does not.[22] Loomis does not
consider the possibility that he plays a useful, *irrational* role.

The grail is brought in by a maiden and it receives no
particular sign of respect as it passes through the castle hall.
For these two reasons it can hardly be a receptacle of the
Eucharist.[23]

> Un graal entre ses deus mains
> Une damoisele tenoit,
> Qui avec les vallés venoit,
> Bele et gente et bien acesmee.
> Quant ele fu laiens entree
> Atot le graal qu'ele tint,
> Une si grans clartez i vint
> Qu'ausi perdirent les chandoiles

Lor clarté come les estoiles
Font quant solaus lieve ou la lune.
Aprés celi en revint une
Qui tint un tailleoir d'argant.
Li graaus, qui aloit devant,
De fin or esmeré estoit;
Prescïeuses pierres avoit
El graal de maintes manieres,
Des plus riches et des plus chieres
Qui en mer ne en terre soient;
Totes autres pierres passoient
Celes del graal sanz dotance.
Tout ensi com passa la lance,
[Par devant le lit s'en passerent]
Et d'une chambre en autre entrerent.
Et li vallés les vit passer,
Ne n'osa mie demander
Del graal cui l'en en servoit ... (vv. 3220–45)

A girl who came in with the boys, fair and comely and beautifully
adorned, was holding a grail between her hands. When she entered
holding the grail, so brilliant a light appeared that the candles lost
their brightness like the stars or the moon when the sun rises. After
her came another girl, holding a silver trencher. The grail, which
went ahead, was made of fine, pure gold; and in it were set precious
stones of many kinds, the richest and most precious in the earth or
the sea: those in the grail surpassed all other jewels, without a
doubt. [They passed before the bed] as the lance had done, and
disappeared into another chamber. The boy saw them pass, but
did not dare to ask who was served from the grail ... (p. 35)

The grail is introduced as 'un graal' (v. 3220). There are no
references to holiness where the vessel is concerned, in Chrétien's version, except in the scene with the hermit — which
may be an interpolation.[24] Meanwhile, there is probably
some connection between Arthur's cup and the grail, and
some attention must be paid to the possibility that the grail
is a female symbol.[25] It should also be noted that while the
grail is not apparently a food-producing vessel, it has some
connection with food: the grail — and not the lance —
passes through the hall as each dish is served:[26]

... Qu'a chascun mes que l'on servoit,
Par devant lui trespasser voit
Le graal trestot descovert ... (vv. 3299–301)

Another important point is D. D. R. Owen's, that Chrétien may not even have thought of the grail as a radiant object: Owen argues that, while the passage describing the entry of the maiden with the grail is ambiguous, there is inadequate support for the interpretation that it is the grail which is radiant and some support for the interpretation that it is the maiden who is radiant.[27] Owen comments that a great brightness 'i vint' (v. 3226) and there is no necessary implication that this comes from the vessel itself. The 'an vint' of the A text (v. 3214) is scarcely more precise, since it merely indicates some unspecified source of brightness, and this could be the grail, the maiden or the circumstance of their entry into the hall. The structure of the passage gives some support to the interpretation that the light has a direct connection with the maiden. She seems to be the main subject of interest at the point where the account of the radiance occurs: she is briefly described there (v. 3223), and she is the subject of the temporal clause which provides the context of the light's appearance (v. 3224); moreover, 'Aprés celi' (v. 3230) significantly refers to her and not to the grail ('After her came another girl ...'). A full description of the grail comes late in the passage and in it there is no further reference to radiance. Chrétien describes feminine beauty in terms of light elsewhere in his work: for example, in Cligés,

> Et la luors de sa biauté
> Rant el palés plus grant clarté
> Ne feïssent quatre escharboncle ...[28]

And the radiance of her beauty lighted the palace more brightly than four carbuncles would have done ...

D. D. R. Owen adds that it is interesting that two near-contemporaries of Chrétien, the First Continuator and Wolfram von Eschenbach, both of whom knew his work, do not refer to the grail itself as radiant. Wolfram gives the radiance to the grail-bearer, Repanse de Schoye: her face, we are told, was so bright that all thought dawn was breaking: 'ir antlütze gap den schîn, / si wânden alle ez wolde tagen' (ll. 235, 16–17).

Arthur C. L. Brown, supported by Helen Adolf, suggests a link between 'graal' and the Old Irish 'criol', which reached

French via Breton or Welsh. 'Criol' — like the modern English fisherman's 'creel' (not noted by Brown) — meant basket or box and it appears twice in a list of treasures and talismans; moreover, Queen Medb possessed one.[29] One more important point is the possible help — not evidence — provided by the Old Irish *Baile in Scáil*,[30] a work frequently cited in this connection. The *Baile in Scáil* recounts how King Conn of the Hundred Battles and his companions meet a horseman who is at first hostile, and who then invites them into his palace. There, a beautiful princess fills a golden cup with red ale and asks, 'Who shall this cup with the red ale be given to?' (She uses the word 'dergflaith' and there is a play on words since it means both red ale and red sovereignty.)[31] The horseman, who is a supernatural being, replies, 'Give it to Conn of the Hundred Battles' and he prophesies the length of Conn's reign. Prophecies as to the reigns of succeeding kings follow. In this story at least, the woman serves the cup to him who is, or will be, king.

As the lance and the grail pass through the castle hall, the questions Perceval should ask, and fails to ask, come into his mind. Gorneman's advice to beware of talking too much is given as his reason for not asking them. Perceval's cousin suggests another reason: ' "this has come upon you because of the sin against your mother, for she has died of grief on your account" ' (p. 39);

'Por le pechié, ce saches tu,
De ta mere t'est avenu,
Qu'ele [est] morte del doel de toi.' (vv. 3593–5)

The questions are 'Why does the lance bleed?' and 'Who is served from the grail?' (' "demandastes vos por coi Ele sainoit?" ', vv. 3552–3; ' "did you ask why it bled?" ', p. 38, and 'Ne li vallés ne demanda Del graal cui on en servoit', vv. 3292–3; 'the boy did not ask who was served from [the grail]', p. 36). The cousin puts the question about the grail another way and joins it with a question about the small silver trencher: she says to Perceval, ' "Did you ask them where they were going?" ' (p. 39; ' "Demandastes vos a la gent Quel part il aloient issi?" ', vv. 3568–9). Asking the questions would have healed the king and restored him to the rule of his land (p. 39):

'Que tant eüsses amendé
Le buen roi qui est mehaigniez
Que toz eüst regaaigniez
Ses membres et terre tenist ...' (vv. 3586–9)

The restoration of the king to the rule of his land echoes the
move at Arthur's court: '"... my greatest enemy ... has
now contested my land"' (p. 11; '"... li pire anemis que
j'aie ... M'a chi ma terre contredite"', vv. 945, 947). Perceval's father, moreover, lost his land upon being wounded:
'"Your father ... was wounded through the leg, so that he
was crippled. Then his great land and his great treasures ...
all went to perdition ..."' (p. 6);

'Vostre peres ...
Fu parmi la jambe navrez
Si que il mehaigna del cors.
Sa grant terre, ses grans tresors ...
Ala tot a perdition ... (vv. 435–8, 440)

It is important to note that, in Chrétien's *Perceval*, both
questions — concerning the lance and concerning the grail
— are of equal importance. The later, Christianised, tradition of the quest for the Grail can lead to our forgetting this.
The Loathly Lady gives rather more words to the lance:

'Chiez le Roi Pescheor entras,
Si veïs la lance qui saine,
Et si te fu si tres grant paine
D'ovrir ta bouche et de parler
Que tu ne poïs demander
Por coi cele goute de sanc
Saut par la pointe del fer blanc;
Ne del graal que tu veïs
Ne demandas ne n'enqueïs
Quel preudome l'en en servoit.' (vv. 4652–61)

'You entered the house of the Fisher King and saw the lance that
bleeds, but it was so much trouble to you to open your mouth and
speak that you couldn't ask why that drop of blood sprang from the
tip of the white head, nor did you ask what worthy man was served
from the grail that you saw.' (p. 50)

How would the questions work? In a magical plot, the
answers to them will probably be that the lance bleeds

because the king is being continually wounded by the hero, and that it is the king who is served from the grail.

Let us look at the evidence which might guide us as to who is served from the grail. That it is the king who is served from the grail is hinted at by the words of the Loathly Lady above, as they appear in the A text:

'Et le graal que tu veïs,
ne demandas ne anqueïs
quel riche home l'an an servoit.' (A text, vv. 4635–7)

The one who is served from the grail is a man of position — as the T text's 'preudome' also suggests. 'Riche' and 'preudome' are, not surprisingly, words used to describe the Fisher King (Perceval's cousin describes him as 'riche' twice in both A and T texts and he is a 'preudome' at the Grail Castle in both texts). But these arguments are superfluous, since it is unlikely that the man of position served from the grail would be any other than the lord of the castle in which the grail is kept. The hermit's words, ' "I believe the rich Fisher King is the son of the king who is served from the grail" ' (p. 69; ' "Et del riche Pescheor croi Qu'il est fix a icelui roi Qu'en cel gr[a]al servir se fait" ', vv. 6417–19, T text) will be ignored here, because, as I discuss below, the episode with the hermit is probably irrelevant to the Perceval story under examination. For the present, it is sufficient that the hermit's words are in puzzling conflict with the words of Perceval's cousin and the Loathly Lady, which make it quite clear that the Fisher King is *the* king: no mention is made of the Fisher King's father.[32] It can be further conjectured that he who is served from the grail may be one who is honoured by the owner. The serving must mean that something would be given by the girl grail-bearer. Possibly it is the girl who is given, with all she is queen of. Or it might just be the sovereignty: the woman serves the cup to him who is, or will be, king.

There is a suggestion in the words of both Perceval's cousin and the Loathly Lady that the two objects — the lance and the grail — and the two questions about them, might be directly related to the two results of putting the questions: the healing of the king and his regaining the rule

of his land. Thus, the lance question would be concerned
with healing the king and the grail question with the
sovereignty. The cousin says, '"he would have regained the
use of his limbs and the rule of his land"' (p. 39; '"Que toz
eüst regaaigniez Ses membres et terre tenist"', vv. 3588–9)
and the Loathly Lady says, '"the rich king who is so distress-
ed would now have been quite healed of his wound and
would have held his land in peace ..."' (pp. 50–1):

> 'Li riches rois, qui or s'esmaie,
> Fust ja toz garis de sa plaie
> Et si tenist sa terre en pais ... (vv. 4671–3)

It is also probably correct to see the grail as linked to the
snatched cup of wine at Arthur's court. In each case, it seems
we have a vessel containing a drink of ritual significance to
do with the possession of the kingdom; in each case, too, a
woman — one, at least, a queen — is associated with the
vessel. There is compelling internal and external evidence to
suggest that the snatched cup and the wine spilt on the
queen express theft of the sovereignty. The question which
Perceval must ask, as to who is served from the grail, may
well be concerned with reparation for the theft through the
acknowledgement of the true owner (as perceived in the
hero's fantasy).

So far, the hero will have been a thief in his thoughts. He
will see his desire for sovereignty as taking a father's place,
and taking the father's queen as an essential part of this
seizure. Hence his leaving Blancheflor, through whom he has
achieved sovereignty; it will be in order to deal with his
guilt. There is a linking of queen and land in the move at
Arthur's court, as there is also in the Beaurepaire move ('la
terre et la pucele', v. 2911), and the idea of restoring the
Fisher King to the rule of his land, as well as to health,
appears quite suddenly, and apparently inexplicably, in the
two words of the cousin: '"terre tenist"' (T text, v. 3589; A
text, v. 3575). The king's dominion is not given any of the
attention given to his health in the moves at the Grail Castle
and with the cousin. The dreamlike move at the Grail Castle
will be concerned, under cover of deep disguise, with the
hero's feelings of guilt, in combination with his desires, and

the questions point to answers which declare the wrong
which is being done to the king and state the ownership by
the king of the sovereignty.

Perceval's sin against his mother is clearly a magical
reason for his failure to ask the questions. This explanation,
given by Perceval's cousin and aptly called 'irrational and
primitive' by Margaret Fitzgerald Richey,[33] expresses the
hero's belief that he is wronging the mother and failing to
confront the grief he is causing her.

Subsequent events reveal that the hero knows the answers
to the questions — as indeed he must do. If he feels guilt,
then he must know the answers. In the moves following the
Grail Castle move, he seems to be entirely occupied with
removing guilt, and he makes no further attempts to adventure with women or challenge the king. There is no immediate return to Blancheflor. Instead, the hero passes into a
move with the cousin, a female character closely associated
with the mother, who impresses upon him the importance of
asking the questions and restoring the king. She is holding
in her arms the decapitated body of her lover, killed as a
result of the hero's thieving activities (the jealous Proud
Knight, seeking revenge on the hero, has killed this lover). In
the Grail Castle, the hero contemplates the wounded king
and now, it seems, he contemplates the mourning queen.
There is a suggestion of a pietá in the scene: a suggestion of
a mother mourning her son is compounded with the woman
mourning her lover. The lover/son must be the hero, who is
the object of the Proud Knight's revenge for having usurped
his position. The mourning woman tells Perceval that his
mother has died of grief on his account. Perceval then rides
off into a move with the tent girl and the Proud Knight. His
leaving the cousin to follow the Proud Knight's tracks im-
plies that he will avenge the death of the cousin's lover on
the Proud Knight; the cousin has hinted at this revenge —
recommending the road the Proud Knight has taken and
adding, '"But I don't say that, so help me God, because I'd
have you go after him — though I wish him as much ill as if
it were me he'd killed"' (p. 40; '"Ne por che ne l'ai je pas dit
Que je weille, se Diex m'aït, Que vos en ailliez apréz lui, Si
volroie je son anui Autant com s'il m'avoit ocise"', vv. 3649–

53). Using the Proud Knight characters, the hero absolves himself in a ritual — this ritual disguised as an exoneration of the innocent woman involved — and he then announces this self-exoneration to Arthur by sending the Proud Knight to tell him; the king's love is reaffirmed and he sets out to find the hero. The following move, where the king and Perceval meet again, is devoted to Arthur's acclamation of the hero, who has discarded his Red Knight character. Next, the Loathly Lady arrives at court to remind him that he has not relieved the suffering of the king. Declaring himself innocent has not achieved a resolution.

I have rushed on to show the pattern as it seems to be emerging, and must now retrace my steps to examine much detail still outstanding. The answer to my fifth question, as to how the mourning cousin can become so absorbed in Perceval's affairs, is now apparent. She is absorbed in his affairs because his misdeeds are the cause of her mourning. It is quite appropriate that she should be conversing with Perceval about the Grail Castle, holding a beheaded lover in her arms. Conversing with the cousin, the hero has a vision of his own death — vengeance having been taken — and, through this cousin's words, a vision of the mother's death and of the king unrestored as a result of his behaviour towards the mother. At this point it is interesting to recall the lines describing the hero's feelings when he has won sovereignty at Beaurepaire:

> Et si fust soie toute quite
> La terre, se il li pleüst
> Que son corage aillors n'eüst;
> Mais d' autre ore plus li sovient,
> Que de sa mere au cuer li tient
> Que il vit pasmee cheoir ... (vv. 2914–19)

The land would now have been his, entirely and undisputed, had his heart not been elsewhere; but he was thinking more of someone else, for his heart was fixed on his mother whom he had seen faint and fall ... (p. 32)

He leaves to see his mother and arrives at the castle of the wounded king, and afterwards at a meeting with the mourning woman.

My sixth question, as to why Perceval in his red armour is not recognised by anyone at Arthur's court, is also answered here. While Perceval's red arms are referred to by Clamadeus and by the Proud Knight when they arrive at Arthur's court (T text, v. 2848, A text, v. 2846; T text, v. 4017, A text, v. 3999), these arms have vanished in the move where the hero is acclaimed by King Arthur; there is no mention of them. The Red Knight armour would have no importance for the hero here: after all, he is not being the Red Knight in this move. There will be no snatching of the queen: he has absolved himself as snatcher of the queen. Indeed, recognition of himself as the Red Knight is not desired here. Recognition is placed instead where Perceval tells Gawain that, since he has broken Kay's right arm, he has avenged the laughing girl struck by Kay. Gawain recalls the message Perceval sent to the king — that he will avenge the girl — and duly recognises him. The revenge itself — which is really the vindication of the prophecy that the hero will be the finest knight — is not achieved here, since it was achieved during the first move at Arthur's court when he killed the invincible Red Knight; but the hero will wish to emphasise it here because this is the move in which he is to receive particular recognition from the king, as part of his self-exculpation ritual. Hence the delay of the revenge: it has not really been delayed at all; the evidence suggests that the hero has reserved it for this additional use in his second move at Arthur's court.

A detail of this move not yet examined is the incident at the beginning where Perceval broods over the three drops of blood on snow, left by a goose wounded by a falcon. The red and white remind Perceval of the colours of his beloved's face and he is lost in thought all the early morning. In the magical plot, the hero will now be thinking of himself as being sought by the king to be acclaimed after his self-exculpation ritual, and it is possible that the wounded goose plays a role at this magical level, expressing the hero's renunciation of the woman; its position at the outset of the move increases the possibility. Accordingly, I shall conjecture that the hero thinks of the woman in terms of a bird that has escaped the swoop of a falcon. It is wounded but the

falcon has flown off, 'not wanting to attack or assail it' (p.
45): '. . . si s'en parti, Qu'il ne s'i volt liier ne joindre' (vv.
4182–3, T text; the same words are used in the A text, vv.
4162–3). The verbs 'liier' and 'joindre' suggest, fundamentally, bind and join. The assailant swooped down
upon the bird but did not want a union. The material has
been developed by Chrétien — if it is indeed part of the
magical plot — and the courtly love treatment of the hero's
thoughts of the woman develops the theme of desire (which
would be present in the magical material) while having no
concern with renunciation. This is typical of what happens
when an author develops magical material.

Further details still undealt with take us back to the Grail
Castle. Why is the sword which was presented to Perceval
unused in battle and untrustworthy? Why the *Fisher* King?
And what is the ritual function of the questions?

First of all, the sword. It is the cousin who warns Perceval
of its untrustworthiness, just as he is considering avenging
the beheaded knight — that is, when he is embarking on a
ritual to save himself from this vengeance, which means to
save himself from his own sense of guilt. It is also the cousin
who tells Perceval that the sword has never spilt a man's
blood. These two items of information, one very surprising
because we feel the Fisher King could hardly have given
such a sword in good faith, and the other incongruous because Perceval has spilt so much blood, are given us quite
suddenly, at the moment when the hero is going to clear
himself of guilt instead of attending to the suffering he feels
he is causing the king. The cousin's very words seem to
encapsulate the hero's dilemma. She has told him of his
guilt and now she comments on such a sword being in his
possession: ' "But where did you get that sword that hangs
at your left side, which has never spilt a man's blood and
has never had occasion to be drawn?" ' (p. 40):

> 'Mais ou fu cele espee prise
> Qui vos pent a[u] senestre flanc,
> Qui unques d'ome ne traist sanc
> N'onques ne fu a besoig traite?' (vv. 3654–7)

' "I know very well where it was made and I know very well
who forged it. Beware! Don't ever put your trust in it. It'll

betray you, I promise you, when you find yourself in a great battle, for it'll fly into pieces"' (p. 40):

> 'Je sai bien ou ele fu faite
> Et si sai bien qui le forja.
> Gardez ne vos i fiez ja,
> Qu'ele vos traïra sanz faille
> Quant vos venrez en grant bataille,
> K'ele vos volera en pieces.' (vv. 3658–63)

The cousin's words express a decided link between the innocence of the sword and its being quite untrustworthy. There is also a stress on the importance of the maker, although whether this importance touches more on the innocence of the sword or on its untrustworthiness is obscure in the text. At this point in his story, the hero is concerned with his guilt, while, at the beginning of the Grail Castle move, when the sword is presented to him, he is concerned with establishing his innocence.

In the Grail Castle, the king learns from the writing on it that the sword sent to him by his niece is 'of such fine steel that there is only one way it could ever be broken, which no-one knew except the one who had forged and tempered it' (p. 34):

> ... Qu'ele estoit de si bon achier
> Que ja ne porroit depechier,
> Fors que par un tot seul peril
> Que nus ne savoit fors que cil
> Qui l'avoit forgie et tempree. (vv. 3139–43)

The niece wishes the sword to be put to good use where it is bestowed:

> '... Mais ma dame seroit molt lie
> Se ele estoit bien emploïe
> La ou ele sera donee.' (vv. 3151–3)

The king seems to have no doubts as to how Perceval will use the sword and he presents it to him saying it is intended and destined for him ('"Vos fu voëe et destinee"', v. 3168) and that he very much wishes him to have it ('"Et je weil molt que vos l'aiez"', v. 3169). The sword is new because it is the last the smith will ever make: he is about to die. There is nothing sinister about the king here, but the sword seems

to express the vision of the hero's innocence and worthiness
which the hero desires and which he also desires to be
entertained by the king — while, at the same time, there is
an important, special flaw, just one, in this vision, known to
the maker. The existence of this flaw in the splendid vision is
stated in writing, as also is the detail that only the maker
knows how the man for whom it is destined will fail (that is,
break the sword). This maker who knows the hero's flaw is
about to die. There is already a suggestion, as Helen Adolf
points out,[34] that the three swords of the smith who is about
to die express the three sons of whom the hero is the third.
Helen Adolf argues that the sword stands for the person. I
agree, and have already added the suggestion that the bestowal of the sword by the Fisher King may be a recognition
of sonship by the king and also by the mysterious niece.
While I do not find useful Helen Adolf's conclusion that, in
one of Chrétien's sources, Perceval was the son of a clever
artisan, I believe the hero is the son of this maker (smith /
father) who knows where his innocence is flawed.

It must be important that this sword has been sent by the
king's niece, and that this niece is beautiful ('"qui tant est
bele"', v. 3146) — as her uncle is somewhat unnecessarily
told. She wishes the sword to be put to good use and the
king has the choice as to who will put it to good use. Blancheflor is niece to Gorneman. It is possible that the king's
bestowal of the sword which the hero is to put to good use
for a mysterious, beautiful woman expresses a ritual declaration that the king regards as innocent the hero's activities in relation to the queen. But this is stepping into speculation, beyond firm evidence. To return to firmer ground,
the hero ceases to trust the sword in the following move
with the cousin, for it is flawed: after his move in the Grail
Castle, the hero knows his declaration of his innocence is
flawed and that this flaw is known to the king. Only recourse
to the king can repair it.

As he leaves the cousin to pursue the Proud Knight, the
hero's sense of his innocence is fragile: the sword expressing
his worthiness cannot be trusted as he fights to establish his
innocence. Perhaps it is not surprising that he does not —
apparently — use it. However, the sword does drop out of

the story in an astonishing way: it seems to be quite forgotten when the hero fights the Proud Knight to establish his innocence. We are not told which sword Perceval uses, although the fact that it does not break suggests that it is the Red Knight's sword. It would make sense in the magical plot that the hero was using the Red Knight's sword to establish an innocence he did not believe in, but why does the text not say so? The interpolation in the T text, having Perceval use and break the Fisher King's sword and then draw the Red Knight's sword to establish his innocence, makes good sense in the magical plot.

Why is the king at the Grail Castle a fisherman? On his way from Blancheflor to the mother, the hero's way is barred and he is diverted to the Grail Castle by thoughts of the wounded king. The imagery used is of the river which cannot be crossed and the wounded king in a boat upon it who directs the hero to his castle for the night. It is impossible to tell how much of this material was inherited by Chrétien and how much invented, but Chrétien may well have given the king the occupation of fisherman, since he might seem in need of an occupation in the place where he intercepts the hero and there are few so suitable for a crippled king living by a river. Chrétien's development of his material may have begun here, but, on the other hand, the explanation given in the text for the occupation — that it is a pleasure accessible to a crippled sportsman (vv. 3516–33) and ' "That's why he likes to live in this house just here; for in all the world he could never find a retreat so suited to his needs" ' (p. 38) — has the air of a rationalisation of baffling inherited material. Whether or not Chrétien invented all the fisherman material, this material has no function in the magical plot. Many have turned to Irish literature for clarification of the Fisher King: Cúchulainn, making his journey to Forgall's dun in order to woo Forgall's daughter Emer, spends a night with Roncu, the fisherman of King Conchobor,[35] and, moreover, there is evidence that the Welsh god Nodons was a fisherman.[36] Some such tradition could have become attached to the hospitable, mysterious king, while, in the magical plot, he is essentially a king who has lost health and lands. It is likely that, as in the case of the grail, the fisherman detail has

become exaggerated in importance during its subsequent
career in tradition, linked enigmatically to a mystical figure
as it is, and the attention it has received in more recent
years from scholars of myth and ritual may also have exaggerated its importance. There are no more than two references to 'the Fisher King' in the material which is definitely
by Chrétien: these are those of the cousin, who refers to '"le
riche Roi Pescheor"' (v. 3495) and '"li Rois Peschiere"' (v.
3520). Otherwise the king is thus referred to in the episode
with the hermit, which is likely to be an interpolation.[37]

What is the ritual function of the questions? I have discussed the answers to the questions and shall now look at the
function of the Grail Castle in the plot as a whole. How
would the ritual of asking the questions actually work? In
this move, the hero seems to be seeking a feeling of his
innocence and of the king's love and esteem, while he is
confronted by the suffering he believes he is causing the king
and also by the woman with the grail whose duty it is to
serve the king. Why does the hero wonder who is served
from the grail, when he must know? It is likely, even from a
superficial view, that the king will be the one who is served
from the grail, and, in the magical plot, the hero is convinced that it is the king who owns the woman and the
sovereignty. The failure to speak the questions (the hero does
think of them) seems to be a failure in acknowledgement:
speaking the questions would restore the king. The hero does
not restore the king; instead he seeks to restore himself.

Wishing to know the answer as to who is served from the
grail, when he already has an answer in his mind, and
desiring a queen and sovereignty, does the hero have in
mind that, as in the case of Conn of the Hundred Battles, the
king will tell the grail-bearer to 'Give it to Perceval' and
then prophesy his reign?

Helen Adolf rightly says that 'Failures are not the theme of
primitive stories'.[38] My own studies have suggested that
magical stories always bring about some kind of resolution
for the hero. It is likely that the ritual of asking the questions
has the power to bestow sovereignty upon the hero of *Perceval*, the plot culminating in his marriage to Blancheflor. For
the marriage to Blancheflor, we have the strong internal

support, though not evidence, of Perceval's repeated promises to return to Blancheflor (vv. 2926–61, T text; vv. 2922–
55, A text). D. D. R. Owen points out, from his own very
different approach, that, by the end of the Perceval adventures proper, Chrétien has used and adapted almost all the
material in his model (which is principally the Fair Unknown story), and what is left is likely to suggest to him a
twofold dénouement: it will involve the putting of the 'un-
spelling' questions, whereby Perceval's worth and nobility
will be conclusively recognised, and this will be followed by
his marriage to Blancheflor.[39]

I believe it is possible that the romance was intended by
Chrétien to take Perceval straight back to the Grail Castle,
on the summons of the Loathly Lady or in some other way.
The coherent magical plot which I have traced ends with, or
just before, the arrival of the Loathly Lady at Arthur's court
and her words to Perceval, and I cannot myself believe that
Chrétien attached the Gawain sequence here. The Perceval
story had reached a critical point and all that remained was
for the hero to return to the Grail Castle, find a resolution to
his lance and grail thoughts by asking the questions, and
then to return to Blancheflor. A skilled writer like Chrétien
would be unlikely to attach the Gawain material here, and I
agree with D. D. R. Owen that this was probably done after
his death by the First Continuator or someone else perhaps
close to Chrétien. Chrétien may have been working concurrently on *Perceval* and on a *Gawain* at the time of his death,
or he may have failed to complete these two works for other
reasons. It seems to me that two unfinished works have been
joined together, and that this has been done quite roughly in
the scene with the Loathly Lady. D. D. R. Owen argues that
the Gawain episodes do not, as many maintain, provide
either a foil or complement to the Perceval sequence.The
stories of Perceval and Gawain are too different in tone and
theme, the Perceval sequence being a 'serious romance' and
the Gawain sequence a 'heroic burlesque'.[40] Owen points out
that, while there have been sensitive attempts to show that
the duality is part of a grand scheme, if the two sets of
adventures were complementary and the romance one and
indivisible, Chrétien would have introduced more parallels

into the two sections in order to point the contrast. He also observes that the *Conte du Graal* has a quite uncharacteristic length, Chrétien's three completed romances all having approximately 6,800 lines, while the Perceval and Gawain sequences have about 4,600 lines each. I agree that more than 9,000 lines is a less credible length for the *Conte du Graal* than is 4,600 for a *Perceval* with two or three moves to go before its completion. Moreover, a magical story, reaching its climax, would not suddenly become much more light-hearted and delay the resolution of its conflicts for many thousands of lines of adventures not concerned with these conflicts. The Gawain episodes are largely adventures with women, and the hero of the Perceval sequence — who could, incidentally, quite readily become Gawain for a while in a single magical plot — does not need escapades with women at this point, nor are they really possible until he has attended to his anxieties relating to the king.

Where the episode with the hermit is concerned, I agree with D. D. R. Owen that it is probably an interpolation on the part of 'the pious interpolator'.[41] Owen believes that Chrétien the artist could not have produced such a clumsy scene as this. He points out that the scene does violent injury to the time sequence: both Perceval and Gawain set out at the same time, but Perceval has been away five years in his scene inset in the adventures of Gawain, while Gawain has been away three days. Owen also shows that the solemnly doctrinal tone of the episode conflicts with Perceval's mother's tone when she is giving similar advice, and that the hermit's instructions are largely surplus to Perceval's needs. He adds that it is quite wrong that the elderly Fisher King should be declared the young Perceval's cousin, and that the grail is here presented as a sacred object, in conflict with its obviously secular character in the scene of its first appearance. More serious still is the way this episode answers the question about the grail, doing so, furthermore, without Perceval's asking the question: the quest for the grail has now entirely lost its point. Stylistic study to ascertain a different author is made difficult by the fact that the interpolator would be very familiar with Chrétien's style and influenced by it, while the subject matter is so different from anything else in Chrétien that this would account for some differences. D. D. R. Owen discusses how this interpolation is probably linked to the one which appears in some manuscripts of the First Continuation (A, L, M, Q and U), where the Fisher King's Christian explanation of the lance to Gawain receives the addition of a Christian explanation of the grail. Owen thinks this is the earliest stage in the legend that Joseph of Arimathea caught Christ's blood in the grail, which was then brought to England. The entirely Christian significance of the hermit's grail means that it plays no part at all in the magical plot I have found.

The hermit's being an interpolation would also explain the cousin's silence on the relationship between Perceval and the Fisher King, which we first hear of from the hermit. A character with her information about both Perceval's family and the Fisher King must also have had that information, and, if it were being expressed at the verbal level by Chrétien, she would have expressed it. The relationship is there, of course, in the magical plot, but it does not have to be referred to at the verbal level. The discrepancy lies at the verbal level, where there appear to be two separate policies.

To return to the putting of the questions, D. D. R. Owen believes that this would lead to the conclusive recognition of Perceval's worth and nobility. I myself think it a possibility that the ritual of asking the questions has the power to bestow sovereignty upon the hero. Perhaps the bestowal of the sword helps to show what a second visit to the Grail Castle would contain: with the gift of the sword the hero is distinguished, it seems as a son, to the highest degree. However, the vision of the hero's innocence and worthiness expressed by the sword has a flaw known to the father. When the hero has dealt with his lance and grail thoughts, there will be no flaw. Asking the questions, whether or not answers are given, would act as a ritual acknowledgement of the king and of the hero's own guilt – by contrast with the rituals the hero has hitherto enacted, in which he usurps the king's position and at the same time establishes a feeling that he is innocent and loved by the king. The hero could not attain a resolution unless he acknowledged that he was wounding the king and that the king was sovereign. He must restore the king, to whom he owes love and loyalty, to his rule. Having done this, his feeling of his innocence would be established and the king's acknowledgement of him would not be flawed as was the sword. The hero would now have the feelings necessary for him to have the king bestow sovereignty upon him in his turn, an acknowledgement of worth without a flaw. After this the hero would be free to return to Blancheflor, marry her and govern her dominion.

What is the explanation for the Loathly Lady? In magical thought, seeing someone as ugly can be a defence against finding her beautiful, because she is taboo, as is the case in *The Weddynge of Sir Gawen and Dame Ragnell*[42] and — possibly — *Sir Gawain and the Green Knight*. Other fears on the part of the hero can also give rise to the ugly appearance of a character. Why should she be ugly, this character who returns the hero to his lance and grail thoughts after his false victory at Arthur's court? The hero would have to have fears, and probably desires concerning her, for her to be so. His thoughts would have returned to the woman and these thoughts summoned him to the Grail Castle once more. It fits, in a sense, that she should be ugly, and yet I wonder, too, whether the hero has sufficient fear of the woman at this point — taboo though he sees her to be: his anxieties relate to what he feels he has done to the king. If the Loathly Lady is not an expression of the feelings about women in this plot, then she cannot be a part of it. Whether or not she is a part of the plot in this sense, she is an anomaly in that we would expect from previous events in the plot that the cousin — or the Fisher King — would summon, or remind, Perceval in some way. A new character, apart from a messenger, would not be expected at this stage. The summoning itself fits entirely: Perceval has to be summoned to the Grail Castle at this point and the Loathly Lady's words are entirely in tune with the plot. I am inclined to believe that Chrétien's Perceval romance breaks off before the Loathly Lady's arrival, in spite of the necessity of the summons and despite the more awkward 'join' at line 4684 in the T text (line 4660 in the A text), where the Loathly Lady drops the cause of the Fisher King and introduces other causes which begin Gawain's adventures. Come what may, I am certain the Perceval romance ends either just before the summons (at line 4602, T text and 4578, A text) or when the Loathly Lady drops the subject of the Fisher King.

It remains to trace the moves of Chrétien's *Perceval* proper. The plot seems to have nine moves as far as it goes: an initial home move with the mother, the move in the tent, the Red Knight move, the Gorneman move, Beaurepaire with Blancheflor, the Grail Castle, the move with the cousin, the tent girl again and finally the move at Arthur's camp. Each move is concerned primarily with either a 'queen' or a king: these parent figures tend to be divided from each other, either one or the other being the chief concern of each move. The progression of moves seeks to resolve the conflict between desire and guilt, through the ritual arrangements of characters representing the hero and the king and queen — the mother, the Proud Knight couple, Arthur's court, the Red Knight, Gorneman, Blancheflor, Clamadeus and so forth. Advice, praise and prophecies are used as magic words and it is likely that the questions about the lance and grail would have similar power to bring about the hero's final victory. That here we have a magical plot seems clear: meaning, meanwhile, has to be less clear (even though some interpretation can be supported by ample contextual evidence), because of its multiple, confused and disguised nature — and also because the plot is incomplete. Even in the best conditions, the bold attempts at interpretation that have to be made in the exploration of a plot likely to prove magical cannot be entirely satisfactory. The critic can only struggle to see that they are accurate enough to identify a magical plot correctly and trace the hero's use of magic.

Throughout this study, I have been prepared to find that the Grail Castle is an addition to the Perceval story; the English tail-rhyme version does not include it. There is nothing to prevent Chrétien deepening the story at the magical level by adding such a move: this is something an outstanding writer might conceivably do, although I have never come across the addition of a move. Writers tend to adhere faithfully to the move sequence of a magical plot they are re-creating. Shakespeare, however, syncopates the Hamlet plot, omitting moves,[43] and alterations occur in *Peredur*, for

reasons which I discuss in a separate chapter. The most
likely verdict where the Grail Castle is concerned is that
Chrétien inherited it with the rest of his plot. The Grail
Castle takes its place as the sixth move in the sequence,
following the move at Beaurepaire: the hero leaves Blancheflor, through whom he has attained sovereignty, in order
to deal with his guilt. He fails to find a feeling of his innocence at the Grail Castle because he is concerned with restoring himself rather than with restoring the king. In-
creasingly, in the subsequent moves, the hero seeks to establish a feeling that he is innocent, in the same way as he does
at the Grail Castle. A second visit to the castle, to ask the
questions, is probably the missing resolution of his conflict.
The kindly, wounded Fisher King must also be seen in relation to King Arthur in the Red Knight move: there are
important differences in the roles of these moves, but, fundamentally, in both the hero seeks to establish a spurious
innocence, while paying no attention to the king's suffering.

It is not difficult to see why the Grail Castle catches the
mind. Chrétien has given us a profound retelling of the
Perceval story, where aspiration conflicts with guilt, so that
its pursuit is accompanied by a struggle for a sense of innocence. This powerful material can readily be used to express
religious feeling, where a sense of sin conflicts with a yearning for ideal goodness. Yet perhaps this is the place to recall
Pauline Matarasso's comment that 'at the very heart of the
Grail legend there lies a grave ambivalence in that the relics
of the Last Supper and the Passion are made to appear
responsible for the malefic enchantments and perils afflicting King Arthur's kingdom, while the sacred lance and the
miraculous sword of King David, the "sword of the spirit",
appear at times in the light of weapons of vengeance and
Nemesis'.[44]

CHAPTER THREE

SIR PERCEVAL OF GALLES

The English *Sir Perceval of Galles*[1] makes an interesting study in relation to Chrétien's *Perceval*. It is a tail-rhyme romance belonging to the second half of the fourteenth century — two centuries later than Chrétien's *Perceval* — which gives us a version of the story used by Chrétien, without the Grail Castle and also without the courtly treatment of the French romance. As an English tail-rhyme romance, it addressed a wider audience than Chrétien did — an audience associated with the courts, as the romance audience always was, but one reflecting the larger courts of the fourteenth century. A major question about the English version is its appearance two centuries after Chrétien's without any mention of the grail: this study can do no more to address this question than show the Grail Castle to be irrelevant in its magical plot.

I find that this romance has eight moves, these taking rather a different course from those of Chrétien's version, but nevertheless suggestive of the course which Chrétien's unfinished work might have taken. The first six moves are as follows: with the mother; with the sleeping lady; with the Red Knight at Arthur's court; with the Gorneman character; with Arthur again, where the king longs for Perceval and, receiving news that he is going to the aid of the lady Lufamour, sets off to support him; and, finally, the Lufamour move, culminating in Perceval's marriage to Lufamour, in the presence of Arthur. There are then two additional moves in which the hero deals with his guilt. This guilt is in relation to the mother — that is, it is concerned with incest — while, in Chrétien, it is mainly, though not entirely, in relation to the king.

I shall begin by looking at differences in the presentation of the male characters in the English version. The hero presents himself as a simple lad, living in humble circumstances, while really nephew to King Arthur without knowing it. Arthur is immediately devoted to him because he is reminded of his dead brother-in-law as soon as he sees him. The Red Knight, meanwhile, killed Perceval's father fifteen years previously, and for the past five years, he has been bursting into Arthur's court, calling every knight a coward, drinking the king's wine and taking the gold cup away on each occasion; when referring to his killing of Perceval's father, the king calls him a thief ('"a theffe"', l. 555). Perceval's behaviour towards Arthur is openly aggressive (this disguised by the humorous treatment of the lad as bucolic and a figure of fun): he says he will slay the king if he does not knight him, and, when the king speaks of his love for the lost knight Perceval resembles, Perceval tells him to stop rambling and get on with making him a knight. This version is more explicit in that aggression against the father is placed in a position parallel with that against a king uncle, and the acknowledged hero, Perceval, is placed in more obvious parallel with the unacknowledged hero, the Red Knight. Moreover, the king's love for the hero is explained in the text as arising from their being blood relations. There is, evidently, little guilt about the king in this version: Perceval scorns to return to court after killing the Red Knight, proclaiming that he is as great a lord as Arthur:

'I am als grete a lorde als he;
To-day ne schall he make me
  None oþer gates knyghte.' (ll. 814–16)

The hero's next move, with the Gorneman character, is also more clearly visible in this version. This Gorneman character does no more than acclaim the killer of the Red Knight. The Red Knight was his greatest enemy ('"moste foo"', l. 899) and he killed his brother fifteen years earlier (ll. 921–2). Links with King Arthur are obvious. The hero is concerned with acclaim, not with being made a knight, and he uses the Gorneman character for this role, rather than return to court.

The connection between Perceval's mother, who is
Arthur's sister, and the other women characters is also made
clearer in this version, so little transformed by courtly treatment. The night before he leaves his mother, we are told, 'All
þat ny3te till it was day, The childe by þe modir lay ...'
(ll. 417–18). In the next move, he kisses the Black Knight's
sleeping lady in bed. Moreover, the mother gives him a ring
as a sign of recognition and he exchanges it with the ring of
the Black Knight's lady when he kisses her. The ring of the
Black Knight's lady is later described as protecting its wearer in battle (ll. 1857–64), and the lady Lufamour's decision
that Perceval is worthy to govern and to be her husband is
made upon his slaying enormous numbers of the sultan's
men besieging her (ll. 1310–12).

There is a fourth woman character, the witch mother of
the Red Knight, whom Perceval meets after killing the Red
Knight and scorning to return to Arthur. She mistakes him
for her son and says she can heal him, but he kills her and
throws her into the fire consuming her son's body. This
detail seems to be part of the Red Knight move, perhaps
strategically placed after Perceval's claim that he is as
great a lord as Arthur: in which case, it would probably
express the removal of his being identifiable as the Red
Knight and emphasise that he is the remover of that
character.

The marriage to Lufamour takes place at once, upon the
elimination of the lover seeking to take her by force; and,
afterwards, the hero does not depart, to a Grail Castle or
anywhere else, to deal with thoughts about a wounded king.
The Lufamour move has, however, been preceded by a move
at Arthur's court, in which the king hears of Perceval's
adventure in Maydenlande and travels there to see him. The
hero has thus armed himself with the king's love and support for the Maydenlande adventure. The king witnesses the
destruction of the character seeking to snatch the lady (a
detail which parallels the destruction of the snatcher of
Arthur's cup) and then he seals the wedding with his approv-
ing presence.

The hero has seized sovereignty in six moves, arranging
his characters into the steps necessary to bring this about.

But two complicated moves concerned with guilt in relation to the mother follow.

Setting out to find his mother, Perceval encounters the Black Knight's lady, who is tied to a tree because her lover judges her faithless. He exonerates her through the defeat of her Black Knight – which means that the hero exonerates himself of whatever the exchange of rings means. The entrance into the final move is marked by an extraordinary detail, indicative of the deep disguises assumed. The exoneration relating to the Black Knight couple cannot be sealed because the rings cannot be exchanged again: the Black Knight has given the mother's ring to the giant brother of the sultan. Why should the Black Knight give the ring to the giant? One would expect him to keep it as compensation for the loss of his lady's ring or as evidence as to who took his lady's ring, or, again, so that he can exchange the rings back again if he ever finds the culprit. And if he has to give it away, why give it to the giant? In this final move, Perceval slays the giant and then finds that the giant has tried to press the ring on his (Perceval's) mother, its original owner, while beseeching her to be his lover. She has gone mad with grief, thinking he has acquired it through slaying her son. Perceval then seeks her out, on foot, abandoning his Red Knight armour for the goatskins in which he was clad as her son.

The giant is linked to the sultan by being his brother and also by his being overcome by Perceval. The sultan and the Red Knight are overcome by Perceval in parallel manoeuvres concerned with establishing the hero's innocence (manoeuvres which simultaneously bring about desires which the hero does not see as innocent). In the sultan, the hero seeks to eliminate the idea that he is seizing the lady, even as he does take her wrongfully (so he believes). Now he uses another such character, placing him in the position of laying siege to the mother, rather than to Lufamour, and eliminates him. This character's being a giant will be an expression of the hero's view of his behaviour — monstrous, threatening and formidable to overcome.

The rings are more difficult to disentangle. Perceval's giving the mother's ring to the Black Knight's sleeping lady suggests that the hero links the woman from whom he steals a kiss with the mother. Meanwhile, his taking the sleeping lady's ring expresses the hero's ownership of her; and the ring's protection of him in battle must express the hero's sense of the power the ownership of the woman gives him to acquire sovereignty. The exchange of rings, using the Black Knight's lady as an intermediate step between the mother and Lufamour, is therefore an essential ritual for the bringing about of the marriage with Lufamour. The Black Knight's giving the giant the ring expresses a link the hero sees between his behaviour at the Black Knight couple's hall and the behaviour of the giant. The hero is the monstrous suitor, and here we must remember that this ring is a recognition token, seemingly the means by which the mother will recognise her son:

> His moder gaffe hym a ryng,
> And bad he solde agayne it bryng:
> 'Sonne, þis sall be oure takynnyng,
> For here I sall þe byde'. (ll. 425–8)

The mother's grief upon seeing the ring in the hands of the giant must mean that the hero thinks of her as recognising him, and therefore as distraught over his behaviour. He has already destroyed the giant. The action which brings about the end of the story is the discarding of the Red Knight guise to seek the mother out, on foot and in goatskins as her son. Upon this, the hero can conjure up a vision of their joyful reunion, and, as her son, he takes her to his 'Qwene' (l. 2277).

The hero has to return to being the mother's son before he can find a resolution, and this is similar to my speculation as to how Chrétien's version would end: by asking the questions the hero would restore the king and return to being his son. Sovereignty could only be well and truly acquired at this point, in Chrétien's version, but the tail-rhyme hero's acquirement of sovereignty in his Lufamour move does increase the possibility that the hero of Chrétien's version would finally take over his sovereignty with Blancheflor, supported by the king.

The tail-rhyme Perceval takes his mother to his 'Qwene'.

Chrétien's Perceval promises Blancheflor and her people
that if he finds his mother alive he will bring her back with
him, and from that day forward will be lord of the land; if he
finds her dead, he will return likewise:

> ... il met en covenant,
> S'il trove sa mere vivant,
> Qu'avec lui l'en amera la
> Et d'enqui en avant tendra
> La terre, ce sachent de fi,
> Et se ele est morte, autresi. (T text, vv. 2927–32)

In Chrétien's more profound version, the mother is dead —
according to Perceval's cousin, who links the wrong Perceval
has done his mother with his failure to ask the questions in
relation to the king. It seems that in Chrétien's plot the
questions about the king, with no special resolution of guilt
over the queen-figure, are the ritual which will enable the
hero to keep his promise to Blancheflor.

CHAPTER FOUR

PARZIVAL

Margaret Richey points out that 'With Chrestien, the story moves between two disparate worlds, outwardly united by the polish and grace of his easy-flowing style, but inwardly of a different order, one crass and fantastical, the other courtly'. She goes on, 'Wolfram's world is always that of the chivalric life, into whose atmosphere those fantastical elements ... are absorbed. Chrestien creates an illusory sense of unison by sheer magic of style, while Wolfram creates a real and organic unison by breathing a stronger humanity into the characters, and especially by giving full significance to the destiny of the hero, which becomes the controlling theme'.[1] I now wish to find out whether Wolfram von Eschenbach's overriding chivalric and other themes do indeed eclipse the magical plot of Chrétien, or whether they create an overlay, the result being, in a sense, two stories — one a magical story faithfully re-created, and the other the author's own imaginative creation. These can exist side by side, in harmony with one another. If the magical plot survives, the overlay will be dependent upon it, as is the case in Chrétien's version and *Hamlet*. If the magical plot is eclipsed, all the original magical details will be transformed to play other roles in the author's imaginative plot, as is the case in Chaucer's *The Wife of Bath's Tale*.[2] I shall examine the much-studied *Parzival* only so far as to explore Wolfram's treatment of the magical plot in Chrétien's *Perceval*. This chapter is dependent on a reading of my chapter discussing Chrétien's version.

Perhaps the best way to conduct this inquiry is to see first whether the questions I ask of Chrétien's *Perceval* are also relevant to Wolfram's *Parzival*.[3]

1. Where the mother's advice and Perceval's subsequent
behaviour are concerned, the questions are raised by Wolfram's version just as much as by Chrétien's. The mother
advises her son: '"Wherever you can win a lady's ring and
greeting, take it — it will rid you of the dumps."' She
continues that he should hasten to kiss the lady and embrace
her body tightly: '"du solt zir kusse gâhen und ir lîp vast
umbevâhen"' (restrainedly translated by A. T. Hatto as
'"Waste no time, but kiss and embrace her"', p. 75). After
this, she says, '"It will bring you good fortune and raise your
spirits, granted she be chaste and good"' (p. 75).

'sun, lâ dir bevolhen sîn,
swa du guotes wîbes vingerlîn
mügest erwerben unt ir gruoz,
daz nim: ez tuot dir kumbers buoz.
du solt zir kusse gâhen
und ir lîp vast umbevâhen:
daz gît gelücke und hôhen muot,
op si kiusche ist unde guot.' (127, 25–128, 2)

This advice comes oddly indeed from a woman about to die
of grief, and it is also inconsistent with the maternal role
this character plays in the plot, a role requiring, it would
seem, advice similar to the maternal wisdom Wolfram found
in Chrétien's mother. Linda B. Parshall argues that Wolfram
omits 'the mother's warning [in Chrétien's version] not to
offend or force any woman, so that Parzival is not explicitly
disobeying her advice. He does what he is told, though a
tendency to over-literal interpretation traps him in humorous moments ...' Dr Parshall points out that Wolfram does
not follow Chrétien in having Parzival kiss the unwilling
woman an exaggerated number of times.[4] I believe this criticism is looking in the wrong direction: an alteration which
amends one problem, only to increase another, should
prompt closer scrutiny of these problems.

In the adventure with the tent lady, Jeschute, who, in this
version, was a queen before her marriage to Duke Orilus
('"ir liezet küneginne namn und heizt durch mich ein herzo-
gin"', 134, 2–3), Parzival is more violent than Perceval.

diu frouwe lûte klagte:
ern ruochte waz si sagte,

ir munt er an den sînen twanc.
dâ nâch was dô niht ze lanc,
er druct an sich die herzogîn
und nam ir och ein vingerlîn.
an ir hemde ein fürspan er dâ sach:
ungefuoge erz dannen brach.
diu frouwe was mit wîbes wer:
ir was sîn kraft ein ganzez her.
doch wart dâ ringens vil getân. (131, 11–21)

The lady wailed loudly. He paid no attention to what she said but
forced her mouth to his. Wasting no time, he crushed her breast to
his, duchess or no duchess, and also took a ring. On her shift he saw
a brooch and roughly tore it off. The lady was armed as women are:
but to her his strength was an army's. Nevertheless there was quite
a tussle of it. (p. 77)

Dr Richey blames the 'enigmatic brevity' of the mother's
advice for his interpretation of it 'quite simply in terms of
physical force',[5] while my investigation must address the
enigma: in Chrétien, there is conflict between the advice and
the behaviour, and here there is not. Meanwhile, whatever
the mother advises, Perceval and Parzival take the same
action; we find a consistency in Wolfram, where we do not in
Chrétien, due to an alteration in the advice rather than in
the behaviour, even though an alteration in the behaviour
would produce a result with fewer, if any, attendant problems. In Chrétien's version, the mother's advice to Perceval
has a magical purpose: at that level, her point of view is
absent and the hero is probably arranging her sanction of
his wishes. In Wolfram's version, this purpose seems yet
more likely. Not only has Wolfram made less attempt than
Chrétien to introduce the mother's point of view in the
advice she gives, but he also seems to have engaged somewhat more in Parzival's desires than does Chrétien, whose
treatment of the scene in the tent is humorous and critical.
Linda B. Parshall points out the eroticism in the narrator's
treatment of the scene in the tent, the ravishing vision which
we see through Parzival's eyes being part of the reason why
he behaves as he does.[6] I would argue that, while there is
detached treatment of the scene, the effects arise mainly
from the development of the feeling in Chrétien's magical
plot where the hero, under cover of simplicity, takes ritual

possession of the kingdom he desires through the kisses and the ring. Dr Parshall also comments on the discrepancy between the innocent motivation ascribed to Parzival and the impulsive aggressiveness of his actions. 'The irony is complicated in that the listener is repeatedly led to misread Parzival's behaviour.'[7] However, if Wolfram has re-created Chrétien's magical plot, the discrepancy will be present in this plot, rather than arranged by the irony of the author: the discrepancy will be between the aggressive feeling in the move and the innocent motivation arranged by the hero. Even if the mother's advice plays no role in the hero's arrangements for his innocence, his simplicity and rusticity will certainly do so. An author's becoming the 'hero' or 'heroine' can lead him — however large a detached vision he may have — to re-create this protagonist's presentation of him or herself, while characters lacking a point of view in the magical plot can easily be 'framed' by this author.

An equal problem is Parzival's mother's last piece of advice:

> 'du solt och wizzen, sun mîn,
> der stolze küene Lähelîn
> dînen fürsten ab ervaht zwei lant,
> diu solten dienen dîner hant,
> Wâleis und Norgâls.
> ein dîn fürste Turkentâls
> den tôt von sîner hende enphienc:
> dîn volc er sluoc unde vienc.'
> 'diz rich ich, muoter, ruocht es got:
> in verwundet noch mîn gabylôt.' (128, 3–12)

'You must learn another thing, my son. Arrogant bold Lähelin has wrested two lands, Waleis and Norgals, from your Princes. By rights they should subserve you. Turkentals, one of your Princes, was killed by him, and he killed your people or took them prisoner.' 'I will avenge this, mother, if God pleases. My javelin shall wound him yet!' (p. 75)

Wolfram gives us no reply from the mother. Yet she has not had him trained, and she has even prepared fool's clothing for him, to protect him by preventing him from being taken seriously by combatants. How can she ask him now to take this revenge? Margaret Richey says that the Lähelin passage is inconsistent with the mother's solicitude for the boy's welfare and safety, and with 'the overwhelming grief which surely left no room for the thought of anything so worldly as the loss of the conquered lands'. She continues, 'One might say that a sudden involuntary sense of neglected duty impelled her to tell this much of the family history against her will; but there are no grounds for assuming any such touch of psychological subtlety, and would it not then have been more obvious for her to have told the boy something about his father?'[8] The Lähelin theme is never developed and the reason for its inclusion is hard to guess. I can only suggest that the passage may have seemed appropriate to Wolfram at this juncture because the theme of thief is a prominent one in Chrétien's plot. A further detail suggesting that Lähelin may have magical significance as a thief is the hermit Trevrizent's asking Parzival whether he is this thieving Lähelin (473, 28–474, 4).

2. To turn to the second group of questions — concerning Arthur's court and the Red Knight — Chrétien's attempted rationalisation of the inaction of Arthur's knights does not reappear in Wolfram's version. Instead, Wolfram has attempted considerable rationalisations in other areas. One of these is the re-creation of the Red Knight in King Ither, but the development of this character is accompanied by an emphatic faithfulness to its magical role. The behaviour of the king and queen is also modified to rationalise the scene. Other telling effects of the rationalisations are to be found in the discrepancies created by the author's moral treatment — an excellent indicator that a magical plot is in use.

King Ither explains his snatching behaviour to Parzival thus:

'ich reit für tavelrunder,
mîns landes ich mich underwant:
disen koph mîn ungefüegiu hant
ûf zucte, daz der wîn vergôz
froun Ginovêrn in ir schôz.
underwinden mich daz lêrte.' (146, 20–5)

'I rode to the Table Round and claimed my lands. My clumsy hand snatched up this cup, and so the wine was spilt into my lady Ginover's lap. This I did to assert my title.' (p. 84)

Ither also tells Parzival:

> 'ine hânz ouch niht durch roup getân:
> des hât mîn krône mich erlân.
> friunt, nu sage der künegîn,
> ich begüzzes ân den willen mîn,
> aldâ die werden sâzen,
> die rehter wer vergâzen.' (146, 29–147, 4)

'Nor did I do so for the sake of plunder: my Crown exempts me from the need. Now, friend, tell the Queen that I splashed her without intent, in the presence of nobles who forgot their weapons.' (p. 84)

Ither does not need to steal ('"durch roup getân"'), for he is a king. Meanwhile, the king and queen are not so extraordinarily upset as in Chrétien's version, and stress is laid on the king's sadness that he lacks the affection of this kinsman (Wolfram makes Ither a kinsman of the king), rather than on his being cowed by an unworthy enemy:

> 'ich muoz doch sus mit kumber lebn
> ân alle mîne schulde,
> sît ich darbe sîner hulde.
> ez ist Ithêr von Gaheviez,
> der trûren mir durch freude stiez.' (150, 6–10)

'Even now, and through no fault of mine, I am denied his favour and lead a wretched life of it. He is Ither of Gaheviez and has shattered all my happiness.' (p. 86)

King Ither is friendly to Parzival and a kinsman of his too, and, when Parzival goes out to fight him, our attention is focused on the knightly demeanour of Ither and the uncouth behaviour of the youth in response.

Margaret Richey points out that the 'discrepancies between old and new are imperfectly solved'.[9] I would add that the Red Knight's ennoblement, both as king and as more courteous knight, does not alter his magical role of snatching sovereignty ('"disen koph ... ûf zucte"', 146, 22–3), a process in which the queen is curiously involved. The chief discrepancy lies between the queen's words after Ither's death, that he '"did but acclaim his heritage and was accorded — death!"' (p. 90; '"sîns erbeteils er gerte, dâ man in sterbens werte"', 160, 9–10), and the king's words that the conflict with Ither is no fault of his and the loss of his favour has shattered all his happiness. Both these statements make entire sense, taken together, at the magical level of Chrétien's plot, where the hero is concerned with a heritage which he feels has to be seized from one to whom he is bound by bonds of love, but, at a rational level, the king would be expected to take responsibility if the issue were a matter of a kinsman's heritage, especially if he desired the favour of this kinsman. Meanwhile, Ither's being described in the text as kinsman to Arthur, and also to Parzival, emphasises his role at Chrétien's magical level, where the Red Knight is unacknowledged hero and therefore son to the king.

The various details relating to the moral treatment might be given satisfactory explanations, but the way they hang together suggests piecemeal treatment rather than a fundamental moral scheme. In this version, the court grieves over the killing of the Red Knight, while, at the same time, there is no condemnation of Parzival's action. Then the narrator tells us, 'Later, on reaching years of discretion, Parzival wished he had not done it' (p. 91; 'sît dô er sich paz versan, ungerne het erz dô getân', 161, 7–8). Trevrizent tells Parzival that he has sinned in killing a kinsman and one whom all wrong-doing saddened because he '"was the very balm of constancy"' (p. 242; '"Missewende was sîn riuwe, er balsem ob der triuwe"', 475, 21–476, 2). Yet when Arthur sets out to seek Parzival, we are told that Parzival has done Arthur 'the honour of saving him from a grave predicament by slaying Ither with his javelin' (p. 147):

... und im solh êre bôt
daz er in schiet von kumber grôz,
dô er den künec Ithêren schôz ... (280, 10–12)

The narrator's use of the word honour ('êre', 280, 10) in a description of the court's opinion of Ither's slaying relates to the lack of condemnation at the court immediately after the slaying, while it does not relate entirely satisfactorily to the court's grief and praise for Ither at that time and it does not relate to the narrator's own high praise for Ither's faithfulness — calling him 'the negation of all that is perfidious' (p. 88; 'der valscheit widersatz', 155, 11). Most striking, the idea that Parzival has done Arthur an honour in killing Ither does not relate to the comments of the narrator and Trevrizent that Parzival has sinned. These problems cannot be explained by there being a fluctuating narrator persona in *Parzival*.[10] In Chrétien's magical plot, and in his treatment of it, there is never any regret or condemnation over the killing of the Red Knight; the hero's guilt concerns the king and queen only. Wolfram has introduced these feelings and moral judgements, superimposing them on a plot where quite opposite feelings are being expressed. Linda B. Parshall's argument, that Arthur's court accepts Parzival's killing of Ither in a way the audience cannot,[11] points out the dichotomy here, while not observing that the dichotomy may also be present in the audience's response. For, if Chrétien's magical plot is present, the members of the audience may engage in the narrative at two levels, that of the hero and that of Wolfram's chivalric themes. Wolfram bestows 'triuwe', with its rich combination of qualities — faithfulness, constancy, affection, instinctive kindness and fellowship[12] — on the Red Knight, while he also emphasises the Red Knight's magical, quite contrary, role in the plot, where his death at the hands of Parzival will be essential to the hero for the establishment of his innocence in the eyes of the king.

David Blamires argues[13] that the death of Ither marks the end of Parzival's primitive innocence. Ither represents the idea of 'mannes triuwe', which is translated by Hatto as 'manly faith' (p. 91). By killing Ither, Parzival shows his own lack of this knightly quality. When the deed is done, Parzival puts on Ither's clothing, of which the colour is the red of blood and thus of sin.[14] Such an imaginative transformation would be in touch with the fantasy in Chrétien's plot, where the hero, in becoming the Red Knight, embarks more deeply on adventures which he sees as stealing from the king. However, Ither, Wolfram's ennobled Red Knight, wears the armour which is the colour of sin before Parzival dons it. At the level of the author's imaginative organisation of the romance, this is a minor point, since the sin can be seen as combined with noble qualities; but at a magical level, what-

ever the red armour may mean, it will mean the same about
every wearer of it, and a second character's taking it from
the first in order to wear it will express an identification
with the first character. The continuing operation of Chrétien's magical plot in *Parzival* must create conflict with the
author's imaginative aims in bestowing knightly virtues
on the Red Knight and in subjecting his slaying to moral
scrutiny.

3. To turn to the third question — Why does Perceval
postpone avenging the laughing girl? — Wolfram's treatment only sharpens the problem. He develops the characters
of Keye and the laughing girl (whom he calls Cunneware), so
that audiences respond sympathetically to them, and he also
has Parzival dismayed by the plight of Cunneware and Anta-
nor when they are chastised by Keye. We are told that
Parzival reaches for his javelin while the chastisement is
taking place, but cannot get near Keye because of the throng
(153, 18–20). But the throng would disperse after the
chastisement ended, in time for Parzival's return to court.
Parzival's final defeat of Keye is just as inconsequential as
Perceval's, being incognito on the part of both knights and
also being in response to further provocation on the part of
Keye, this time directed against Parzival himself.

4. Where the fourth question is concerned — why Arthur
should be so 'worked up' about Perceval — Wolfram's version, very far from dealing with the problem of Arthur's
inexplicable and excessive love for Perceval, intensifies it by
having the whole court admire the youth to an extraordinary extent. There is much idealisation of Parzival, a great
deal of this having to do with the author's chivalric themes.
Parzival has hardly entered Arthur's court, on the first occasion, when we are told:

> sus wart für Artûsen brâht
> an dem got wunsches het erdâht.
> im kunde niemen vîent sîn. (148, 29–149, 1)

And so the boy in whom God had contrived perfection was brought
into Arthur's presence. To dislike him was not possible. (p. 85)

Chrétien's treatment of his fantasy material (in which the
hero himself magically arranges the love and admiration of
the king) is more down-to-earth and also gently ironic:

Nus qui le voit nel tient a sage,
Mais trestot cil qui le veoient,
Por bel et por gent le tenoient. (T text, vv. 976–8)

No-one who saw him thought him wise, but all who saw him
thought him handsome and fair. (p. 11)

5. In the case of the fifth question — concerning the grief-
stricken cousin's surprising interest in Perceval's concerns —
this cousin, called· Sigune by Wolfram, and described as
niece of the grail king, seems outwardly more bizarre in
Parzival than in Chrétien, and yet, on close scrutiny, Chrétien's cousin is the more extraordinary. Perceval meets his
cousin just once, with her newly-slain lover in her arms, and
it is remarkable that she concentrates so entirely on Perceval's affairs in the circumstances. Parzival, however, meets
her three times, and on each occasion she is mourning this
lover: the first time he is newly dead, clasped in her arms;
the second, he is embalmed and still clasped in her arms,
and the third, he is in his tomb while she weeps above it
(138, 21–3; 249, 15–17; 435, 21–2). When Parzival meets
Sigune for the first time, the lover has just been killed by
Orilus, at about the same time that Parzival embraces Orilus's wife Jeschute. Orilus links the slain man with Parzival
when speaking to Jeschute afterwards about his own exploits at Arthur's court and about his sister, Cunneware,
who has the role of laughing prophet at the court in this
version:

'... ir munt kan niht gebâren
mit lachen, ê si den gesiht
dem man des hôhsten prîses giht.
wan kœm mir doch der selbe man!
sô wurde ein strîten hie getân,
als hiute morgen, dô ich streit
und eime fürsten frumte leit,
der mir sîn tjostieren bôt:
von mîner tjoste lager tôt.' (135, 16–24)

'... Until she sets eyes on the most illustrious man in the world her
mouth will never wear a laugh.
   'If only that man would come my way! There would be some
fighting here like this morning's, when I fought a prince who chal-

lenged me and did him some mischief! — My lancethrust stretched
him out dead!' (p. 79)

These extraordinary reflections on the part of Orilus make
best sense as an elaboration of the detail in Chrétien's
magical plot where the hero has a vision of himself as the
slain lover/son, vengeance having been taken by the husband
he has challenged. Why otherwise should Orilus speak of
wishing to kill the unknown most illustrious man in the
world, the sight of whom will bring joy to his 'sweet' sister
(135, 15)? Signe, too, links the slain man with Parzival, for
she tells him the dead knight has been a defender of his
(Parzival's) kingdom and '"slain on your account"' (p. 81;
'"durch dich erslagen"', 141, 2), by Orilus, an aggressor
against Parzival's kingdom. What Signe tells Parzival at
this first meeting is relevant to her mourning, and, on the
second occasion they meet — after the Grail Castle adventure — the conversation does not seem outwardly so
extraordinary as in Chrétien, since the lover is not newly
killed; Signe's seeming to be engrossed in Parzival's concerns is acceptable. On the third occasion they meet, Signe
is supported by the grail while she mourns, and she assists
Parzival in his seeking of it by advising him to find Cundrie
(the Loathly Lady).

R. S. Loomis points out discrepancies in these meetings.
At the first meeting, Signe tells Parzival explicitly that
Orilus is the slayer not only of her lover but also of Parzival's paternal uncle, and Parzival vows vengeance. At the
second meeting, Signe seems to be interested only in Parzival's adventure at the Grail Castle and in the treacherous
sword. Parzival rides away without a word about revenge on
Orilus. Then he comes upon the tent lady, compels Orilus to
acknowledge her innocence and sends him to Arthur. There
is not a word about Orilus's crime in killing Signe's lover,
and nor is there about Parzival's obligation to mete out
justice to the culprit. At the third meeting between Parzival
and Signe, though Orilus's crime is mentioned, the obligation to punish him is again forgotten. Parzival takes no
vengeance on the slayer of his uncle and of his cousin's
lover.[15]

However, Wolfram's extension of the theme of Sigune can
be seen to produce fresh detail which hangs together well as
magical material in tune with Chrétien's plot. In this apparent magical material, the cousin's role would seem to be
that of a woman closely associated with the mother, who is
suffering and mourning as a result of the hero's behaviour.
The three conversations would seem to bring out the particular magical concerns invested in her by the hero. Initially, his thoughts of stealing the queen (in the guise of the tent
lady) give rise to a vision of a mother grieving over her son,
slain for this theft by the man with a prior right to the
queen. As in the case of Chrétien's version, the vision is
pictorially reminiscent of a pietá,[16] where a mother mourns
her son; and the conversation is about the newly-wronged
husband and about his victim, who has been a loyal defender of Parzival's kingdom. The loyal defender of Parzival's
kingdom would be the hero himself, against whom Orilus is
seen as an enemy. Meanwhile, the woman is not only grief-
stricken but angry – when, at the second meeting, she learns
that the hero is not (to give a magical interpretation) doing
anything about his relationship with the king. From these
visions of her come the impetus, first for the hero's establishment of his innocence and then for his asking of the question, expressing his acknowledgement of the king's suffering
and of his own behaviour.

Over and above the possible re-creation of magical material, Wolfram has developed Sigune as a faithful woman —
unlike, as the narrator comments, so many fickle women —
and her 'triwe' is emphasised ('hœrt mêr Sigûnen triwe
sagn', 253, 18; 'Rather hear more about Sigune's fidelity',
p. 134), while it is Sigune who accuses Parzival of failure
in this quality ('"ir truogt den eiterwolves zan, dâ diu galle
in der triuwe an iu bekleip sô niuwe"', 255, 14–16; '"You
showed your venomous wolf-fangs when the canker took
root in your integrity and grew apace!"', p. 135).

6. Where the failure of Arthur's court to recognise Perceval as the Red Knight is concerned, Wolfram does not tackle
the problem. Instead, he intensifies it by having Parzival
declared an impudent interloper, probably as part of his
development of the character of Keye, giving him good,

knightly motivation for his behaviour. This is an example of
how Wolfram's concerns as an author often do not include
his confronting the irrationality of his material.

Just before this second meeting at Arthur's court, Orilus,
sent to the court by Parzival, gives an account of Parzival's
victory over him, referring to the victor as the Red Knight
twice (276, 4; 276, 21); then the entire retinue speaks of the
Red Knight's valour: 'über al diu messenîe sprach, des rôten
rîters ellen næm den prîs zeime gesellen. Des jâhen se âne
rûnen' (278, 24–7; 'Everywhere Arthur's retainers were
saying that the Red Knight's courage had taken glory for
companion and they did not say so in whispers', p. 146). If
the Red Knight is such a subject of conversation at court,
and the court then travels to seek this Red Knight ('der rîter
rôt', 280, 9), why does Cunneware's servant-lad not realise
that he has come across the Red Knight when he sees him in
his armour (283, 25–284, 3; pp. 148–9)? And why do Segra-
mors, Keye and Gawain all fail to recognise him? Parzival is
described once more as the Red Knight while Gawain brings
him to the court (305, 11). There is no actual moment of
recognition — although there is in Chrétien, when Perceval
says he thinks he has avenged the laughing girl by wounding
Kay (T text, vv. 4466–81; A text, vv. 4442–57) — but the
lady Cunneware receives her avenger with joy (305, 14–18)
and afterwards the king goes to meet Parzival at Gawain's
tent, having heard that the Red Knight has gone there ('. . .
der rôte rîter wære komn . . .', 307, 17–20). Chrétien never
calls Perceval the Red Knight, while Wolfram does so even
at this point where he faithfully re-creates Perceval's not
being recognised by his red arms. In case some doubt is
arising as to whether the Red Knight's armour is conspi-
cuously red or not, we are given a description of King Ither's
armour as so red that the eyes seeing it are themselves
reddened and his shield is redder than fire: 'Sîn harnasch
was gar sô rôt daz ez den ougen rœte bôt . . . sîn schilt noch
rœter danne ein fiur . . .' (145, 17–18, 22).

In Chrétien's plot, the reason why the hero is not recognised as the Red Knight is probably that he has renounced
his Red Knight thoughts in this move (where he is acclaimed
by the king). His having ceased to think of himself as the

Red Knight is sufficient to cause the extinction of the idea at
the magical level, and its extinction indicates that Perceval's
being the Red Knight has no function at the author's imaginative level. This situation appears, in a more startling
way, to be the case in Wolfram's version, where the name
'Red Knight' is reiterated. The magical theme of renunciation appears to be present in this text (although it does not
include the wounded goose material, since Wolfram's falcon
is a female and therefore cannot represent the hero). Side by
side with the theme of renunciation, we find Wolfram's contradictory theme of love: Wolfram expends much poetic
energy developing Parzival's tranced state over the blood on
the snow, under the power of 'minne', while he neglects to
attempt a thorough rationalisation of his material. Margaret
Richey notes that Wolfram has a place for both rough and
smooth,[17] while I would add that it is common to find, in an
author's treatment of a magical plot, imaginative development of parts of the material, while other parts remain
untransformed and often puzzling to the levels of thought
awakened by the author's imaginative treatment. The 'minne' material does not relate closely to what appears to be the
purpose of the move in which we find it, and yet it does
relate: while the hero has renounced the woman and all that
she means for him, the desire is still present.

Leaving the questions about Chrétien's *Perceval* now, I shall
briefly examine those parts of *Parzival* where Wolfram seems
to have made few, if any, fundamental alterations.
    Parzival's stay with Gurnemanz is a free development of
Chrétien's move with Gorneman. The main alterations are
that Parzival stays a fortnight, rather than one night, with
Gurnemanz, he is not knighted by Gurnemanz and, unlike
Perceval, he is desired as a son-in-law, and also son, to
replace the old man's lost sons. Parzival is loved and
acclaimed yet more greatly by Gurnemanz than is Perceval
by Gorneman, and, at the magical level in Chrètien's version, this is the chief role of the move.
    Wolfram's narrative is close to that of Chrétien in his
account of the adventure of the besieged lady, the lady here
being a queen, Condwiramurs, and her home Pelrapeir (in

Chrétien, Beaurepaire). Parzival sets off into this adventure yearning for the daughter Gurnemanz has offered to him. He marries the queen, and becomes king: 'dâ krône truoc Parzivâl' (222, 13). Then he leaves to find his mother and seek adventure; he is reunited with his wife only upon becoming king of the grail (799, 1 ff).

While Chrétien's Beaurepaire has an important role in the magical plot, it has been developed in the spirit of chivalry, which is probably the reason for Wolfram's exceptionally close adherence to it. Margaret Richey comments that its being conceived in the spirit of the age of chivalry means that it is 'therefore free from those primitive elements which Wolfram found it necessary to adjust or modify'.[18] It is not, in fact, in the least free of them, but it has lent itself to a transformation which makes them inconspicuous. A recognition of its primitive purposes is essential for an understanding of Chrétien's Grail Castle, and inability to see more than the chivalric surface can lead to a special difficulty with the Grail Castle because Perceval's failure to ask the questions can — on a superficial view — seem out of keeping with the chivalric hero at Beaurepaire and more consistent with Perceval's earlier, untaught condition.

Jessie Weston comments that the names Condwiramurs and Cunneware are 'suspiciously' alike.[19] However, David Blamires points out that 'Condwiramurs' is intended by Wolfram to mean 'to lead, or bring, love,' the origins of the name being French 'conduire' and 'amor(s)'.[20] Whether the names of the woman characters are linked or not, Wolfram's alterations — or, as always, possibly his additions from another source — all suggest Wolfram's engagement in some of Chrétien's magical material, where the female characters express a vision of one queenlike woman, linked with the idea of the sovereignty, in the hero's mind. These alterations include Condwiramurs's being a queen, three other women characters' (the mother, the tent lady and the grail bearer) being queens, now or in the past, in their three separate episodes, and the offering of Gurnemanz's daughter who would make Parzival son and heir to her father.

Wolfram's only significant alteration to the second meeting with the woman in the tent is that Parzival swears

Jeschute's innocence on holy relics in Trevrizent's cell. It is
described as a charitable deed on Parzival's part because it
proves Jeschute's innocence, and it might, with even greater
power, prove the hero's at the magical level, where — in
Chrétien's plot — this is his concern. Another addition is
that the ring is returned to Orilus and he puts it back on
Jeschute's finger. In a magical plot, this may help to reinforce the renunciation apparent in the next move. Or it may
simply be appropriate imaginative treatment of the reconciliation between husband and wife which is given much
attention by Wolfram. Finally, the detail that Orilus is an
aggressor against Parzival seems to bring out meaning
which is only latent in Chrétien's magical plot, but its function is restricted to the first meeting with Sigune. It is not a
feature in Wolfram's treatment of the two scenes with Orilus
and Jeschute which are taken from Chrétien's plot. R. S.
Loomis comments that the wanton slayer of the lover of
Perceval's cousin gets off far too easily with a promise to
surrender at Arthur's court — Perceval even forgets to re-
proach him for the crime[21] — but, at a magical level, the
function of Orilus's 'surrender' at Arthur's court is simply to
declare the hero's innocence, and valour, to the king.

Wolfram's plot will only be magical if he has re-created
his magical sources totally: he may add irrelevant material,
or he may modify, elaborate, syncopate or simplify the plot,
but there must be a complete structure of moves. It does
appear that Wolfram has preserved the essential details of
Chrétien's magical plot, below his overlay, in many of the
adventures of Parzival, but these details might all be entirely transformed by overriding imaginative concerns. Wolfram
completes Chrétien's unfinished romance, and, in such circumstances, his own imaginative vision could take over,
eclipsing the magical purposes of Chrétien's plot. Wolfram's
Grail Castle should provide crucial evidence.

At Wolfram's Grail Castle there are several important
alterations, omissions, additions and emphases. Some of
these are described in my note section[22] and they will
also be referred to as they arise in the discussion that
follows.

Wolfram seems to intensify Chrétien's magical material and

to bring out latent features. He emphasises the suffering of
the king and he places the injury firmly in the testicles. His
single healing question directly asks the nature of the suffering. The king (called Anfortas) is also identified as Parzival's
maternal uncle. Furthermore, Wolfram brings out the importance of the woman who bears the grail: she is a queen
and the king's sister, Repanse de Schoye, and she it is who is
radiant, rather than the grail. There is a great presence of
women at Wolfram's Grail Castle, while at Chrétien's such a
presence is scarcely felt: Parzival's first comment on the
Grail Castle to Signe is that he saw great wonders there
and many fair women: 'grœzlîch wunder ich dâ sach, / unt
manege frouwen wol getân' (251, 26–7).

Wolfram's chief explanation for Parzival's failure to ask
the question is that he has been lacking in 'triuwe' (that is,
lacking in a sense of fellowship and instinctive kindness):[23]
Signe, Cundrie (the Loathly Lady) and the hermit Trevrizent all accuse him of this (255, 13–16; 316, 2; 488, 28–30).
Gurnemanz's advice against asking questions is also given as
an explanation (239, 10–13). Hugh Sacker points out that
Wolfram is criticising the courtly obsession with outward
form ('zuht', 'fuoge') at the expense of inner feeling: Parzival
is thinking more about the propriety of his own behaviour
than about the distress of his host.[24]

The critics tend to concentrate on Wolfram's courtly treatment of his material, while certain questions about his Grail
Castle have not been asked. The imperfect rationalising and
imaginative activity of an author — bestowing new functions and characteristics on characters and other story elements whose roles and attributes continue to be conceived
fundamentally in magical fantasy — can have startling
effects. Wolfram's concern with Parzival's lack of 'triuwe'
and compassion is an appropriate imaginative transformation of the magical material in Chrétien's plot, but it also
has the effect of making more obtrusive the extraordinary
situation of the grail king. Only Parzival can cure him, and
he can do it by asking the king to tell him, it seems, about
his humiliating condition. He already knows the answer —
the hermit having told him specifically (479, 12) — and a
more general question about the king's suffering, with the

prime aim of expressing sympathy, would make more sense
and be more compassionate.

This brings us up against another important consideration: the question as the hermit gives it to Parzival is a
significantly different one from the question with which Parzival heals the king (Wolfram completes the romance). The
hermit's question is '"hêrre, wie stêt iwer nôt?"' (484, 27),
translated by Zeydel as '"Sir, how does your trouble
stand?"'[25] and by A. T. Hatto (p. 246) as '"Sire, what ails
you?"'; and Parzival finally asks the king, '"œheim, waz
wirret dier?"' (795, 29), translated by Zeydel as '"What
afflicts thee, uncle dear?"'[26] and by Hatto (p. 395) as '"Dear
Uncle, what ails you?"' The noun 'nôt' means affliction,
distress or grief, and the verb 'wirret' does not suggest a
physical wound so much as a state of being disturbed, confused, troubled or thrown into disarray. Signe's words, that
the hero should have had compassion on his host and in-
quired about his suffering (or plight) — '"und het gevrâget
sîner nôt"' (255, 19) — do not tell us much more. A. T. Hatto
gives the hermit's '"wie stêt iwer nôt?"' and Parzival's
'"waz wirret dier?"' the same translation ('"what ails
you?"'), but the hermit's question appears to be asking how
the king's trouble is, which would be a more appropriate
question. The problem lies in the question which Parzival
actually asks.

However, this question receives no answer anyway: instead, it instantly heals the king, in accordance with what
Chrétien's Perceval is told by his cousin and the Loathly
Lady (T text, vv. 3584–7; 4670–2). The commonplace,
potentially intrusive, question has amazing power, and until
Parzival asks it, no amount of love and care from the king's
people can relieve his agony. At the imaginative level, too
much is being required of the king, of Parzival and of the
question: why should the relief of the king's agony have to
wait for a single person and such a question? Could it be
that we accept the situation because, in the magical plot,
both the hero's vision of himself and his feeling of guilt take
on these proportions? In Chrétien's plot the question about
the bleeding lance is not really a question, for the hero
knows that his own behaviour is the answer. If Wolfram's

plot is magical, the answer, at that level, would be a problem for the hero rather than the king: the king would be no
more than a figment of the hero's guilt, and all the feelings
would be the hero's.

The moral problem apparent in Chrétien's presentation of
the Fisher King's situation — that the king can be restored
to health and rule by two apparently easy questions which
have not been asked by anyone although the society of the
romance is presented as chivalrous — is met, deliberately or
not, by Wolfram's introduction of the grail prophecies (as
described in my note 22), which give Parzival the designated
position of being the one character who can heal the king
through asking the question. However, the idea of anyone's
being especially called by God to make an apparently unre-
markable (if not impertinent) inquiry about a sick person's
health, and be supernaturally rewarded for making it, has
potentially comic effects. It alerts one to the possibility that
the author's exalted themes are bound up in a magical plot.

It is particularly important to consider in detail whether
overriding concerns on the part of Wolfram have caused the
meaning of Chrétien's questions — 'Why does the lance
bleed?' and 'Who is served from the grail?' — to be lost in
the same way that Chaucer's imaginative concern with the
creation of the Wife of Bath eclipses the magical concerns of
the Loathly Lady tale she tells. Wolfram's changing Chrétien's questions into a single and apparently very different
question, asking the king what is afflicting him, may still be
faithful to Chrétien's magical plot. Chrétien's questions are
important for an understanding of the Grail Castle's role in
his plot — even though, alas, we have no firm evidence for
the answers to them. Margaret Richey argues that neither of
the two questions, as stated by Chrétien, has any logical
bearing upon the healing of the grail king, even though we
are told that the effect of the questions will be the healing of
the king and the restoration of peace and security to his
land. Thus Wolfram (Dr Richey continues), ignoring the
restoration of peace aspect, and concentrating on the healing, gives us 'a single question expressing sympathy and
interest with suggestion of a spiritual power to heal'.[27] Linda B. Parshall comments that 'The posing of the question

demonstrates Parzival's changed awareness of the Gral's significance, as the intimate compassion of his words reflects the depth of his own real love and kinship'.[28] Thereupon Anfortas is healed by God. Wolfram's question is thus interpreted by the critics as an imaginative question, one concerned with the suffering of another, while Chrétien's questions I have found to be concerned with the magical resolution of the hero's guilt.

But how much does Wolfram's question, asking the king what is causing his suffering, express actual concern over this suffering — even though the question follows Parzival's prayer before the grail that the king might be healed? I am here questioning not Wolfram's conscious intentions as an author, so much as the content of the very few words in this all-important question. Can we feel without any doubt that 'Uncle, what ails you (afflicts you)?' or even 'Uncle, what is distressing you?' — placed though the question is in the context of Parzival's spiritual journey and prayer — is an expression of a healing sympathy which can raise a stricken man and prove the questioner worthy of the position of supreme knight? The question would, at the level of Chrétien's magical plot, be thoroughly pertinent, because, there, the hero has to confront what he feels he is doing to the king, but, if it is to fulfil its role in Wolfram's imaginative themes, it needs to have a rather different direction. As it stands, it is a frail vehicle for the conveyal of a heartfelt compassion, being enigmatic in that respect, rather flat and over-curious. Has Wolfram re-created the magical purposes of Chrétien's questions at the expense of his imaginative concerns?[29] Behind the hero's confrontation with his guilt, in Chrétien's magical plot, is his desire for the sovereignty, and Wolfram's Parzival is to be king of the grail, once he has healed Anfortas by asking the question from his heart. How unequivocal is the motivation given to Parzival by the author, consciously or unconsciously? Are we all colluding with desires for Parzival on the part of Wolfram? Both A. T. Hatto and Edwin Zeydel translate the question — '"œheim, waz wirret dier?"' — with an added endearment: '"Dear Uncle, what ails you?"' and '"What afflicts thee, uncle dear?"', presumably on the authority of the hermit that a successful question would spring from Parzival's 'triuwe' (483, 19–30; 488, 28–30). Edwin Zeydel may also have been influenced by his search for a rhyme; and Parzival's addressing the king as 'uncle', rather than 'herre' (the address in the hermit's question), together with his use of the familiar pronoun rather than the hermit's formal one, may have encouraged the translators to include the endearment. But there is probably an element of love behind the magical question 'Why does the lance bleed?', and this could be part of a magical purpose behind '"œheim, waz wirret dier?"', acting as the greatest influence of all on the words chosen by the translators.

Whether there is an element of love at the magical level of Chrétien's plot or not, it does seem as if Wolfram may be requiring his question to carry a meaning it cannot possibly carry. Meanwhile, his choice of the verb 'wirret' for Parzival's question is intriguingly apt for a magical level of meaning. In Chrétien's magical plot, the hero confronts his belief that he is wounding (castrating?) the king, but this wounding, expressed as physical, is as much felt by the hero to be spiritual: the grief and defeat of the kings are more often the theme than their physical pain.

Wolfram's single question, operating as it does together with a grail which has the power to bestow a supreme sovereignty on Parzival, seems to be a precise re-creation — however idiosyncratic — of Chrétien's two questions, in terms of function. Wolfram endows both his question and his grail with certain magical powers. The question brings instant health to the stricken king —

swaz der Franzoys heizt flôrî,
der glast kom sînem velle bî ... (796, 5–6)

The lustre which the French call 'fleur' entered his complexion ...
(p. 395)

— and Parzival immediately becomes, as previously announced by a grail inscription, ruler over the grail:

da ergienc dô dehein ander wal,
wan die diu schrift ame grâl
hete ze hêrren in benant:

Parzivâl wart schiere bekant
ze künige unt ze hêrren dâ. (796, 17–21)

No other Election was made than of the man the Gral Inscription
had named to be their lord. Parzival was recognised forthwith as
King and Sovereign. (p. 395)

Chrétien's question about the lance — 'Why does the lance
bleed?' — is, I believe, identical in meaning with Wolfram's
question — '"œheim, waz wirret dier?"' — in so far that
these questions both express an inquiry about the king's
suffering, and both — in expressing the interest of Perceval /
Parzival, not of anyone else — have the power to heal the
king. Meanwhile, the function of Chrétien's question as to
who is served from the grail seems to be closely connected
with the function of Wolfram's grail. The grail in *Parzival*
has the power to bestow the highest status and splendour on
Parzival — *when* he has asked the question about the king's
suffering. This may very well be the intended role of the
grail question in Chrétien. There is some compelling evidence in what we have of Chrétien's magical plot that the
grail is concerned with the possession of sovereignty.

If Wolfram's version includes a complete magical plot and
that magical plot is identical fundamentally with Chrétien's,
what about all the many differences in detail that we find
between the two Grail Castles, not yet discussed?

While Wolfram emphasises the suffering of the grail king,
true to the magical concerns in Chrétien as well as to his
own imaginative concerns, his grail king is wounded in pursuit of a woman: how can he, therefore, have been wounded
(at a magical level) by the hero? This alteration by Wolfram
may have arisen partly from his religious transformation of
the grail and from ideas of chastity involved, and partly
from the idea of the injury in the testicles (which is magical
material in Chrétien). No difference would be made to any
meaning at the magical level, where only an injury inflicted
by the woman character herself could make the difference
(the wounding activity of a female character could not express the hero's wounding activity). Wolfram's introduction
of the pursuit of a woman has the status of an addition and
this addition helps to make the replacement of Anfortas by

Parzival as king more acceptable at the imaginative level. Wolfram's giving the wound a venomous character is another of his appropriate intensifications, but not necessarily for magical purposes. Other differences in detail concern the lance and the sword. The lance in Wolfram's version is dripping with blood, rather than bleeding, which seems to express the action of the wounder rather than the suffering of the wounded. The accompanying lamentation, however, emphasises the suffering. The sword, presented at the end of the evening, rather than at the beginning, is the king's personal sword, the sword he was using when he was wounded. It may be irrelevant at a magical level that the sword was present at the king's wounding in the service of Orgeluse — although we must note that Wolfram's used sword cannot express innocence as does Chrétien's unused one. What is important is that the king honours Parzival as a son, and that this would have been the moment, other chances having been missed, to ask the king how he had been wounded. This is strongly felt at the author's imaginative level, but, if Chrétien's magical plot has been faithfully reproduced in *Parzival*, we have a unique twist to the magical situation in Wolfram's version, that the sword which was present at the wounding is bestowed upon him who inflicted the wound and this would emphasise the need for the question expressing the hero's acknowledgement of this wounding.

In Chrétien's plot, one outcome of the putting of the questions is to be the restoration of the king's rule ('"terre tenist"', v. 3589, T text) — whether or not the hero is also to attain sovereignty — while, in Wolfram's version, there is no mention of the restoration of the king's rule and no restoration takes place, for the deliverer (Parzival) succeeds Anfortas upon healing him, as the grail decrees. This has much to do with Wolfram's religious and chivalric themes, but, if Wolfram has created a magical plot, the heaven-sent decree in the inscription on the grail would give necessary power to the hero's thoughts of replacing the king. In Chrétien's plot, it is likely that the power the hero needs to acquire a sense of his own sovereignty is to be obtained by his acknowledgement of the king's sovereignty and of his own guilt.

Decided links may be discerned between Wolfram's religious material and Chrétien's magical material. Parzival is to achieve the kingship of the grail (sovereignty) on attaining absolute goodness (a sense of his innocence, all guilt resolved), and it is suddenly made easy for him because he finds favour with God. In Wolfram's creation of Parzival's second visit to the Grail Castle, it is no longer an unknown knight who is expected and no longer is there any uncertainty as to whether, when he comes, he will prove unworthy. Wolfram has Parzival and his wife and son called by name in the grail prophecies. Moreover, Parzival is told to ask the question and also told that his question will cure the grail king.[30] Wolfram's material seems to transfer us from the primitive material, where the hero's magical tactics have powers limited by the power of his guilt, on to another magical level where struggle and uncertainty are removed by the use of Christian magic. The hermit takes away the hero's sins ('wand in der wirt von sünden schiet', 501, 17), after he has confessed them and repented, and sovereignty and goodness are bestowed by means of a magical use of God. Wolfram re-creates Chrétien's powerful conflict — between aspiration, attainable only when a sense of innocence is achieved, and an opposing sense of guilt: the conflict lends itself easily to the expression of religious feeling, where a sense of sin conflicts with a yearning for ideal goodness. In his resolution, which Wolfram invents in the absence of Chrétien's resolution, he uses magic words and rituals as Chrétien would have done, but magic words and rituals with all the power of the medieval church behind them.

Wolfram completes Chrétien's unfinished plot, and I am persuaded that his faithfulness to it throughout ensures his continued faithfulness in his conclusion of it. However, his re-creation of the magical material is highly idiosyncratic. He has built up a striking magical structure of his own, using Christian magic through the hermit, and also the powers of God employed through the inscriptions on the grail, for the establishment of Parzival as supreme, ideal knight. Powers are established to bring about perfect virtue, supreme sovereignty and ideal happiness for Parzival. The result is the contrast between Parzival's first visit to the Grail

Castle and his second, where all uncertainty has gone and he knows not only what to do but that upon doing it he will become king of the grail. The hero's guilt is dispelled and his sovereignty is prophesied.

Wolfram gives Chrétien's plot the outcome that the hero succeeds the king, and he does this in such a way that the material acquires omnipotent powers to bring about the hero's desires. The magical prophecy brought about by divine inscription on the grail, and reported by the hermit, pronounces that the hero's failure during his first visit to the Grail Castle was included as a possibility in a set of preordained events in his career, the hero being the one chosen who has only to ask the question to heal the king and then himself to take the place of the king by decree from on high (483, 19–484, 30; pp. 246–7). This decree dispels all idea of usurpation or theft.

Cundrie's announcement of the inscription proclaiming that the hero is to be lord of the grail (781, 3–782, 30) has a particularly interesting magical form. An examination of it will show how it has powers to bring things about in the mind. Its most significant content (the bulk of it) is as follows:

'ôwol dich, Gahmuretes suon!
got wil genâde an dir nu tuon ...
nu wis kiusche unt dâ bî vrô.
wol dich des hôhen teiles,
du krône menschen heiles!
daz epitafjum ist gelesen:
du solt des grâles hêrre wesen.
Condwîr âmûrs daz wîp dîn
und dîn sun Loherangrîn
sint beidiu mit dir dar benant ...
wær dir niht mêr sælden kunt,
wan daz dîn wârhafter munt
den werden unt den süezen
mit rede nu sol grüezen:
den künec Anfortas nu nert
dîns mundes vrâge, diu im wert
siufzebæren jâmer grôz:
wâ wart an sælde ie dîn genôz? ...'
si sprach 'nu prüeve, Parzivâl.

der hôhste plânête Zvâl,
und der snelle Almustrî,
Almaret, [und] der liehte Samsi,
erzeigent sælekeit an dir.
der fünfte heizt Alligafir,
unde der sehste Alkitêr,
und uns der næhste Alkamêr.
ich ensprichez niht ûz eime troum:
die sint des firmamentes zoum,
die enthalden sîne snelheit:
ir kriec gein sîme loufte ie streit.
sorge ist dînhalp nu weise.
swaz der plânêten reise
umblouft, [und] ir schîn bedecket,
des sint dir zil gestecket
ze reichen und zerwerben.
dîn riwe muoz verderben ...
du hetes junge sorge erzogn:
die hât kumendiu freude an dir betrogn.
du hâst der sêle ruowe erstriten
und des lîbes freude in sorge erbiten.'

'O happy you, son of Gahmuret! God is about to manifest his grace
in you! ... Now be modest and yet rejoice! O happy man, for your
high gains, you coronal of man's felicity! The Inscription has been
read: you are to be lord of the Gral! Your wife Condwiramurs and
your son Loherangrin have both been assigned there with you ...
Had you known no other good fortune than that your truthful lips
are now to address noble, gentle King Anfortas and with their
Question banish his agony and heal him, who could equal you in
bliss?' ... [Cundrie then named seven stars in a heathen tongue]
'Now take note, Parzival', she said. 'The loftiest planet Zval and
swift Almustri, Almuret and bright Samsi point to good fortune in
you. The fifth is called Alligafir and the sixth Alkiter, while the
nearest to us is Alkamer. I do not pronounce it in a dream: these
planets are the bridle of the firmament, checking its onrush; their
contrariness ever ran counter to its momentum. You have now
abandoned care. All that the planets embrace within their orbits,
whatever they shed their light on, marks the scope of what it is for
you to attain and achieve. Your sorrow is doomed to pass away ...
You raised a brood of cares in tender years: but the happiness
which is on its way to you has dashed their expectations. You have
won through to peace of soul and outlived cares to have joy of your
body.' (pp. 387–8)

The chief, thematic content — in terms of the romance as a whole — of the earlier part of Cundrie's speech is the making of statements: Parzival is to be sovereign of the grail, his wife Condwiramurs is to be joined with him in this position, he is hailed as the crown of human salvation, and he is to heal Anfortas with the Question. God is about to manifest his grace in Parzival. The second half of Cundrie's announcement is concerned chiefly with the statement that Parzival has abandoned care. The final couplet has a particular interest. Linda B. Parshall thinks the implication is that Parzival has already achieved 'his personal peace with God', which is the satisfaction of the soul ('"der sêle ruowe"'), and is now ready for the entirely distinct satisfaction of the body ('"des lîbes freude"'), which the grail can offer him. The specific powers of the grail are worldly, not spiritual: the dispensation of food (238, 13–17; p. 126); the sustaining of life and youth (469; p. 239) and the dispensation of the good things of earth that Paradise once provided (470; p. 240).[31]

The magical process which can be seen here is a conjuring up of supreme and permanent sovereignty and happiness by decree from God, this decree given in the form of writing — which is invested with magical power — inscribed on the grail — which is also invested with magical power. The language takes on the power of magic words: observe the power of the couplet, '"daz epitafjum ist gelesen: du solt des grâles hêrre wesen"'. Words expressing happiness are reiterated in the first half of the announcement, and they appear in exclamations and commands expressing how happy Parzival is or must be. The second half of the announcement takes on, even more strikingly, the form of a spell. Seven 'stars' (that is Saturn, Jupiter, Mars, the Sun, Venus, Mercury and the Moon) are named in Arabic, which is given its medieval name 'heathen' ('heidensch'). Their movements ordain that Parzival has now abandoned care, and this abandonment of care is stated four times: '"sorge ist dînhalp nu weise"'; '"dîn riwe muoz verderben"'; '"du hetes junge sorge erzogn: die hât kumendiu freude an dir betrogn"'; and, finally, '"und des lîbes freude in sorge erbiten"'. The repetition of the statement, together with the incantation using the 'stars', dispels the hero's anxiety. The incantation

employs the magic number seven, and the names of the
heavenly bodies in a tongue which bestows upon them the
power of the occult, and, above all, it employs astrology:
movements of heavenly bodies have determined that the
hero's care is now over.

The final couplet is a telling one. At the magical level, it
announces that the hero has won through his anxiety to have
joy of his body. The association of Condwiramurs with Parzival's destiny, in Cundrie's announcement, together with
the couple's reunion after the long separation, suggests an
important meaning of the final couplet. Parzival's taking
Condwiramurs, together with the grail crown, is ordained by
God. In the Perceval magical plot, the hero leaves the
woman (called significantly Lufamour, Condwiramurs or
Blancheflor) through whom he achieves sovereignty, in order
to deal with his guilt: the separation ends when the guilt
is resolved. The inclusion of Condwiramurs in Cundrie's
announcement is essential, and it is interesting that Wolfram clearly includes a magical statement that the queen
may be enjoyed. In his magical sources for the Perceval
story, she is shadowed by thoughts of incest.

Wolfram has enormously developed the episode with the
hermit Trevrizent (based on the visit to the hermit in Chrétien's *Perceval*, which is probably an interpolation), and this
development seems to include his giving it a role in a magical plot — a role it does not have in Chrétien. Do the Gawain
adventures likewise have any particular role in Wolfram's
magical plot? Wolfram follows Chrétien's narrative quite
closely and it does not seem that the Gawain episodes do,
concerned as they are with comparatively light-hearted
adventures with women. However, Gawain's story in *Parzival* ends with his marriage to Orgeluse (in Chrétien, l'Orgueil-
leuse), who is dangerous to woo, material not entirely
irrelevant to the Perceval fantasy, and, meanwhile, Wolfram's chivalric concerns include this material. There is material in *Parzival* which has nothing, or little, to do with
the magical plot of *Perceval*, but this material does not alter
Wolfram's magical plot; it only delays its progression.

Where Wolfram's first two books are concerned, they are a
free development of Chrétien's brief account of Perceval's

father — which Chrétien has the mother tell her son. Wolfram creates his own material for these first two books,[32]
and this material is an imaginative development of brief
magical material in Chrétien. Parzival's father appears to be
parallel to Parzival, being a younger son who did not inherit
from his father and who is '"set on"' (p. 19) winning queens
and their kingdoms; this career ends with his being killed by
a king, and at this point Parzival takes over. Where the
magical plot is concerned, the first two books have no more
force than material which, in one way or another, helps to
enhance the hero. They contain no hint of the wounded king
theme apparent in the father of Chrétien's Perceval, nor of
the related magical idea, in the English *Sir Perceval of Galles*,
that the hero's father has been killed by the Red Knight.
Wolfram's re-creation of the Perceval magical plot begins at
Book Three.[33]

This re-creation makes an exceptionally informative study
for the student of the magical plot, particularly in the areas
of authorial alteration and development at the magical level.
Emerging with remarkable clarity is the extent of Wolfram's
engagement at the magical level. Every text containing a
magical plot challenges the critic anew, and perhaps Wolfram's version of Chrétien's *Perceval* impresses upon us most
forcibly how much this is the case.[34]

CHAPTER FIVE

PEREDUR

As in the case of my study of the Welsh version of the Ywain story (*The Lady of the Fountain*), this study of *Peredur*[1] can only be a limited one, but I believe it is useful, even without the Welsh language, to consider the work briefly, in the light of my findings where the French, English and German versions are concerned, in order to raise some questions and make some comments.

Welsh scholars disagree over whether or not Chrétien's version was a source for *Peredur*. Many hold that the Welsh and French versions are end-products of a common source, while others still hold the view that the Welsh storyteller knew the tale through Chrétien and adapted it for a Welsh audience, using the techniques of Welsh storytelling and Welsh material already in his possession.[2] There is also disagreement over the structure of *Peredur*. Some have followed Thurneysen in dividing the work into four sections based on the relationship between the parts of the Welsh text and parts of Chrétien's *Conte du Graal*: I(*a*) from the beginning up to Peredur's second meeting with King Arthur; I(*b*) the story of Peredur and Angharad Law Eurawc; II from the adventure with the one-eyed giant up to the marriage with the Empress of Constantinople, and, finally, III, the rest of the story, starting with the Loathly Lady.[3] Other scholars argue that we must find a fresh understanding of the text in its entirety.[4] Among the themes seen as unifying the different parts of *Peredur* is that of sovereignty — in this case, sovereignty in a political sense rather than as a state of mind: it has been argued that *Peredur* is concerned with the gaining of a kingdom lost upon the father's death.[5]

While I see the force of the arguments that we should not
bring inappropriate modern responses to bear and see *Peredur* as 'une oeuvre ... assez mal composée',[6] my own
findings where Chrétien's *Perceval* is concerned make me
intensely interested in the fact that the distinct story of
Angharad Law Eurawc is attached at the very point where
the magical plot in Chrétien's *Perceval* breaks off and the
distinct story of Gawain is attached. Moreover, in finding
that the plot of the English version forms a complete magical structure of a different, though parallel, kind to that of my
conjectured grail plot, I am the more interested that the
Welsh version breaks off at the point where Chrétien's version breaks off and does not supply an ending in any way
similar to the one I conjectured as likely for Chrétien's grail
story. There may, nevertheless, prove to be a complete
magical plot in *Peredur*, as is the case in Wolfram's version.

This question cannot be addressed, however, until I have
examined the plot of the first section, Thurneysen's I(*a*). This
section corresponds more closely with Chrétien's plot than
does the plot of *Sir Perceval of Galles*. The most striking
variations are found in the treatment of the characters who
correspond to the Fisher King and Gorneman in Chrétien.
Peredur spends a night with a grey-haired, lame, fisherman
uncle who feasts him, tests his prowess and acclaims him,
and then he spends a night with a grey-haired, handsome
uncle who feasts him, tests his prowess and acclaims him.
The first uncle gives Peredur advice which is identical to
some of Gorneman's advice to Perceval (that he should leave
his mother's words and regard the uncle as his teacher, and
that, if he sees what is strange to him, he must not ask about
it but wait to be told). With this uncle, he is tested by means
of a fight with sticks and shields. The second uncle tests him
by having him strike a column in half with a sword and then
join them together again. He does not entirely succeed in
this second test and the uncle prophesies that he will be the
greatest warrior when his full strength is reached. This test
is followed by the 'grail' scene as it appears in this version: a
huge spear, with three streams of blood along it, is brought
in, and a salver with a man's head on it, surrounded by
blood. There is lamentation. No questions are expected or

asked, and Peredur takes his leave the next morning. The
events in the castle are not related to any suffering on the
part of the uncle. In the light of my findings where Chrétien's version is concerned, I have some matters to raise.
First of all, the second part of the advice given to Peredur
counsels against asking questions, while no questions are
involved in the 'grail' scene of this version. (That Peredur
does not ask and the uncle does not tell him is mentioned,
but the matter is not brought up at all in the following scene
with the character corresponding to the mourning cousin in
Chrétien, and the uncle is not in need of the questions, in
any case.) Moreover, Chrétien's Gorneman advises Perceval
against talking too much, rather than against asking questions; the advice is related to Perceval's not asking the
questions at the Grail Castle by being given as the reason
at that point in the narrative. The Welsh advice is more
explicit about not asking questions concerning things that
seem strange, and this in a context where such questions
have no role. Furthermore, I have found that the advice has
the status only of a superficial rationalisation in Chrétien's
plot and is therefore not a likely candidate for transmission
in any other tradition than a literary tradition. I have also
found the fisherman detail to have no very profound role in
Chrétien's plot, and here it is attached to the 'wrong' uncle.
The lameness has followed suit, but neither uncle appears to
be suffering, while, in Chrétien's plot, the king's suffering is
— in great contrast to the fisherman detail — essential to the
plot. I shall return to the different treatment of the Grail
Castle. Two important matters appear to be emerging: the
plot of *Peredur* has quite different feelings at the magical
level from those apparent in Chrétien's plot, while, at the
same time, I think there is evidence that the Welsh storyteller knew Chrétien's version.

There are important differences in the treatment of the
female characters. The first move with the tent lady shows
how the emphasis in this version is on affirming the
sovereignty of the queen-figures. The tent lady welcomes
Peredur graciously and she is seated in a golden chair, with
a frontlet of gold and sparkling stones, rather than asleep in
bed. Peredur kneels to kiss her, and, as Glenys Goetinck

points out,[7] it is more than likely that he kisses her hand.
This scene is in interesting contrast with the advice given by
the mother in this version: she tells Peredur that he should
make love to any fair lady he sees, even though she does not
desire him, for this will make him a better and nobler man.

The adventure with the character corresponding to Chrétien's Blancheflor (the black, white and red maiden) is in a
position different from its crucial position in Chrétien's plot,
coming not immediately before the visit to the 'grail' castle,
but after it. In harmony with the tent lady move, it is concerned with restoring the lady's dominion, without any
accompanying mention of love or marriage where Peredur is
concerned.

The meeting with the character corresponding to Chrétien's cousin — Peredur's foster-sister — follows the 'grail'
move, as in Chrétien, but no sovereignty move corresponding to Chrétien's Blancheflor move appears anywhere in the
text preceding it. A version of Chrétien's Red Knight move,
however, does appear in the text preceding it. Peredur's
encounter with his foster-sister takes place in a forest. He
hears a woman shrieking and finds her trying to put a dead
man on a horse, shrieking each time she fails. He asks her
why she is shrieking and the exchange between them is as
follows: '"Alas, thou accursed Peredur", said she, "small
relief from my affliction did I ever get from thee." "Why",
said he, "should I be accursed?" "Because thou art the cause
of thy mother's death. For when thou didst set out against
her will, pain leapt within her, and of that she died. And
inasmuch as thou art cause of her death, thou art accursed.
And the dwarf and the she-dwarf thou sawest in Arthur's
court, that was the dwarf of thy father and thy mother. And I
am a foster-sister of thine, and this is my husband whom the
knight that is in the clearing in the forest has slain ..."'
Peredur says he will '"exact vengeance"' and he does so by
defeating the knight, making him marry his foster-sister,
and then sending him to Arthur's court to tell Arthur it was
Peredur who overthrew him '"in service and honour to
Arthur"' and to say Peredur will not go to Arthur's court till
he encounters the tall man (Cei) '"to avenge the injury
to the dwarf and the maiden"'. Cei is rebuked by Arthur and

the household 'for driving away from Arthur's court a lad as
excellent as Peredur', and Arthur says he will search the
wilderness of the Island of Britain for Peredur until he finds
him (Jones and Jones, pp. 193–4). It is interesting here that,
while the husband is — presumably — newly dead, the
foster-sister addresses herself immediately to Peredur's
affairs and speaks of her affliction as if it is connected with
Peredur and of long duration. Her first thought is that Peredur has caused his mother's death. As in Chrétien, the
thoughts creating this scene seem to be of a queen mourning
her son's behaviour, but the details here are different: Chrétien's lover/son is absent and we have a husband killed; this
situation is immediately repaired by the remarriage of the
mourning queen. It seems that the hero makes good the
killing of the queen's husband, restoring the husband and
declaring his innocence through doing so. In the magical
plot, the killer must be himself, but the absence of suffering
in the kings (Arthur and the second uncle), and the emphasis
on affirmation of the queens, suggest that reinstatement is
the important element here.

Peredur's second meeting with the tent lady is yet another
reinstatement of the queen. In this version, the tent lady's
knight is not the killer of the knight mourned by the woman
relative (the plot has two knights of the clearing). At the
magical level, these two knights are distinct, for, in this plot,
we have two wives reinstated (the foster-sister and the tent
lady), while, in Chrétien, we have a vision of a lover/son
killed by an avenging husband, and his innocence 'proved'
against the husband (this involving the two moves of the
mourning cousin and the battle against the tent lady's
knight).

The witches of Caer Loyw seem to have no role in the
magical plot. This particular plot could not include warrior
women who attack other women (the witch who trains Peredur attacks a countess), nor malignant women who
are responsible for the severed head of the 'grail' scene (an
explanation given in the last part of *Peredur*), and nor could
it include women who are destined to be destroyed in battle
by Peredur (the destiny of the witches). In this magical
plot, the female characters will all express the particular

aspects of the queen-figure at the centre of its theme of sovereignty.

The final move in section I(a) of *Peredur* seems to carry out the same function as its counterpart in Chrétien. There is no problem over recognition in this version since red armour is not involved in the role of the knight who seeks to snatch the sovereignty. Here, the musings of Chrétien's Perceval over the woman he loves reappear, although no love for the black, white and red maiden is expressed in her move. This presents no problem at the magical level, but the sex of the pouncing hawk and the killing of the bird both do; a female hawk cannot represent the hero, and the killed duck cannot play the role in the plot that Chrétien's goose may possibly play.

The sequence of moves before us clearly lacks the tension apparent in Chrétien's magical plot. The hero challenges the king and loves the black, white and red maiden, but these elements receive less emphasis than the kingly and queen-like roles these characters play in affirming Peredur and being treated in return as sovereign. Only the foster-sister suffers, but her marriage is immediately restored. The placing of the move with the black, white and red maiden after the move with the second uncle is also an indication that the plot is not concerned with conflict between desire and guilt in the sense that Chrétien's plot is. The moves in *Peredur* do not seem to be highly charged magical steps in a struggle. The additional material of the witches might also, in this case, be seen as an indication of lack of tension.

This lack of tension may offer some explanations for the baffling differences between the Welsh 'grail' move and Chrétien's. There is no suffering and there are therefore no questions to be asked. The severed head, which appears instead of the grail, does not seem, in this context, to express either aggression or guilt (aggression, if it is the king's head and guilt, if it is the hero's): the feelings in the context do not appear to be strong enough to produce such a vision. Without a completed sequence of moves, it is difficult to discover the role of the severed head; in the case of Chrétien's unfinished plot, rich detail compensates, to some extent, for the lack of an ending. I can only observe that lack of tension in a magical plot allows modifications and playful additions; and that Chrétien's Grail Castle cannot be relevant here — as it cannot be relevant in the English version — for there is no guilt in relation to the king. The severed head may, in some way, be a playful alternative.

While the initial plot breaks off where Chrétien's 'Perceval' breaks off, the redactors of *Peredur* have supplied much additional material. The section numbered II by Thurneysen (which is the third sequence, beginning with Peredur's asking the black man who it was who put his eye out, and ending with the marriage to the Empress of Constantinople) appears to be concerned with the acquisition of sovereignty and can be an indication of the nature of the material in the initial sequence before us. It certainly provides something approaching the continuation up to the hero's victory which is required by the initial sequence, and this must be the good reason why we find it in this text. It is a series of adventures where women are won in combat and renounced (magically) until the hero marries the empress, and its lack of deep conflict is in harmony with the initial sequence. It is, nevertheless, a distinct plot in which the hero aspires to the empress, rather than the black, white and red maiden, and it is divided from the initial sequence by the story of Peredur's winning of Angharad Law Eurawc. Peredur's declaration of love to the maiden Angharad Golden-hand (Jones and Jones, p. 207) scarcely fits into the sequence created by sections I(*a*) and II, in which the female characters represent sovereignty and are renounced, in some way, until the hero finally achieves the empress.

It is interesting to glance at the last part of *Peredur* — Thurneysen's section III[8] — for further consideration of the 'grail' material. In section III, Peredur returns to the castle of the manifestations — the uncle there is now lame, so lameness seems to be transferred to the 'right' uncle — in order to hear a yellow-haired youth's explanations for the manifestations. In particular, the yellow-haired youth explains that he was the Loathly Lady (who appears, in *Peredur*, at the beginning of section III) and that the head belonged to a cousin slain by the witches of Caer Loyw. This material will have its own explanation elsewhere than in the magical plot of section I(*a*), but my interest here, in the light of Chrétien's plot, is that we have such a return to the 'grail castle' in order to receive explanations. The desire for explanations is very much the experience of audiences of the unfinished Grail story. At the magical level of Chrétien's plot, explanations are not needed: the meaning of the questions is that the hero has an action to perform, not explanations to receive (profound material absent in *Peredur*).

The magical plot of *Peredur* is a very different plot from that of Chrétien: the powerful conflicts of Chrétien's plot do not reappear here, and the comparative light-heartedness of the re-creation must be one of the many reasons for the differences apparent in this version. However, I do find a number of indications that the Welsh storytellers and red-actors involved used Chrétien, or some intermediate text, as their source for the parts called sections I(*a*) and III by Thurneysen.

PART THREE

CHAPTER SIX

GAWAIN AND THE GREEN KNIGHT

When I first studied the plot of *Sir Gawain and the Green Knight*,[1] I was interested in its relationship to dream material, in particular to Martin's beheading dream.[2] Upon coming to it again, after my experiences with plots such as those of *Hamlet*, *Jane Eyre* and the Ywain, Perceval and Apollonius texts, I came with a conviction that the magical plot was essentially a series of rituals — albeit created at a level of thought close to that of dreams — and I have therefore emerged with rather different results.

However, in spite of my increasing experience of the magical plot as ritual, *Sir Gawain and the Green Knight* continued to present me with difficulties, and it was only when I studied the plot of Emily Brontë's *Wuthering Heights* that I felt I was beginning to understand the nature of the rituals in the Green Knight plot. In the Introduction to this book, I distinguish certain types among the plots I have come across, and these are illustrated by my studies of the Apollonius and Ywain plots, and by the various Perceval plots. *Sir Gawain and the Green Knight* does not belong to any of these types. There is no attainment of any kind of sovereignty for the hero, since the acknowledgement of the lord's right, also present in Chrétien's *Perceval*, is ultimately paramount, whereas, in *Perceval*, it is part of the hero's quest for sovereignty. Moreover, *Sir Gawain and the Green Knight* differs from *Hamlet*, where there is also no attainment of sovereignty, by clearly not being devoted, from beginning to end, to the purification of the hero's feelings: much of the text is devoted to the enjoyment of these feelings, threatened though they are throughout by thoughts of punishment.

If the Green Knight plot is magical, then it is a series of rituals. In which case, what is the ritual function of the beheading game? What is it bringing about in the mind? As in the case of *Hamlet*, the critic is faced with the problem that a magical plot is concerned with the hero's wishes and yet the outcome of the adventure does not seem entirely desirable. The exchanges of winnings must also have a ritual purpose and one which is parallel to that of the beheading game, because both are bargains, concerned with an exchange between the hero and the Green Knight. The adventure is remarkably enclosed by these bargains, the beheading game providing the outer fence and the exchanges of winnings providing an inner fence, round the temptation scenes. When I considered the plot of *Wuthering Heights*, I felt that 'fence' (defence) might be the right word, for the defences of Emily Brontë's plot are clear. The Heathcliff story is followed by a replay, substituting a tamed Heathcliff in Hareton and re-establishing the family — a process which legitimises the adventure. The story is defended not only by this rearguard, but also by its presentation from the outset: it is filtered through two layers of narrator, the respectable Lockwood and his informant the upright Nelly Dean, who is often shocked and who weighs everything up according to accepted values. The punitive, moralising religion of the ` period, which threatened the adventure, is also dealt with at the outset: it is presented in the guise of the unpleasant clown Joseph, and in the sermon of Jabes Branderham (dreamed by Lockwood), against which even Lockwood rebels. This dream is followed by Lockwood's dream of Catherine sobbing ' "Let me in — let me in!" '[3] I think it is correct to see an analogy here between the two plots: both appear to be a journey into forbidden experience (or experience felt to be forbidden) for the fulfilling enjoyment of that experience before retreating from it; the journey is made possible by a great number of safeguards placating the powers-that-be. In *Sir Gawain and the Green Knight*, the safeguards are the two bargains — the beheading exchange and the exchanges of winnings — which acknowledge the lord's right.

Of course, all magical plots might be regarded as providing the conditions in which suppressed feelings can be given full play: the difference here is one of emphasis. In *Wuthering Heights* and *Sir Gawain and the Green Knight*, the energies of the magic are channelled more into providing safeguards than into bringing about a victory for the heroine's or hero's desires. The focus of interest is the extended enjoyment of present feelings, rather than a reaching out for new, enhanced feelings about the self, and these feelings are felt to be dangerous. Hence the provision of exceptional defences, with the heavy use of rituals to placate the powers-that-be, over and above the usual disguises.

I shall now conduct a new exploration of *Sir Gawain and the Green Knight*, and shall begin by surveying questions and comments of scholars over the years, in the light of those questions and comments considered in the preceding studies of this book, for I must seek to establish once again the presence of a magical plot in this text. But first I shall supply an outline of the plot.

1. On New Year's Day, King Arthur keeps his vow not to begin the feast before he has seen a marvel. As he waits, a huge knight comes riding into the hall, his clothing, horse, skin and hair all green in colour; he is also carrying a mighty axe and a holly bough. This knight challenges any of the company to a game: the knight accepting the challenge must deal him a blow with the axe and receive a blow from him in return a year later. The court is silent with amazement and the Green Knight laughs at them. Enraged, Arthur seizes the axe but his nephew, Gawain, who has been sitting next to Guinevere, asks for the adventure. He strikes off the green head with a single blow, and the Green Knight rises, picks up his head, reminds Gawain to keep his appointment at the Green Chapel a year later, and leaves the hall.

2. The year passes, and after All Saints' Day Gawain sets out from Camelot in search of the Green Chapel. He searches in vain through a wintry wilderness full of perils until he comes upon a castle. It is Christmas Eve and the lord of the castle entertains him hospitably, while he is also welcomed by the beautiful lady of the castle and another lady who is ancient, hideous and not made known to Gawain. When Gawain wishes to resume his quest on St John's Day, the host persuades him to remain three days longer, until New Year's morning, since the Green Chapel is nearby. For the entertainment of Gawain, he suggests that they play a game: each evening host and guest will exchange whatever they have

gained during the day. On the first day, the host hunts female deer
in the forest, while his wife visits Gawain as he lies in bed and
makes amorous advances; Gawain resists, but, eventually, he cour-
teously accepts a kiss from her. This he exchanges for the flesh of a
doe, killed and cut up by the lord. On the second day, the host
hunts a dangerous boar, and the lady visits Gawain as he lies in
bed, once more, this time telling him that he is strong enough to
force her: Gawain accepts two kisses from her, these being exchanged for the boar's head. On the third day, the host hunts a wily
fox, which is pursued with cries of 'thief', while the lady visits
Gawain with naked breasts and back; she persuades him to receive
three kisses and also a green belt, which he accepts because she
tells him it will protect him, and he thinks of his ordeal the next
day. The host, on his return, hands Gawain the fox's skin, which
was torn off the animal upon capture, and Gawain gives the three
kisses in return, but not the green belt. The following day, Gawain
rides over the wintry hills into a wild valley, where he finds the
Green Chapel, which turns out to be a hollow, grassy mound. As he
explores the mound, he hears the sound of an axe being sharpened
and the Green Knight appears. Gawain flinches a little as the axe
descends and the Green Knight withholds the axe, reproaching
him. The next blow is a feint, and, when the Green Knight swings
the axe a third time, he only wounds Gawain slightly in the neck.
Springing up to defend himself, Gawain discovers that the Green
Knight is none other than his friendly host. The lord of the castle
tells him that he is Bertilak de Hautdesert and that he himself
planned the temptations at his castle; he knows all about Gawain's
conduct. The slight wound punishes him for his lapse in perfect
fidelity to his troth, his concealment of the green belt. The whole
scheme of the Green Knight has been devised by the hideous old
woman at the castle, who is Morgan the Fay and Gawain's own
aunt, her aim being to test the knights of the Round Table and to
frighten Guinevere. The host invites Gawain to return to the castle,
but Gawain is too ashamed to accept. Returning to Arthur's court,
he wears the green belt as a baldric in token of his fault, and the
lords and ladies, who comfort him, wear similar green baldrics in
his honour.

   G. V. Smithers has written that the perennial task confronting the critic of a medieval work 'is to see its surface
meaning in its true relation to the buried meanings or *vice
versa*. Among other things, this is because a received story is
likely to embody more than one stratum of motivation; and

the ostensible or explicit motivation will not necessarily be the essential one'. In the case of *Sir Gawain and the Green Knight*, Smithers judges that the traditional framework 'happens to be contained in (and thus to harmonize with something of) the English poet's conception of what was at issue: both are aimed at the testing of a hero and at showing him to be first among heroes'.[4] J. A. Burrow cites Rochester in *Jane Eyre* as an example of the problem of the tester in stories where truth belongs to the fantasy world of myth and folktale: how could Rochester subject the woman he loved to such an ordeal as his test? 'Despite all Charlotte Brontë can do, the behaviour of tester and heroine alike is implausible; and the whole episode remains in the mind as a piece of dream-work — one of the fantasies which the author spins round the person of her hero ... When high romance (courtly or hagiographic) begins to give ground before lower, more realistic forms of presentation, cracks appear in the façade, and the conduct of both tester and hero begins to present problems.'[5] These two critics of *Sir Gawain and the Green Knight* have described the problem before us perfectly, but they have placed a ball and chain upon the task of dissecting it by making assumptions about meaning, in particular, by assuming that the Green Knight story is about a test.

1. The vexed pentangle will be the subject of the first — though not the chief — of my assembled questions. Norman Davis notes that this pentangle is treated as so important that the narrative is delayed for it, but the subject is never returned to, not even when we would expect it — when we want to know about the relationship of the pentangle to the green belt.[6] P. M. Kean remarks on the continuing obscurity of the pentangle passage, in spite of lengthy critical discussion: little light has been thrown on its elusive phrasing and insistence on virtues which do not, after all, seem very important in the story, as it develops.[7]

2. Norman Davis comments in a similar fashion on Gawain's devotion to the Virgin. Gawain prays to her to guide him to shelter (ll. 737, 753–8) — a prayer answered by the appearance of Bertilak's castle — and he has her image on his shield (l. 649); when he is severely tempted, she protects him. Then she is never mentioned again: Gawain gives no

thanks for her care of him and we hear no more of his devotion.[8]

3. J. A. Burrow says that the chief source of problems in *Sir Gawain and the Green Knight* is the marvellous. The Green Knight's magic is referred to the traditional magic arts of Morgan le Fay, so they are not open to question, but what about the marvellous elsewhere in the poem? Gawain arrives at the Green Chapel 'decked out like a savage with talismans of every description. His helmet is circled with diamonds, which "keep the bones and members whole"; his coat-armour is set with "virtuous stones"; his shield bears the image of Mary on one side and the magic pentangle on the other; and he carries round his waist a magic life-saving belt'. Burrow continues that the poet 'blithely assumes ... the Green Knight can have no difficulty in cutting off [Gawain's] head, if he so wishes; and he never bothers to justify this assumption by explaining, say, that Gawain forfeited the protection of Mary and the pentangle when he trespassed against truth, or that the lady tricked him over the belt'. There is an 'uncertainty of boundary between the natural and marvellous'.[9]

4. The Green Knight's magic is referred to the magic arts of Morgan le Fay, but Morgan's role in the plot is far from clear. G. V. Smithers says, 'We should all be glad to know just how Morgan la Fée came to be in the poem, and just how much her presence in it meant to the author'.[10] She is 'a distinctly pallid presence in this poem as it stands; she makes little impression at the one point where she is introduced in person, and she fades from one's mind as the story progresses'.[11] J. A. Burrow asks how Bertilak comes to play the part of the Green Knight — and why. Morgan's well-known hatred for Guinevere, Arthur and the Round Table is given as the explanation for the adventure, but we are not told how she could persuade Bertilak to consent to her schemes.[12] Marjory Rigby writes: 'The relationship between Bertilak and Morgan is left undefined, as is Bertilak's nature. If Morgan is evil, must not Bertilak, her instrument, be evil? Yet he appears attractive in his generous praise of Gawain and in his delight at Gawain's success.'[13]

5. G. V. Smithers points out that, in French and German

analogues to *Sir Gawain and the Green Knight*, Gawain's virtuosity in conversation with ladies is followed by unhesitating acceptance or wooing of the lady concerned when they are in bed together. The English author has replaced this aspect of *courtoisie* with the Christian morality which excludes it. But the more important question, for my argument, is Smithers' point that the English author has introduced an inconsistency into the action: 'Gawain's rejection of the lady's advances at the later stage makes something like nonsense of his display of courtly talk at the earlier one, or at least dilutes it into a mere gesture that is no longer a part of the total character within which his two forms of response at two points were indissolubly fused in a single trait ... In depicting Gawain's exchanges with the lady, our poet has dealt with the contradiction between the courtly ideal of amorousness and the Christian ideal of chastity by drastically limiting the scope of the former in Gawain's conduct', leaving it 'a mere code of external manners'. These things, Smithers concludes, add up to substantial indications that the poet's concern is with spiritual, Christian and ecclesiastical values, and therefore with the spiritual rather than the secular aspect of the knightly ethos as embodied in Gawain.[14]

6. Burrow comments that the poet's attitude to the lady in the temptation scenes is 'somewhat ambivalent'. In the second scene, 'he openly shares with the audience the knowledge that she is testing the hero' (ll. 1474–5; 1549–50). In the first scene, he does indeed hint that she does not love Gawain by saying that she behaves as if she does (l. 1281), but, in lines 1549–50, 'he rather pointedly suggests that the lady's thoughts are not entirely absorbed in her purpose of leading Gawain into sin ('what-so scho þoȝt ellez')', and, at the beginning of the third temptation, he goes further, in giving love as her motivation:

> Bot þe lady for luf let not to slepe,
> Ne þe purpose to payre þat puȝt in hir hert,
> Bot ros hir vp radly, rayked hir þeder ... (ll. 1733–5)

Burrow says that the poet seems to be cheating here, rather as he does over Bertilak's laughter on learning that it is

Gawain whom he has in his house (l. 909). Or perhaps he does not, 'with absolute consistency, imagine the lord and lady of Hautdesert as mere agents of Morgan le Fay — feeling no special interest in that side of the matter'.[15] Marjory Rigby says that 'neither the audience nor the hero knows what the lady is about ... When the lady is pressing Gawain hardest the poet retreats behind the veil of reportage. When she "Nurned hym so neȝe þe þred" [urged him so near the limit] (l. 1771), what was she saying to him? The poet leaves it to our imaginations. When the lady arrives with her hair adorned and neck and breast exposed the poet does not state that she has made herself look as seductive as possible; we may understand as much, if we wish. The explanation of her conduct [that Bertilak sent her to test Gawain, l. 2362] comes as a surprise'.[16]

7. Lines 1283–7 suggest that the lady knows Gawain is obliged to face the blow from the Green Knight:

'Paȝ I were burde bryȝtest', þe burde in mynde hade.
Þe lasse luf in his lode for lur þat he soȝt
    boute hone,
   Þe dunte þat schulde hym deue,
   And nedeȝ hit most be done.

The lady appears to be thinking that, even if she were the most beautiful of women, he would feel the less love because of the disaster to which he is hastening, the blow which will strike him down, and must, of necessity, be dealt. Norman Davis discusses the dilemma for the editor of preserving the text, while not — in so doing — spoiling the suspense (a dilemma leading to his punctuation of the above lines). Meanwhile, the story as presented has given the lady no opportunity to know the object of Gawain's journey, so — as Norman Davis comments — 'it would be a serious flaw in the handling of the plot'.[17]

8. Why should the return blow of the axe be a reason for Gawain's not accepting the lady's advances? Making love need not prevent him from keeping his appointment at the Green Chapel, but the appointment may mean that he is not in the mood for love. He does, however, enjoy other delights provided by the castle, including the lady's company else-

where than in his bedchamber, so why should he not enjoy dalliance, which would be in full accordance with his 'cortaysye'? Fidelity to his word (that he will keep his appointment) could be interpreted as the matter he has on his mind preventing his making love, but the poetry of lines 1283–7 stresses his fear and seems to bring together significantly the love, on the one hand, and the disaster and blow, on the other ('luf', 'lur' and 'dunte'). This deeper situation is also suggested in lines 1773–5, which are cited by G. V. Smithers[18] as the poet's own acknowledgement of the potential contradiction between the values of *courtoisie* and of Christianity bestowed upon his Gawain:

> He cared for his cortaysye, lest craþayn he were,
> And more for his meschef ȝif he schulde make synne,
> And be traytor to þat tolke þat þat telde aȝt.

The dilemma between being a boor ('craþayn') and a sinner is clear here, and so is a dilemma between 'cortaysye' and honourable behaviour towards a host, but we are also told that Gawain cares more about the disaster to himself ('his meschef') if he were to be a traitor to the owner of that house. There is an underlying echo of the linking, in a single thought, of the 'luf', the 'lur' and the 'dunte'.

9. Why is the Green Knight associated with a 'chapel'? G. V. Smithers notes that the association is one suggesting that the Green Knight is a hermit, and yet we know that his other characteristics deny this: 'That he should be given both the function and (by his name ['de Hautdesert']) the abode of a hermit is so bizarre as to require explanation'. Gawain confesses to him and is absolved:

> 'Þou art confessed so clene, beknowen of þy mysses,
> And hatz þe penaunce apert of þe poynt of myn egge,
> I halde þe polysed of þat plyȝt, and pured as clene
> As þou hadez neuer forfeted syþen þou watz fyrst borne ...'
> (ll. 2391–4)

Smithers explores the evidence for the Green Knight's being a combination of two figures — the shapeshifer of *Bricriu's Feast* and the hermit in Arthurian stories in Old French prose ('Hautdesert' relating to the 'haut hermitage' in *La*

Queste del Saint Graal) — but points out the problem that the Green Chapel is a mound. He suggests that the Green Chapel is a sinister inversion of the orthodox Arthurian chapel in the wilds, and that the Green Knight's hermitage appears only as a part of his name because he is a combination of two 'utterly incompatible persons' and therefore cannot contain all the attributes of each. Smithers also points out that the Green Chapel is mentioned by name early in the story (ll. 451, 705), long before the sequence in which it appears: this could mean that the poet worked out the Green Knight's dual character beforehand, but it 'might ... encourage the suspicion that the Green Chapel was inherited from an antecedent version'.[19]

10. G. V. Smithers probes further into the 'incongruous part played by the Green Knight'. He asks, 'Why is the Green Knight (of all people) represented as hearing a "confession" by Gawain at their last meeting? ... Gawain's final conversation with the Green Knight is represented as a confession to that somewhat ill-qualified person'. The Green Knight declares Gawain to be purified from his transgression, and to have received his penance from the point of the Green Knight's axe. Smithers suggests that the answer to this 'puzzling' feature may be the spiritual and ecclesiastical values with which the poet has invested the story.[20]

11. G. V. Smithers goes on to ask why Gawain makes a 'confession' at all at that point (at his last meeting with the Green Knight), since he has already gone through an orthodox form of confession the day before leaving the castle (ll. 1876–84). He suggests that the poet 'came to regard this confession as being in some way connected with the one which Gawain had made to the more orthodoxly qualified priest of the castle ... in which he had suppressed all mention (so far as we are told) of the girdle', and he comments, 'What is arresting in this poem is the means by which the supernatural has been made to serve the purposes of the Christian faith'; the author has 'taken the sting out of it', leaving us only with a sense of the strange and sinister.[21]

12. J. A. Burrow asks how Gawain's going to confession at Bertilak's castle fits in. The pentangle passage 'does not encourage the segregation of "chivalric" from "Christian"

virtues; for it links them together', so Gawain's confession
and absolution without confession of the belt will not do. It
'flies in the face of the pentangle passage'. The poet makes
no comment, unless the reference to Doomsday, which has
'an odd effect', is a comment (one understood only in retrospect, when we know the encounter has constituted 'a kind of
personal Doomsday' for Gawain). Burrow then makes an
extremely important point — that, 'when the time for his
judgement comes, Gawain does *not* find himself "clene",
despite the poet's assurance. The priest's absolution does not
save him from bitter shame and remorse — any more than
the lady's girdle saves him from the axe'.[22] It is interesting
to examine the two confession passages in the light of these
comments. The lines describing the first are as follows:

Syþen cheuely to þe chapel choses he þe waye,
Preuély aproched to a prest, and prayed hym þere
Þat he wolde lyste his lyf and lern hym better
How his sawle schulde be saued when he schuld seye heþen.
Þere he schrof hym schyrly and schewed his mysdedez,
Of þe more and þe mynne, and merci besechez,
And of absolucioun he on þe segge calles;
And he asoyled hym surely and sette hym so clene
As domezday schulde haf ben diȝt on þe morn.

These lines come immediately after those describing Gawain's hiding of the belt, and there is an urgent desire for
absolution, an appeal to the priest for mercy ('and merci
besechez, And of absolucioun he on þe segge calles'). The
reference to Doomsday which Burrow feels has 'an odd
effect' gives a particular force to the absolution: Gawain is
absolved and made as clean as if the next morning is to be
Doomsday. The confession to the Green Knight follows the
Green Knight's statement that the hiding of the belt has been
a small lapse in loyalty (' "lewté" ', l. 2366), and, this time,
we hear the confession itself:

'Corsed worth cowarddyse and couetyse boþe!
In yow is vylany and vyse þat vertue disstryez ...
For care of þy knokke cowardyse me taȝt
To acorde me with couetyse, my kynde to forsake,
Þat is larges and lewté þat longez to knyȝtez.

> Now am I fawty and falce, and ferde haf ben euer
> Of trecherye and vntrawþe: boþe bityde sorʒe
>   and care!
>   I biknowe yow, knyʒt, here stylle,
>   Al fawty is my fare;
>   Letez me ouertake your wylle
>   And efte I schal be ware.' (ll. 2374–5; 2379–88)

Here, the emphasis is not on the desire for absolution, but on
the desire to confess.

13. Gawain confesses to cowardice and lack of fidelity
('"vntrawþe"'), in relation to his withholding of the belt,
and, in view of these confessions — which would seem, on
the face of it, to be a full confession — it comes as a surprise
that he also confesses to covetousness and treachery. Norman Davis comments on '"couetyse"' that the 'word seems
inappropriate', but that the definition of avarice, in medieval treatises on the sins, was very wide: though the belt has
not been wrongfully acquired, having been given to Gawain,
his failure to exchange it for the Green Knight's winnings
might be held to be a branch of '"couetyse"'.[23] I think this is
going too far to accommodate a problem, and that the detail
of the confession, in all its ambiguity, must be given close
attention. What is the status of '"trecherye"' in it? Whatever punctuation is chosen for its context, its inclusion is less
direct than that of '"couetyse"', but it is significantly linked
with '"vntrawþe"', a relevant fault in this confession.

These questions point to situations in the text similar to
those found in the previous texts studied, but the presence of
these situations does not inevitably mean that the text includes a magical plot. There can be a number of reasons why
cracks appear in a text combining a traditional story and an
author's treatment of it, and not every traditional story is
one I would describe as magical. The cracks have to be
examined closely, and I shall begin by surveying the types of
crack apparent.

First of all, there appear to be gaps at the level of the
Christian treatment: Gawain receives an absolution from a
priest which seems to have no role in the plot (since Gawain
does not find himself 'clene' at the Green Chapel), and the

pentangle and Virgin similarly seem to have no profound role; they do not reappear in the romance when we expect them.

There seems to be some inconsistency, too, in the courtly treatment. It is likely that this is due to the poet's concern with Christian values, but a lack of consistency in the Christian treatment makes it important to include this problem here.

The explanation for the adventure is, meanwhile, quite incoherent in terms of the characterisation apparent in the text, as these explanations often are. We are asked to accept that the *Gawain*-poet's strangely 'pallid' Morgan le Fay wins the consent of a character as strong, wholesome and generous as Bertilak to a scheme of a mean nature which has nothing to do with him. We are also asked to accept that the lady's role has been arranged by Bertilak (1. 2361), to further this scheme, and also — a more important consideration here — to overlook the fact that this is not entirely a sufficient explanation for the line giving her the motivation of love: 'Bot þe lady for luf let not to slepe ...'.

The commentators' observations as to the poet's inconsistent and enigmatic treatment of the lady are interesting. There are other possible explanations for the ambiguities (as to whether she is a dispassionate tester or not, and whether she knows the object of Gawain's journey). She could, anyway, quite well be both a tester and a woman enjoying the job, without this creating a problem in the poet's scheme, and since her husband is involved in the object of Gawain's journey, we can accept that she is well informed without there having to be any indication in the text. Nevertheless, problems over a character's motives, and over how much a character knows, are typical where a magical plot is present. Characters not representing the 'hero' or 'heroine' will have no mind of their own, and the motives and knowledge which *are* present (those of the hero or heroine) can be invisible to the rational mind. In this case, the ambiguities do not necessarily present a problem, but they should be borne in mind. A matter which must be addressed, however, is the apparent close relationship between the love and the blow. If I addressed the problem by applying the model of the magical plot, I

would have the following result. The lady and the blow
would have equal status as figments of the hero's thought,
and the kind of links detected between them — the
lady's knowing about the blow and the poetic links between
'luf', 'lur' and 'dunte' — would indicate the connection and
something of its nature. That Gawain's love is affected by
thoughts of the blow would make entire sense at a magical
level, where there tends to be an idea of the primal triangle,
and such a meaning could also explain the suggestion that
there is a theme of chastity, unsatisfactory but haunting the
temptation scenes. The commentators' favoured theme of
fidelity would, meanwhile, be in harmony with such a
magical theme, because the magical theme would include
concern that there should be no theft from the lord of the
castle. The hero would be concerned not to 'be traytor to þat
tolke þat þat telde aȝt', for such treachery would give rise to
the blow.

The questions relating to the two confessions would also
seem to be solved by the point of view supplied by the
model. Within a magical plot, the two confessions would
have entirely different roles. The first confession before the
priest would not have the role of a true confession: its role
would be a magical, protective one, strategically placed after the temptations and hiding of the belt, and before the
meeting at the Green Chapel, and concerned entirely with
the absolution, couched in language with magical power:
'And he asoyled hym surely and sette hym so clene As
domezday schulde haf ben diȝt on þe morn'. A magical hero
would arm himself with the sense of his innocence which
this Christian magic bestows, just as he arms himself with
the talismans noted by Burrow — some of these also Christian material in origin. By contrast, the confession at the
Green Chapel would be a true one, because a false or incomplete confession could not bring about the end of the story —
a magical hero has to find a solution to all his guilt. The
second confession would, like the first, have a magical function — in a magical plot this must be the case — but the
magical function would be quite different. It would not be
protection against punishment but the removal of the guilt
through a ritual which acknowledged the sins and provided

magic words of forgiveness (' "I halde þe polysed of þat ply3t, and pured as clene As þou hadez neuer forfeted syþen þou watz fyrst borne" ' (I hold you cleansed of that offence and purified as clean as if you had never transgressed since you were first born). Far from being 'ill-qualified' to hear Gawain's confession and grant absolution, the Green Knight would be the very character who must do this. The problem of ' "couetyse" ', meanwhile, would disappear: it would make perfect sense as one of the sins — referring to the lady, rather than only to the belt (and thus more in accord with the Commandment, Exodus, 20, v. 17). Discussing the meaning of ' "couetyse" ', G. V. Smithers points out that it may mean merely 'desire for something owned by someone else',[24] and this meaning has a particular force in the familiar magical situation of the primal triangle.

I see a remarkable linking of two strands quite separate in origin: the poet's Christian treatment and the purposes of the plot — which I regard as magical. The plot is a powerful vehicle for the themes of fidelity and loyalty which evidently concern the poet, and, meanwhile, his Christian material appears sometimes to be used magically. I would add to G. V. Smithers' point concerning the arresting way in which the supernatural has been made to serve the purposes of the Christian faith, that equally arresting is the way the Christian faith has been made to serve the purposes of the supernatural (that is, in the context of my study, the magical). However, if there is a magical plot here, the poet's additional material (the Christian material) will be dependent on the plot. This would account for some gaps in the Christian material (although the problems relating to the first confession, the pentangle and the Virgin disappear if we see these details as having magical roles). Altogether, *Sir Gawain and the Green Knight* is an extraordinarily coherent work.

The Green Knight plot evidently has a strongly ritual nature, its magical subject a conflict between desire and guilt which culminates in ritual punishment (' "penaunce apert of þe poynt of myn egge" ', l. 2392), and confession, followed by an absolution (exorcism) expressed in words of magic power (ll. 2393–4). Magical ritual or not, it is unlikely that G. V. Smithers is right in saying that 'the whole point of the story [used by the *Gawain*-poet] is to establish the primacy of Gawain among knights'.[25] Such a comparatively simple purpose is found in the plot of *Bricriu's Feast*,[26] and an examination of the two plots shows the difference between a magical plot such as I have indicated and a traditional plot, magical or otherwise, devoted to the subject Smithers suggests. The Bricriu plot is a series of tests, with the prime aim of establishing the supremacy of Cúchulainn, and it is a celebration of Cúchulainn rather than an expression of feelings which require penance.[27] An author developing a traditional plot, breathing into it themes of his own, would probably find the Green Knight plot, with its deep conflicts, more profound and inspiring material to work upon than the Bricriu plot.

Although *Bricriu's Feast* is a quite different kind of story from the Green Knight story, we can learn much from comparing the beheading exchange in each. It is evident from the detail of both the actions and the attributes of the challenger that the beheading element in *Sir Gawain and the Green Knight* is the same kind of material as the beheading element in *Bricriu's Feast*. The challenger in each is contemptuous of those he challenges: the Green Knight describes Arthur's knights as beardless children (l. 280) and accuses them of cowering with fear (l. 315), while Cú Roí, as the churl, refers to Cúchulainn as a pitiful stripling and says to him, '"No doubt you fear death, wretched fly"'.[28] In *Bricriu's Feast*, the two other contestants for the champion's portion behead the churl and then fail to come back the next night for the return blow; Cúchulainn then fulfils the bargain, and the churl, having brought the axe down with the blade turned up, proclaims him supreme warrior of Ériu. In *Sir Gawain and the Green Knight*, where there are two bargains (those of the beheading theme and of the temptation theme), the Green Knight refers only to the temptation theme bargain when the return blow is over, but he warmly acknowledges Gawain's arrival on time at the tryst, upon their meeting there (ll. 2241–2). The details relating to the dealing of the return blow are also similar. In *Bricriu's Feast*, Cúchulainn's neck can only reach half way across the block,

and the churl says, ' "Stretch out your neck, you wretch" ';
' "You torment me" ', Cúchulainn replies, ' "Kill me quickly" ', but the churl insists that he make his neck long enough
for the block, and he does so.[29] In *Sir Gawain and the Green
Knight*, the details are explained in terms of the fulfilling of
the temptation theme bargain, but they are, in fact, close to
those of *Bricriu's Feast*. The Green Knight's first blow is
interrupted by Gawain's flinching and by the Green Knight's
reflections on his cowardice, and the second blow menaces
without descending, in order to test Gawain's ability not to
flinch. After the second raising of the axe, Gawain says
angrily, ' "Wy! þresch on, þou þro mon, þou þretez to longe" '
(l. 2300). A manhood test (perhaps taking the form of the
flinch, the test blow and finally the reprieve because the hero
has fulfilled the bargain and without flinching) appears to be
taking place. Afterwards, the details are explained as a series
of reprieves in relation to the fulfilling of another bargain,
one belonging to a sequence in which love is linked to fear of
the blow. The lord of the castle explains that Gawain has
been reprieved because he kept the bargain of the exchanges
of winnings, giving the lord his gains — except that he failed
to give him the green belt, and consequently received a nick
in the neck. Over and above these reprieves at two levels of
meaning, one in relation to the beheading game bargain and
the other in relation to the temptation theme bargain, the
nick in the neck is described as a penance by the Green
Knight, the word linked to his announcement of absolution.
The evidence for all these threads of meaning is found in the
words of the Green Knight.

In a magical plot, all the events are arranged by the hero,
and the challenge here is therefore Gawain's, not the Green
Knight's — if, indeed, it has the active role of a challenge, at
the magical level. The reason why the hero arranges the
beheading game should be made clear by the meaning of the
events at Bertilak's castle, since the events at Bertilak's castle will form a second move, playing out the feelings in the
initial move at Arthur's court in fuller detail. The chief
feature of the beheading game in tradition is that the ogre
reprieves and honours the hero who keeps the terrifying
bargain. There does not appear to be a challenge on the part

of the chief character; rather, the game is used to establish
the quality of this character. In *Bricriu's Feast*, Cúchulainn's
supremacy is established. This is clearly not the prime aim
of *Sir Gawain and the Green Knight*, but the motif of the
successful test might nevertheless be used by the hero.
Chiefly, the return blow in the Green Knight plot is an
acknowledgement that Gawain has honoured the bargains
(an acknowledgement present in *Bricriu's Feast*) and it also
provides the ritual in which the hero's penance can be performed (this penance, together with Gawain's confession at
the Green Chapel, leading to the Green Knight's absolution).
Since the events are arranged by the hero, it is quite possible
that the beheading exchange, in which the return blow is
established in tradition as a reprieve for the gallant hero,
has been chosen to provide a reassuring framework for an
adventure felt to be an infringement of the rights of an
all-powerful being.

How might the adventure be infringing these rights? The
adventure at Bertilak's castle now requires scrutiny. A
second bargain surrounds it, presumably supplying a further
reassuring framework. The adventure itself can have no
other interpretation, at the magical level, than that the hero
conjures up the lord's lady to his bedside and enjoys
thoughts of her making sexual advances to him. He presents
himself as entirely passive and loyal in these scenes, the
nature of his involvement concealed by our not realising
that the hero himself is arranging all the events. His enjoyment is affected by thoughts of a blow: Gawain feels less
love because of the disaster to which he is hastening, and the
blow which will strike him down; he cares more about the
disaster to himself if he were to be a traitor to the owner of
the house. (At the Green Chapel, he does find that he has
been a traitor.) Meanwhile, the bedchamber scenes are
accompanied by the hunting scenes, the descriptions of these
keeping us informed as to what the owner of the house is
doing at each stage of the temptations. In a magical plot, the
status of these must be that they are thoughts in the mind
of the hero as he enjoys the lady. The hunted female deer
tremble as the lady makes her first entrance, and they are
cut up after she kisses Gawain and leaves. The monstrous,

savage boar charges and is pursued, in the lines before the lady enters for the second scene, in which she tells Gawain that he is strong enough to take her by force if he wishes; the boar is then beheaded after her two parting kisses. The fox is called 'thief' before the lady's third entrance, with naked breasts and back, and flayed alive after Gawain has received and concealed the belt. Exact interpretation is difficult, but the hero's fear of punishment at the hands of the lord is clear, and the three kinds of quarry express his feelings and how he judges them, as his scenes with the lady progress.[30]

The role of the exchanges of winnings in such a context as this is clear. They are rituals providing tokens for the lord that the hero has not been a traitor. The lord, for his part, shows the hero what will happen to him should he be one: he displays the head of the boar and the skin of the fox. It would be important that Gawain's kisses are warmly given and warmly received. At the Green Chapel, the Green Knight gives the honouring of this bargain as the reason for Gawain's reprieve.

As so often, I can feel clearer about the function of the plot — in this case, that it makes possible an adventure into experience felt to be forbidden — than I can about meaning beyond this. The problems of the Green Knight plot are also made severe by there being only one good text and one poorer one, the tail-rhyme version.[31] The chief problems of the plot are the roles of the belt and the Green Chapel. I shall present an explanation for them here which fits exceptionally well with the other detail in the text, but which still has the status of a hunch because the elucidation of magical material requires a great deal of contextual evidence, more than we have in the texts available.

Gawain is told by the lady that the belt will protect him, but it appears to do the reverse: the hero's penance and confession are both concerned with the lady's belt. Meanwhile, the confessions to covetousness and treachery must refer to the lady. What can be the role of the belt? As the belt's failure to protect goes unmentioned in the text, and its seemingly ineffective protective properties are unlikely to have been introduced by the author, it is best to begin by assuming that the belt has a protective function in the magical plot. Disguise could be this function, for the belt certainly does have the effect of disguise: it takes the lady's place in the confession. Meanwhile, in the Green Knight's explanation, we are told that the belt, like the kisses, belongs to him. This could be a disguised statement, the lady really being referred to, and yet I wonder whether there is, concealed here instead, a closer relationship to the kisses with which the belt is linked, the belt being the lady's permission for the journey to the Green Chapel? This magical permission would be arranged by the hero, of course, since the lady cannot be an independent giver at the magical level. Why should the hero arrange this magical permission for his journey to the Green Chapel? The tryst at the Chapel is to take place in any case, and its role, I have decided, is defensive, rather than a continuation of the adventure. However, there must be some explanation for the Green Chapel, and one which would logically fit the context tentatively suggested here is the one which I brought forward in my first study of the plot, that the Chapel has a sexual interpretation, being a vision of woman's genitals. This interpretation would give us a more powerful story: the Green Chapel's being a step further in the sexual adventure would mean that the adventure deepens in the very place where the hero yields up to the lord what he owes to him. The interpretation also presents us with a powerful image parallel to the images in Bertilak's castle. The sharpening of the axe as Gawain explores the green mound parallels the events in the bedchamber and hunting scenes (and also the connection made at the verbal level between the love and the blow): as the hero thinks sexually of the lady, there are visions of the lord preparing to strike and going through activities suggestive of punishment. These sexual interpretations of the belt and the Chapel make excellent sense in the context of the increasing kisses and undress in the bedchamber, and the increasing ardour (on the third morning 'Gret perile bitwene hem stod', l. 1768), and in relation to the flayed skin of the thief, displayed as the last act of the exchanges. The display of the fox's skin is significantly the last act of the exchanges, since, in the two previous exchanges, Gawain's kisses are given last, after he has been shown the fate of the animals:

only when the hero has not honoured the bargain does the lord's reply come last. The physical appearance of the Chapel as a hollow, grassy mound is suggestive, though it presents problems, and the lady's action of removing her belt from round her waist also seems to fit, without being finally persuasive. If I settled for the sexual interpretations, the belt would directly have to do with the covetousness, and could still play its protective role as a disguise.

Such interpretations would appear to make the reprieve at the tryst all the more remarkable. However, the safeguards set up by the hero are rituals guaranteed to placate the lord and bring about his forgiveness, and this indicates the terror of the adventure. G. V. Smithers' suggestion that the Green Chapel is a sinister inversion of the orthodox Arthurian chapel gives us a story with less fear, the sexual adventure ending with the departure from Bertilak's castle, and the place of the tryst expressing the hero's fear of the judgement awaiting him there. I find this interpretation acceptable in that it does not leave unanswered questions, but a rejection of the sexual explanation for the belt and the Chapel (a rejection leaving the belt a disguise for the lady and the Chapel a sinister place for the penance and confession) presents us with comparatively loose relationships between the images of the bedchamber and hunts, the exchanges of winnings and the place of the tryst; with the sexual explanations they become close-knit and highly charged.

The description of the Green Chapel is enigmatic, and so is its name. When Gawain finally sees the Chapel, he reflects upon it as the place of the Green Knight's evil devotions ('Dele here his deuocioun on þe deuelez wyse', l. 2192), and feels that this tryst which will destroy him has been imposed upon him by the Devil (ll. 2193–4). Though he reflects upon it in this way, the description preceding these lines tells us that he looks for a chapel and sees no such thing anywhere ('non suche in no syde', l. 2170), except, not far off, in a glade, a mound as it were, a smooth hillock by the side of a stream ('Saue, a lyttel on a launde, a lawe as hit were; A balȝ berȝ bi a bonke þe brymme bysyde', l. 2171–2). Gawain finds it overgrown with patches of grass and hollow within: only an old cave ('nobot an olde caue' l.2182). For all Gawain's

comments, the description itself conveys a peaceful, unthre-
atening scene. It is the name by which this mound is called
throughout most of the length of the romance, before we are
given a description of it, which expresses fear, and this fear
may arise from the hero's feeling that the mound is taboo.[32]
Whatever it represents, why does the mound appear so
peaceful at this terrifying point of the story, when its name,
and Gawain's reflections upon it, and also the accompanying
sharpening of the axe, all belie this? The sharpening of the
axe occurs after the initial vision, when Gawain climbs up to
the roof of the 'rough dwelling':

> He romez vp to þe roffe of þe roȝ wonez.
> Þene herde he of þat hyȝe hil, in a harde roche
> Biȝonde þe broke, in a bonk, a wonder breme noyse,
> Quat! hit clatered in þe clyff, as hit cleue schulde,
> As one vpon a gryndelston hade grounden a syþe. (ll. 2198–202)

If the vision of the mound parallels the conjuring up of the
lady at the bedside, positive and negative feelings will conflict with each other in its description, and, just as the exchanges of winnings make possible the enjoyment in the
bedchamber, so the adventure at the Green Chapel is made
safe — though still not without fear — by its being identical
with the hero's fulfilment of the bargain with the Green
Knight. The fulfilment of the bargain has the power to
confirm his fidelity and cleanse him of guilt.

If I settle for the sexual interpretations of the belt and the
Chapel, I must take into account that this more dangerous
sexual journey, with its accompanying punishment, is an
integral part of the 'outer' defence for the adventure. There
must be an element of challenge to the lord and fear of an
appropriate punishment (whether castration or death) in
this particular version of the beheading game. Yet, compounded with this is the honouring of the lord's right to the
return blow. We are presented with a powerful blending of
conflicting material. The hero fears and desires the blow
which has been ordained by himself to make the adventure
possible. The honouring of the bargain at Bertilak's castle
has prepared the way for the outcome of this blow (since the
reprieve is explained in terms of the exchanges of winnings),
but the hero's step in concealing the belt is a major infideli-

ty, if the sexual interpretation is correct. This major infideli-
ty helps to explain the confessions to covetousness and
treachery, which, otherwise, seem an over-reaction in view
of the yielding of the kisses and the due arrival at the tryst.
The warmth and generosity of the Green Knight are striking,
and Gawain's warm kissing of the lord must be a significant
function of the exchanges of winnings. At the tryst, there is a
piling up of magical arrangements. The acknowledgement of
the lord's right to the return blow is followed by the cleansing penance; the return of the kisses at the exchanges of
winnings is given as the reason for the reprieve; then the
hero makes his confession and is given absolution in words
of magical power. Gawain's shame continues after his confession and absolution, but I believe the contrasting attitudes of the Green Knight and Gawain here have parallel
functions. Both are invested with power to release the hero
from guilt, the lord's words and deeds expressing complete
trust and forgiveness, and Gawain's implying that he re-
nounces the lady and will not forget his transgression. The
lord gives Gawain the belt, and invites him back to his castle
for the rest of the feast; Gawain and the lady will be reconciled. He speaks warmly of Gawain's fidelity ('"þy grete
trauþe"', l. 2470). Gawain refuses to return to the castle and
denounces women, and he says the belt will remind him of
his fault. At Arthur's court, he carries out a further penance,
wearing the belt as a token of his fault, but he also has
Arthur's court wear it as a sign of his honour. With all these
safeguards to release the hero from guilt, how much is the
wearing of the belt also a token of victory?

  I think the defence structures (of the two bargains) play a
more important role than the move structure in this plot:
rather than having steps in a struggle, we have an adventure
made possible by a double set of safeguards. However, there
is a clear entry into a new move with the arrival at Bertilak's castle for the adventure. A repetition of Arthur and
Guinevere in Bertilak and his lady is therefore present. Owing to primal triangle associations, the hero's sexual adventure is haunted by the idea of there being an all-powerful
lord with prior right to the woman. He gains control over
the fear and guilt, which create this lord, by arranging
rituals guaranteed to placate him, bring about his forgive-

ness and free himself from guilt. Over and above the employment of the bargains is a variety of other protective devices, some of which are taken from the Christian religion, but, of these, the first confession, the pentangle and the Virgin do not have any obvious protective function in the plot; Gawain's arrival at the Green Chapel 'decked out like a savage with talismans of every description' does, however, indicate the fear in the plot. While art has created a splendid structure at the magical level, the type of thought is of the same magical kind as that of Martin, when he conjured up the word EMIN on the axe-man's wall and used it to restore his head.

Now that the magical scheme is revealed as organised by the hero, what is the status of the explanation that it is organised by Morgan le Fay? Bertilak can be seen to be central to the scheme — rather than inexplicably involved in arrangements which have nothing to do with him — and how he appears, whether as evil or generous, is dependent on the hero's state of mind. The hero himself is bringing about the enchantments. The explanation that Morgan is behind the enchantments expresses an essential feeling in the plot, that woman, a witch, is responsible for it all, rather than the hero himself. Hence, I believe, is the reason for Morgan's presence. That this presence is such an ugly one by the beautiful lady's side gives us a clue to the hero's vision of the woman: ugliness can be an expression of fear, and it also has a magical role as a defence against the hero's finding the woman beautiful, and, meanwhile, this character is the fascinating Morgan le Fay, Gawain's own aunt, and — since Bertilak's castle is a new move — the queen (represented in the first move by Guinevere); in *The Grene Knight*, she is the lady's mother. The beautiful seductress in the hero's vision appears as two characters, both deeply disguised, the all-powerful mother-figure, and the young woman, firmly separated off from the sinister power of the woman who is felt to be responsible for it all.

In spite of the severe problems of interpretation encountered, perhaps this discussion has established more firmly than my previous investigations the magical nature of the plot used by the *Gawain*-poet.

NOTES

INTRODUCTION

1 See *Sir Gawain and the Green Knight*, ll. 1876–84; 2374–88. This problem of the two confessions, referred to below, in my Introduction, and discussed in Chapter Six, is pointed out by J. A. Burrow in *A Reading of Sir Gawain and the Green Knight*, London, 1965, pp. 105–10.

2 See Wolfram von Eschenbach, *Parzival*, ll. 280, 10–12; 161, 7–8; 475, 21–476, 2. I discuss this contradictory treatment of Parzival's slaying of the Red Knight, Ither, in Chapter four.

3 See Chrétien de Troyes, *Yvain*, vv. 491–511, for the accusation against the innocent Calogrenant. The problem of Yvain's aggression against the fountain knight is referred to below, in my Introduction, and discussed in Chapter one.

4 Tony Hunt, 'Chrétien de Troyes' Arthurian romance *Yvain*', *Medieval Literature, Part Two: The European Inheritance*, Harmondsworth, 1983, particularly pp. 132–3; 134; 139; 140–1.

5 Philip Edwards, in his edition, *Pericles, Prince of Tyre*, Harmondsworth, 1976, pp. 30–1.

6 I discuss 'The Wife of Bath's Tale' in *Magical Thought in Creative Writing*, Stroud, 1983, pp. 82–93. My argument is that the tale of the Loathly Lady has a 'hero' magical plot in which the ugliness of the bride is brought about by the fears of the hero, who sees her as a mother-figure, taboo and powerful. She becomes beautiful when his feelings about her change. Chaucer, however, has his Wife of Bath use the tale to overturn what she sees to be the male view of women and replace it with her own view. He also has this middle-aged character with a liking for young men use it to fulfil her own desires: identified with her Loathly Lady, she makes herself young and beautiful for the bridegroom who submits himself to her. In the magical plot, the Loathly Lady is in the power of the hero's feelings about her — he has, in a sense, cast a spell on her — but he

invests power in her. The Wife of Bath develops this theme of power and places the power firmly in the hands of her Loathly Lady. Chaucer also shares a joke with *his* audience (beyond the Wife's activities with *her* audience): he uses its knowledge of the traditional story so that the fear of incest and of the dominant mother-figure are present and attached to the Wife herself, even though her use of the story has left these magical elements out.

7   I discuss the Tristan story, and other medieval stories, in *Traditional Romance and Tale*, Cambridge, 1976, but these studies need to be revised, as my study of *Sir Gawain and the Green Knight* has been for this present book, in the light of my more recent research. At present, I see myself confined to plots which can be explored through rich textual evidence and excellent questions posed by scholars, because I have to argue the case for the existence of magical plots. Had the lost earlier parts of the versions of Thomas and Béroul — at least — survived, the Tristan plot might have been a good choice for this book.

8   I took the word 'move' from Vladimir Propp, but my moves are quite different from his. Mine are cycles of ritual thought, repetitions of the central concerns of the hero, each of which is a step forward, in some way, towards the achievement of the hero's, or heroine's, desires. For Propp a move is a repetition of the story sequence of leaving home, adventures, victory, return and recognition, which occurs when a fresh act of villainy creates a new initial lack in the home situation. See Vladimir Propp, *Morphology of the Folk Tale*, Austin, Texas, 1968.

9   See Joseph Hall's edition of *King Horn*, Oxford, 1901, which gives us the London, Oxford and Cambridge texts in parallel. Horn takes the name Goodmind ('Godmod') in the London text, Cutbeard ('Cutberd') in the Cambridge text and Cubert in the Oxford text. He also becomes Goodmind ('Gudmod') in *Horn et Rimenild*, and he becomes 'Godebounde' in *Horn Child and Maiden Rimnild*. In the simplified ballad versions, known as *Hind Horn*, the hero does not give himself a new name, but he experiences the seven years' exile over the sea which Goodmind/Cutbeard also undergoes.

10   W. H. Auden, 'The Guilty Vicarage', *The Dyer's Hand and Other Essays*, London, 1963.

11   See Jay Dixon, 'Fantasy unlimited: the world of Mills and Boon', *Women's Review*, Issue 21, July, 1987, pp. 18–19; Ann Barr Snitow, 'Mass market romance: pornography for women is different', *Desire: the Politics of Sexuality*, edited by Ann

Snitow *et al.*, London, 1984; Ann Rosalind Jones, 'Mills &
Boon meets feminism', *The Progress of Romance: The Politics of
Popular Fiction*, edited by Jean Radford, London, 1986. These
romances are written to a formula, often by professional and
academic women for an additional income (see *Women's Review*, Issue 21, pp. 20–1).
12 I discuss *Treasure Island* in *Magical Thought in Creative Writing*,
    p. 27.
13 I discuss *The Lord of the Rings* in *Magical Thought in Creative
    Writing*, pp. 70–81; 107–13.
14 See *Traditional Romance and Tale*, pp. 11–12; 14–15.
15 As in the case of the previous dream, this dream was im-
    mediately recorded as related — on 6 February 1974.
16 I discuss *Jack and the Beanstalk* in *Signal: Approaches to Chil-
    dren's Books*, no. 36, September, 1981, pp. 140–1.
17 I discuss *The Golden Bird* in *Traditional Romance and Tale*, pp.
    39–46, and in *Signal: Approaches to Children's Books*, no. 36,
    September, 1981, pp. 142–4. The hero steals from the kings in
    a way not unlike the way Jack steals from the giants, in *Jack
    and the Beanstalk*. He rides forward from king to king, on the
    tail of the fox. First, he fails to steal a royal object, then he is
    sent by the court which has condemned him to death to
    attempt instead to fetch (steal) another to be given to the king
    in exchange for it, then earns the princess (through the fox's
    labour) at the end of the line of kings, then retraces his steps to
    pretend the exchanges which, through trickery, turn into
    thefts. Having seized the royal objects, which are the golden
    bird, the golden horse and the princess, from the kings (that is,
    from the king), the hero creates two final moves to deal with
    his guilt. Instead of celebrating the successful outcome of the
    adventure, the fox suddenly asks to be killed and have his head
    and feet cut off. The rest of the detail is in the Introduction.
    Upon being killed and mutilated, the fox turns into the brother
    of the princess. The brother of the princess would be heir to the
    throne, but the hero has evidently not taken this prince's place:
    the fox must be an aspect of the hero. The shapeshift may be a
    disguised admission as to the identity of the fox, and also as to
    the identity of the hero (son to the king), but perhaps it also
    declares that the crime is now cancelled out, the thief (the fox)
    having had a right to that which he obtains for the hero. Such
    a statement can make no rational sense, but it can help to free
    a hero from guilt. This story has the standard number 57 in
    many editions of the Grimm collection.
18 I discuss *The Goose-Girl* in *Magical Thought in Creative Writing*,

pp. 17–33. This Grimm story deals with the conflict in the third and final move, as part of the struggle for sovereignty. In the second move, the heroine loses her mother's drops of blood, which speak magic, ritual words declaring her mother's wish that she become a queen, and the horse, later to speak these words, says nothing in protest when the usurping waiting-maid takes over. It speaks the words in the third move, when its head is set up over the gateway; they are then repeated to the king, and, finally, spoken by the chief character, the ack-nowledged heroine, herself. The king's recognition follows. In some versions of the story the chief character is mutilated (see J. Bolte and G. Polivka, *Anmerkungen zu den Kinder- und Hausmärchen der Brüder Grimm*, Leipzig, 1912–32, vol. 2, pp. 278 ff). This story has the standard number 89 in many edi-tions of the Grimm collection.

19 I discuss *Hamlet*, and the versions of Saxo Grammaticus and Belleforest, in *Magical Thought in Creative Writing*, pp. 114–39.

20 I discuss Charlotte Brontë's *Jane Eyre* in *Magical Thought in Creative Writing*, pp. 48–61. The novel has a complex, eight-move plot which cannot be summarised here.

21 Freud's theory of the Oedipus complex has to do with his theories of unconscious phantasy and infantile sexuality, work-ed out during his study of hysteria. A consideration of it should therefore be kept distinct from a consideration of the social reality of the incidence of incest — which appears to be an abuse of power on the part of the parent. For a reassessment of Freud's theories, in relation to the criticisms of social realists, see Juliet Mitchell, *Psychoanalysis and Feminism*, Harmond-sworth, 1975, and, for a critical survey of the research into the incidence of incest, see Sarah Nelson, *Incest: Fact and Myth*, Edinburgh, 1982 and revised edition 1987.

22 See W. W. Lawrence, *Shakespeare's Problem Comedies*, New York, 1931, and G. K. Hunter's edition, *All's Well that Ends Well*, London, 1959. G. K. Hunter comments, 'Helena is, un-doubtedly, in some ways, a fairy-tale heroine, with a back-ground of spiritual or magical power' (p. xlix). W. W. Lawrence concludes that, while Shakespeare was free to make the many changes he made, he was not free — owing to his audience's expectations where a familiar tale was concerned — 'to turn the heroine into a wanton, to question the efficacy of her strategems or to cast doubts upon her ultimate happiness' (p. 67). Lawrence comments that the heroine not only forces an unwilling man into marriage with her, but the husband finally accepts the situation as 'evidence of his wife's courage and

love'; there is no suggestion anywhere that he regards himself as having been 'despicably tricked', and many versions emphasise his pleasure at the outcome (p. 49). The story exalts the cleverness of the woman: her wits 'are more than a match for those of the husband' (p. 47).

23 Boccaccio's version is the ninth novel of the third day in his *Decameron*; pp. 304–14, in the Penguin Classics translation of G. H. McWilliam.The description of Boccaccio's treatment is quoted from W. W. Lawrence, *op. cit.*, pp. 60–1.

24 W. W. Lawrence, *op. cit.*, pp. 61–2.

25 G. K. Hunter, *op. cit.*, p. xxix: 'it is mainly a quality of *strain*, of striving through intractable material for effects which hardly justify the struggle, a quality of harsh discord which seeks resolution, but achieves less than is sought'.

26 I have not published my study of the 'All's Well' story. The plot appears to have two moves. In her first move, the heroine arranges the marriage through the king — who is won as her ally by means of her magical healing powers, acquired by her using medicines inherited from a great physician (magician) father. But the heroine has yet to seal the marriage in the husband's eyes, and she does this in her second move, with the permission and help of a mother-character. Shakespeare brings out some of the magical power here sharply. He not only introduces the countess, Bertram's mother, in the first move, in a role strongly supportive of the heroine, but, in the second move, he develops the detail of the ring (which the heroine must obtain — together with her husband's child — if she is to live as his wife). In Shakespeare's play, the ring is an heirloom expressing Bertram's family and its honour (III.viii); possession of it magically bestows membership of the family. Then there follows the bedding of Bertram, with the consummation and conception. Furthermore, Helena's final question to Bertram, 'Will you be mine now you are doubly won?' (V.iii.308) suggests the power of the dual tasks (obtaining the ring and the child) to bring about this marriage, and Bertram's reply has something of the quality of magic words: 'If she, my liege, can make me know this clearly / I'll love her dearly, ever, ever dearly' (V.iii. 309–10). The repetition of the crucial words, the rhyme emphasising 'dearly', and the addressing of the whole to the king, give power to the declaration and bestow upon it an air of finality.

27 J. S. Mill, 'The Subjection of Women', in *Three Essays*, Oxford, 1975, p. 495. This essay was first published in 1869.

28 Rosemary Jackson, *Fantasy: The Literature of Subversion*, Lon-

don, 1981, pp. 124–5. I am grateful to Edmund Cusick for drawing my attention to the similarity in our arguments.

29 Apart from *Jane Eyre*, I have studied H. Rider Haggard's *She*, in *Magical Thought in Creative Writing* (pp. 37–47); and Christoph von Schmid's *The Basket of Flowers* (translated into English, 1851), together with Elizabeth Wetherell's *The Wide, Wide World*, in 'Morals and magic for Victorian children', *Signal: Approaches to Children's Books*, No. 38, May, 1982, pp. 88–102.

30 Leo Bersani, *A Future for Astyanax*, London, 1978, pp. 189–229.

31 I have not published my own study of *Wuthering Heights*. I believe the Lockwood and Nelly Dean narrations help to distance the fantasy and make it more acceptable to the reader. Leo Bersani comments that these characters seem to be in the wrong novel, while I believe their presence is a deliberate defensive procedure. The story is presented to us by the respectable Lockwood and by the upright, moralising Nelly, who is often shocked and who weighs everything up according to accepted values. Other magical devices are also used to make the first move possible. The forbidding of the experiences is ridiculed away through the use of Joseph, and through the use of the Reverend Jabes Branderham dream. In Joseph, God and religion are voiced by an unpleasant old clown. Where the dream is concerned (Chapter 3), the sequence begins with Lockwood's reading some childhood writing of Catherine's — the significant first words we hear from her: ' "An awful Sunday! ... H. and I are going to rebel ..." '. Catherine then recounts how, as the family could not go to church, the children had to listen to a three-hour sermon from Joseph while their elders did ' "anything but reading their Bibles" '. Later, Catherine and Heathcliff hurled and kicked, respectively, their good books into the dog-kennel. The book in which Catherine had written is entitled 'Seventy Times Seven, and the First of the Seventy-First. A Pious Discourse delivered by the Reverend Jabes Branderham, in the Chapel of Gimmerden Sough'. Lockwood falls asleep and dreams that Joseph is taking him to hear Jabes Branderham preach from the text 'Seventy Times Seven': either Joseph, the preacher, or Lockwood has committed the 'First of the Seventy-First' and is to be publically exposed and excommunicated. Branderham's pious discourse has four hundred and ninety parts, and he has his own 'private manner of interpreting' sin: there are 'odd transgressions' Lockwood has 'never imagined previously'. Lockwood denounces the preacher, calling upon fellow-martyrs to

'"crush him to atoms"', because he, Lockwood, has '"endured and forgiven the four hundred and ninety heads of [his] discourse"' and the '"four hundred and ninety first is too much"'. Jabes Branderham, in return, denounces Lockwood as a sinner because seventy times seven times he has yawned. The whole assembly rushes at Lockwood to beat him, and the rapping noises, as blows miss their aim, become the tapping noises at the window; the dream of Catherine sobbing '"Let me in — let me in!"' follows. I believe the Branderham dream, in which the respectable narrator, Lockwood, is involved in rebelling against an excessively moralising and punitive religion, and in which that religion is caricatured and made ridiculous, has an important magical role, making possible the narration of the Catherine / Heathcliff story.

32 Stephen Prickett, *Victorian Fantasy*, London, 1979. Prickett comments that, in the Gothic, we find a literary medium that does not tell a story so much as offer verbal pictures (pp. 78–9). I am indebted to Edmund Cusick for drawing my attention to this resemblance, in the introduction to his doctoral thesis-in-preparation on George MacDonald, University of Oxford.

33 *Ibid.*, p. 78. Prickett is commenting on Mary Shelley's *Frankenstein*.

INTRODUCTORY STUDY: APOLLONIUS OF TYRE

1 Albert H. Smyth, *Shakespeare's Pericles and Apollonius of Tyre*, Philadelphia, 1898, p. 24.
2 Peter Goolden, *The Old English 'Apollonius of Tyre'*, Oxford, 1958, pp. xiv, xiii.
3 Albert H. Smyth, *op. cit.*, pp. 19, 23, 69.
4 R. M. Dawkins, 'Modern Greek oral versions of Apollonios of Tyre', *Modern Language Review*, XXXVII, 1942, pp. 169–84.
5 Peter Goolden, *op. cit.*, p. xiv. R1 and R2 have been edited in a parallel edition by Alexander Riese, *Historia Apollonii Regis Tyri*, 2nd edition, Leipzig, 1893.
6 Gower's version of the Apollonius of Tyre story in Book VIII of his *Confessio Amantis* is dated 1393. I have used the 1554 edition as it appears in Geoffrey Bullough, *Narrative and Dramatic Sources of Shakespeare*, vol. VI, London, 1966, pp. 375–423.
7 I have used Philip Edwards' edition, *Pericles, Prince of Tyre*, Harmondsworth, 1976. I do not refer to Shakespeare in my

discussion owing to the uncertainties over the play's authorship.

8   I have used the edition of Lawrence Twine's *The Patterne of Painefull Adventures* dated about 1594, as it appears in Geoffrey Bullough, *op. cit.*, pp. 423–82.

9   I have used the edition of Hermann Oesterley, *Gesta Romanorum*, Hildesheim, 1963, tale no. 153, pp. 510–32. The *Gesta Romanorum* has been translated by Charles Swan (revised by Wynnard Hooper), *Gesta Romanorum*, London, 1904.

10   See F. N. Robinson, *The Poetical Works of Chaucer*, London, no date, p. 75, 'Introduction to the Man of Law's Tale', ll. 81–9.

11   G. Wilson Knight, *The Crown of Life*, Oxford, 1947 and London, 1948, pp. 63, 73. While his different approach leads him to discover themes of 'remorse' and 'repentance' in the play, Wilson Knight observes that Pericles in involved in a process of purification through suffering.

12   John Pitcher, in 'The poet and taboo: The riddle of Shakespeare's *Pericles*', *Essays and Studies*, 1982, pp. 18–20, argues for a continuation of the theme of incest in *Pericles* from the first two acts into the final three, where, with the begetting of Marina, 'a new proximity between father and daughter is engendered'.

13   Philip Edwards comments, *op. cit.*, p. 159, note to l. II.iv.2, that the text of *Pericles* shows emphatic juxtaposition of the relation of the two kings, Simonides and Antiochus, and their daughters; and John Pitcher, *op. cit.*, pp. 17–18, argues that Simonides' conduct as a parent is reminiscent of that of Antiochus.

14   That the Diana of Ephesus was different in character from the classical Greek goddess, being a fertility goddess, is evidently irrelevant here.

15   John Pitcher, *op. cit.*, pp. 21–3, has a useful argument that Lysimachus is a thinly concealed surrogate or double for Pericles.

16   Philip Edwards, *op. cit.*, pp. 30–1.

CHAPTER ONE:
YWAIN: CHRÉTIEN'S YVAIN AND HIS COUNTERPARTS

1.   Chrétien de Troyes, *Yvain (Le Chevalier au Lion)*, edited by T. B. W. Reid, Manchester, 1942; *Les Romans de Chrétien de Troyes*, IV, *Le Chevalier au Lion (Yvain)*, publié par Mario Roques, Paris, 1980. Translated by W. W. Comfort in *Chrétien*

de Troyes: Arthurian Romances, Everyman's Library, London, 1914. I have used Reid's edition, and, for translations, have drawn on Comfort and also on Tony Hunt's translations in *Medieval Literature, Part Two: The European Inheritance*, Harmondsworth, 1983, pp. 390–8. I have not used Comfort's translations as freely as I would have liked because I need translations which convey the original more directly.

2 *Ywain and Gawain*, edited by Albert B. Friedman and Norman T. Harrington, Early English Text Society, London, 1964.

3 Hartmann von Aue, *Iwein*, edited by Ludwig Wolff, 2 vols., Berlin, 1968. For translations I have used R. W. Fisher's translation in his *The Narrative Works of Hartmann von Aue*, Göppingen, 1983.

4 *Herr Ivan*, edited by Erik Noreen, Uppsala, 1931.

5 *Owein or Chwedyl Iarlles y Ffynnawn*, edited by R. L. Thomson, Dublin, 1968. I have used the translation by Gwyn Jones and Thomas Jones in *The Mabinogion*, London, 1949 and 1974. I have also used the early seventeenth-century Llanstephan 58 copy, edited and translated by R. L. Thomson, *Studia Celtica*, VI, 1971, pp. 57–89: this copy has considerable verbal independence and some interesting readings.

6 Tony Hunt, 'The medieval adaptations of Chrétien's *Yvain*: a bibliographical essay', *An Arthurian Tapestry*, edited by Kenneth Varty, Glasgow, 1981.

7 Tony Hunt, 'Chrétien de Troyes' Arthurian romance *Yvain*', *Medieval Literature, Part Two: The European Inheritance*, see note 1 above, pp. 126–41.

8 *Ibid.*, pp. 132–3.

9 *Ibid.*, pp. 134–5.

10 *Ibid.*, p. 136.

11 *Ibid.*, p. 139.

12 See Stephen Knight, *Arthurian Literature and Society*, London, 1983, p. 93.

13 *Ibid.*

14 See Tony Hunt, *Chrétien de Troyes: Yvain*, Critical Guides to French Texts, London, 1986, p.45.

15 See Arthur C. L. Brown, '*Iwain*, a study in the origins of Arthurian romance', *Studies and Notes in Philology and Literature*, VIII, Boston, 1903, pp. 125–7. For Wace on the Fountain of Bérenton, see *Maistre Wace's 'Roman de Rou et Des Ducs de Normandie'*, by Hugo Andresen, Heilbronn, 1877 and 1879, vol. 2, pp. 283–4. Wace describes how hunters used to go to Bérenton and draw water: they poured a little water — by chance — on the stone, and rain followed (vv. 6399–408):

La fontaine de Berenton
Sort d'un part lez un perron.
Aler soleient ueneor
A Berenton par grant chalor,
E a lors cors l'eue espuisier
Et le perron desus moillier.
Por co soleient pluie aueir;
Issi soleit iadis ploueir
En la forest e enuirun,
Mais io ne sai par quel raison.

16 Tony Hunt, *op. cit.*, note 14 above, p. 44.
17 Tony Hunt, *op. cit.*, note 7 above, p. 134.
18 Tony Hunt, *ibid.*, pp. 141, 134.
19 Tony Hunt, *ibid.*, pp. 134, 140–1.
20 See Tony Hunt, *ibid.*, p. 141.
21 See Tony Hunt, *ibid.*, pp. 134–5.
22 Tony Hunt, 'The lion and Yvain', in *The Legend of Arthur in the Middle Ages*, edited by P. B. Grout, R. A. Lodge, C. E. Pickford and E. K. C. Varty, Woodbridge, 1983, pp. 90, 94.
23 See A. H. Diverres, '*Iarlles y Ffynnawn* and *Le Chevalier au Lion*: adaptation or common sense?', *Studia Celtica*, XVI/XVII, 1981/82, pp. 153–4.
24 See *ibid.*, p. 155.
25 Arthur C. L. Brown, 'The Knight of the Lion', *Modern Language Association of America*, XX, 1905, pp. 673–706.
26 See A. H. Diverres, *op. cit.*, p. 157.
27 See *ibid.*, pp. 147–8.
28 See Tony Hunt, *op. cit.*, note 7 above.
29 See A. H. Diverres, 'Yvain's quest for chivalric perfection', in *An Arthurian Tapestry*, edited by Kenneth Varty, Glasgow, 1981, pp. 214–28.
30 *Culhwch and Olwen* is translated by Gwyn Jones and Thomas Jones in *The Mabinogion*, see note 5 above. For the meeting with the giant herdsman, see pp. 108–12.
31 *In Gilla decair* is edited and translated by Standish H. O'Grady in *Silva Gadelica*, I, London, 1892, pp. 258–75 (text) and 2, pp. 292–311 (translation).
32 See Arthur C. L. Brown, *op. cit.*, note 25 above, pp. 682–4.
33 Arthur C. L. Brown, *op. cit.*, note 15 above, particularly pp. 62, 70–1.
34 In the translation by Gwyn Jones and Thomas Jones, see note 5 above, p. 158.
35 *Ibid.*, p. 161.

36   Arthur C. L. Brown, *op. cit.*, note 15 above, particularly pp. 82-127.

37   *Serglige Con Culaind 7 Óenét Emire* (The Sick-bed of Cúchulainn and the One Jealousy of Emer) is preserved in the *Book of the Dun Cow*, dated about 1100 A.D. and available in an edition by R. I. Best and Osborn Bergin, Dublin, 1929. The *Serglige* has been edited by Myles Dillon, Medieval and Modern Irish Series, vol. XIV, Dublin, 1953. It is available in translation in *Early Irish Myths and Sagas*, by Jeffrey Gantz, Harmondsworth, 1981, pp. 153-78, and in Lady Gregory's *Cuchulain of Muirthemne*, London, 1902, pp. 210-22.

38   *Imram Brain meic Febail* (Voyage of Bran son of Febal): see Kuno Meyer and Alfred Nutt, *The Voyage of Bran son of Febal to the Land of the Living*, vol. 1, London, 1895, and A. G. van Hamel, *Immrama*, Medieval and Modern Irish Series, vol. X, Dublin, 1941.

39   *Immram Curaig Maíle Dúin* (Voyage of Mael Dúin's Coracle): like the *Voyage of Bran*, preserved as a fragment in the *Book of the Dun Cow*, and more fully elsewhere. Edited and translated by Whitley Stokes in *Revue Celtique*, IX, 1888, pp. 447-95, and X, 1889, pp. 50-95. There are useful introductions to the *Immrama*, and other early Irish stories, in Myles Dillon, *Early Irish Literature*, Chicago, 1948.

40   *Immram Snédgusa ocus Maic Riagla* (The Voyage of Snédgus and Mac Riagla): there are three versions, all preserved in fourteenth-century MSS. The original version, in verse, is edited by A. G. van Hamel, *op. cit.*, note 38 above. The prose version A is edited and translated by Whitley Stokes in *Revue Celtique*, IX, pp. 14-25, and prose version B, again by Whitley Stokes, in *Revue Celtique*, XXVI, pp. 130-70. This voyage is the pilgrimage of two monks of Iona, and the episodes are borrowed in part from the *Immram Curaig Maíle Dúin*.

41   *In Gilla decair*, see note 31 above, pp. 266-7 (text) and 301-2 (translation).

42   For Baron Munchausen's experience of the portcullis incident, see the following (among many editions): *The Travels and Surprising Adventures of Baron Munchausen*, preface by Henry Blanchamp, London, no date, p. 30; *Singular Travels, Campaigns and Adventures of Baron Munchausen*, by R. E. Raspe and others, London, 1948, p. 20; *The Adventures of Baron Munchausen*, illustrated by Ronald Searle, London, 1969 and 1985, p. 30, and *Wunderbare Reisen zu Wasser und zu Lande*, edited by Gottfried August Bürger, Im Insel Verlag, Frankfurt am Main,

1950, p. 25. The incident occurs as the Baron rushes in 'with the flying enemy', and the horse drinks after it, the water pouring out of its belly since its hind quarters have been left behind in the gateway; when the Baron notices the problem, he has the horse repaired.

43 For the predominantly burlesque character of 'La Mule sans frein', see the edition of R. C. Johnston and D. D. R. Owen, *Two Old French Gauvain Romances*, Edinburgh and London, 1972, pp. 1–11. The relevant lines are 465–70 (p. 33, in Elisabeth Brewer's translation, in *From Cuchulainn to Gawain*, Cambridge, 1973).

44 Stephen Knight, *op. cit.*, p. 85.

45 See Arthur C. L. Brown, *op. cit.* note 15 above, pp. 129–32.

46 *Guy of Warwick* is edited by J. Zupitza, Early English Text Society (Auchinleck MS.), Extra Series 42, 49, 59, London, 1883–91.

47 See Stephen Knight, *op. cit.*, pp. 98–9.

48 Tony Hunt, *op. cit.*, note 22 above.

49 See Tony Hunt, *op. cit.*, note 6 above, p. 205.

50 See Erik Noreen, *Studier rörande Eufemiavisorna* III, *Textkritiska Studier över Herr Ivan*, Skrifter utgivna av Kungl. Humanistiska Vetenskaps-Samfundet i Uppsala, 26: 1, Uppsala/Leipzig, 1929, p. 25. Erik Noreen suggests that the curious 'Landewans' arises from Chrétien's lines (vv. 2150–3):

> Par la main d'un suen chapelain
> Prise a Laudine de Landuc,
> La dame, qui fu fille au duc
> Laudunet ...

'Landewans' could represent any of the three proper names in these lines. Noreen also quotes the corresponding passage from *Ívens Saga* (edited by Eugen Kölbing, 1898), the Icelandic abbreviated version of the lost Norwegian version (which was used by the author of *Herr Ivan* — see Tony Hunt, 'Herr Ivan Lejonriddaren', *Medieval Scandinavia*, VIII, 1975, pp. 171–2): after the marriage, the lady gives Iven all her duchy, which had belonged to her father, Laudun — 'gaf hon þá ... allt sitt hertogadoemi, þat er átt hafði Laudun, faðir hennar' (7: 18). It seems most likely that 'Landewans' refers to Laudunet, Laudine's father.

51 The English version of the hero's words to the women is as follows, '"A, God forbede ... Þat þe sister of Sir Gawayn Or any oþer of his blode born Sold on þis wise knel me byforn"' (ll. 2323–6), and Hartmann has, '"nu enwelle got / daz mir diu

unzuht geschehe / daz ich ze mînen vüezen sehe / diu mîns
hern Gâweins swester ist. / jâ wære des, wizze Krist, / dem
künege Artûs ze vil"' (ll. 4782–7; '"God forbid that I should
ever suffer such an improper situation as to see my lord Gawain's sister at my feet! God knows, this would be too much
even for King Arthur"', Fisher, pp. 231–2). The Swedish version
devotes several lines to repeating Ivan's refusal to allow the
prostration: 'Han badh them tagher up standa allæ: / "J skulen
mik ey til fota falla! / . . . Iak vil thet ække hafua aff thik / at ij
skulin fallæ a knæ for mik, / ey bør idher thet vidh mik at gøra,
/ iak vil thet ey se ælla høra"' (ll. 3231–2; 3235–8; 'He bade
them all stand up: "You should not fall at my feet! . . . I do not
wish to have you falling on your knees before me, you ought
not to do it for me, I do not wish to see or hear it"'). The
English version of Yvain's '"Des m'an deffande, Que je ja nule
rien an aie!"' is '"Nai, God forbede þat I sold tak any mede
[reward]"' (ll. 2367–8); the Swedish has, '"Gudh forbiudhe
thet ij alla saka / thet iak skal goz for æro taka"' (ll. 3297–8),
and the German has, '"sône stât niht mîn muot / daz ich ûf
guotes miete / den lîp iht veile biete"' (ll. 4842–4; '"It is not
my intention to sell myself for material reward"', Fisher, p.
232).

52   All three dependent versions follow Chrétien in the use of the
name Knight of the Lion when Ywain is speaking to Laudine
after the rescue of Lunete. The four versions of the reply to
Laudine's request for the knight's name are as follows: '"Ja del
Chevalier au Lion N'orroiz parler se de moi non. Par cest non
vuel, que l'an m'apiaut"' (Yvain, vv. 4613–15); '"I hat þe
knight with þe lyoun"' (Ywain and Gawain, l. 2662); '"Leons
riddara man kallar mik"' (Herr Ivan, l. 3854), and, in Hartmann, '"ich heize der rîter mittem leun"' (l. 5502).

53   See R. L. Thomson's introduction to his edition, op. cit., note 5
above.

54   See A. H. Diverres, op. cit., note 23, and also Brynley F.
Roberts, 'The Welsh romance of the "Lady of the Fountain"
(Owein)', The Legend of Arthur in the Middle Ages (see note 22),
pp. 179–82.

55   It is the view of A. H. Diverres that the Welsh writer, following
Chrétien, omitted the Noire Espine story of the sisters' conflict
over their inheritance for two reasons: first, because he has no
theme of a knight seeking chivalric perfection, the theme in
Chrétien to which the Noire Espine episode belongs, and,
second, because, under the Welsh law of the time, daughters
could not inherit; the situation would be impossible to a Welsh

audience (A. H. Diverres, *op. cit.*, note 23, pp. 156–7). It seems
to some scholars that while omitting the Noire Espine adventure, the Welsh writer made use of its battle.

56   This is the White Book reading; the later Red Book of Hergest
has '"twyllwr bratwr aghywir"', and the Llanstephan MS. 58
has '"megis twyllwr, bradwr"' (p. 78 in R. L. Thomson's edition, see note 5 above), meaning 'like a deceiver, traitor'.

57   R. L. Thomson points out on p. 56 of his edition, note to l. 570,
that this insult was so deadly that the use of it by a wife to her
husband was one of the three occasions on which the Laws
gave him the right to strike her without reparation.

58   See A. H. Diverres, *op. cit.*, note 23, p. 145.

59   R. L. Thomson's translation, *op. cit.*, note 5 above, p. 81.

60   *Ibid.*, p. 83. R. L. Thomson, in his note to l. 658 (p. 58) of his
edition from the White and Red Books, discusses the various
efforts of translators and editors to deal with the problem of
the reading here. Lady Charlotte Guest, in her *The Mabinogion*,
London, 1977, p. 24, alters a word and achieves, 'And the
Countess and all her subjects besought him to remain'. T. P.
Ellis and John Lloyd, in their *The Mabinogion: A New Translation*, Oxford, 1929, vol. 2, p. 59, give a word an unusual sense
and achieve, 'and the Countess offered him herself and all her
dominions'.

61   In R. L. Thomson's edition, ll. 691–2. This is the White Book
reading: the Red Book omits 'bradwr', and so also does Llanstephan 58 (Thomson, p. 82), the meaning in those cases being
deceiver ('dwyllwr'), without the sense of traitor.

62   D. G. Mowatt, 'Tristan's mothers and Iwein's daughters', *German Life and Letters*, XXIII, 1969 / 70, pp. 18–31.

63   Tony Hunt, *op. cit.*, note 7 above, p. 135. Hunt argues that
Yvain's ready acceptance of Gawain's arguments is a sign of
his immaturity and lack of discrimination.

64   The 'primal scene' is defined in the Penguin Dictionary of
Psychology as 'A recollection or confabulated scene from childhood of some early sexual experience, most commonly of one's
parents copulating'.

CHAPTER TWO: CHRÉTIEN'S PERCEVAL

1   Chrétien de Troyes, *Le Roman de Perceval ou Le Conte du Graal*
(T text), edited by William Roach, Geneva and Paris, 1959; *Les
Romans de Chrétien de Troyes*, V and VI, *Le Conte du Graal
(Perceval)* (A text), publié par Félix Lecoy, Paris, 1981. I have

used Nigel Bryant's translation of the T text in *Perceval: the Story of the Grail*, Woodbridge, 1982.
2 See note 3 to Chapter four.
3 See note 1 to Chapter five.
4 See note 1 to Chapter three.
5 Nigel Bryant, *op. cit.*, p. xii.
6 Helen Adolf, 'Studies in Chrétien's *Conte del Graal*', *Modern Language Quarterly*, VIII, March 1947, p. 15.
7 *Ibid.*, p. 15.
8 David C. Fowler, *Prowess and Charity in the 'Perceval' of Chrétien de Troyes*, Seattle, 1959, p. 27.
9 Helen Adolf, *op. cit.*, p. 6.
10 Arthur C. L. Brown, *The Origin of the Grail Legend*, Cambridge, Mass., 1943, p. 126n and p. 178n.
11 Glenys Goetinck, 'Gwenhwyfar, Guinevere and Guenievre', *Études Celtiques*, No. 11, 1964–5, pp. 351–60.
12 Helen Adolf, *op. cit.*, p. 5.
13 *Ibid.*, pp. 12–13.
14 *Ibid.*, p. 8.
15 *Ibid.*, p. 4.
16 *Ibid.*, p. 9.
17 David C. Fowler, *op. cit.*, pp. 32–3.
18 L. T. Topsfield, *Chrétien de Troyes: a study of Arthurian Romances*, Cambridge, 1981, p. 296.
19 Norris J. Lacy, *The Craft of Chrétien de Troyes: an Essay on Narrative Art*, Leiden, 1980, p. 109.
20 D. D. R. Owen, 'From Grail to Holy Grail', *Romania*, LXXXIX, 1968, pp. 31–53.
21 Helen Adolf, *op. cit.*, p. 7.
22 R. S. Loomis, *Arthurian Tradition and Chrétien de Troyes*, New York, 1949, p. 381.
23 See D. D. R. Owen, *op. cit.*, pp. 34–5.
24 See *ibid.* I cite many of D. D. R. Owen's arguments later in the chapter. One point he makes is that the hermit episode does not seem to have been there when the First Continuator was at work, because the Continuator does not take its Christian material into account in the episodes he devotes to Gawain's experiences at the Grail Castle. There are no references to the holiness of the vessel or to the man in the inner room, and the feast which the grail provides in the Continuation contradicts the idea of its carrying a single, consecrated wafer. D. D. R. Owen believes that the Continuator either misread or deliberately developed Chrétien's statement that at each course of the

banquet served to Perceval the grail passed through the hall
before him (pp. 44–5).
25 Helen Adolf, *op. cit.*, p. 7n.
26 Women in this romance seem to be connected with food. Chrétien is fond of describing meals, so it would be risky to make
too much of this point, but perhaps it is significant that food
plays an important part in the adventure with the tent girl and
with Blancheflor, while it does not do so at King Arthur's
court. Perceval takes food as well as kisses and a ring from the
tent girl, and, at Beaurepaire, the struggle with the unwanted
suitor is a time of starvation while the time of food is immediately the time of love: 'The castle cooks were not idle, and
boys lit the kitchen fires to cook the dinner. Now the boy could
sport with his love at his ease; she embraced him, and he
kissed her ...' (p. 28). At the beginning of the romance, Perceval says to his mother, 'Give me something to eat' (p. 6). Wolfram's version, which sometimes brings out latent content in
Chrétien's, has its tent lady ask Parzival not to eat her, but to
find himself some other food; she offers him bread and wine:

> si sprach 'ir solt mîn ezzen nieht.
> waert ir ze frumen wîse,
> ir naemt iu ander spîse.
> dort stêt brôt unde wîn ... (131, 24–7)

27 D. D. R. Owen, 'The radiance in the Grail Castle', *Romania*,
LXXXIII, 1962, pp. 108–17.
28 A. Micha, ed., *Cligés*, 1957, vv. 2709–11. Translated by W. W.
Comfort in *Chrétien de Troyes: Arthurian Romances*, Everyman's Library, London, 1914, pp. 126–7.
29 Arthur C. L. Brown, *op. cit.*, pp. 439 ff and Helen Adolf, *op. cit.*,
p. 7.
30 For the *Baile in Scáil*, see Eugene O'Curry, *Lectures on the
Manuscript Materials of Ancient Irish History*, Dublin, 1861, pp.
387–9.
31 Glenys Goetinck, *op. cit.*, p. 356, and *Peredur: a Study of Welsh
Tradition in the Grail Legends*, Cardiff, 1975, p. 287. Also Myles
Dillon, *Early Irish Literature*, Chicago, 1948, p. 109n. The play
on words was first pointed out by Thurneysen.
32 D. D. R. Owen, in 'From Grail to Holy Grail', see note 20, p. 46,
suggests that 'the pious interpolator', who, he believes, inserted the hermit scene, invented the man in the inner room to
provide an answer to the question as to who is served from
the grail. Perhaps the disappearance of the grail into another
chamber ('Et d'une chambre en autre entrerent', v. 3242, T

text) prompted the idea that the grail passes through the hall on its way to a destination in that chamber.

33 Margaret Fitzgerald Richey, *Studies of Wolfram von Eschenbach*, London, 1957, p. 68.
34 Helen Adolf, *op. cit.*, p. 13.
35 See Arthur C. L. Brown, *op. cit.*, pp 46–7. All we know of this fisherman encountered by Cúchulainn is found in two brief references in the *Tochmarc Emere* (The Wooing of Emer). These are as follows (according to Kuno Meyer's translation in four successive issues of *The Archaeological Review*, I, March–August 1888): '"we slept ... in the house of the man who tends the cattle of the plain of Tethra"' (p. 72) and '"The man, I said, in whose house we slept, he is the fisherman of Conchobor. Roncu is his name. It is he that catches the fish on his line under the sea; for the fish are the cattle of the sea, and the sea is the plain of Tethra, a king of the kings of the Fomori"', p. 152). Cúchulainn's wooing is opposed by Emer's father, who believes he may meet his death through Cúchulainn; he instigates Cúchulainn's training in arms with Scáthach, the Shadowy One, from which he hopes he will never return. Cúchulainn's training with Scáthach is largely a series of victorious encounters with formidable female characters. Cúchulainn then returns to Forgall's dun and seizes Emer; Forgall flees and falls to his death. Emer then spends a chaste night with King Conchobor, before she sleeps with Cúchulainn. Arthur C. L. Brown argues (*op. cit.*, p. 52) that Forgall was originally a giant and that Cúchulainn originally killed him; Emer, moreover, was originally Forgall's wife, and Forgall was in control of the action. Brown believes that there are indications that Chrétien had some sort of connection with the Irish literary tradition: he hears echoes of some of the Irish descriptive names — 'Glend Gaibthech' (glen perilous) and 'Mag n-Dobail' (plain of ill-luck) — in 'fontainne perilleuse' (*Yvain* v. 810) and 'chastel de Pesme-Avanture' (*Yvain* v. 5103). The above evidence for a connection between the Fisher King and the fisherman of Conchobor seems tenuous enough, and it must also be pointed out that there are uncertainties for us in the source material for the *Tochmarc Emere*. Only the first reference to the fisherman, quoted above, is present in the text identified by Thurneysen as representing Version I of the story: this is the text in the Book of the Dun Cow, dated about 1100 A.D. (a text both incomplete and greatly altered below the fisherman reference by a thirteenth-century interpolator). The second reference occurs in Thurneysen's Version III, which is found complete in the Stowe

MS., dated about 1300 A.D. The problem of the sources is discussed by A. G. van Hamel, in the introduction to his edition, published in his *Compert Con Culainn and other Stories*, Dublin, 1933, Volume III of the Medieval and Modern Irish Series, pp. 16–68. Translations tend not to include the fisherman references: two which do are Kuno Meyer's, quoted above, and Lady Gregory's, in her *Cuchulain of Muirthemne*, London, 1902 and 1973, pp. 35–52.

36   See Arthur C. L. Brown, *op. cit.*, pp. 146–7. See also John Carey, 'Nodons in Britain and Ireland', in *Zeitschrift für celtische Philologie*, XL, 1984, pp. 1–22. Carey's survey of the evidence shows that we cannot accept with full confidence the evidence that the name Nodons has the primary meaning of catcher (suggesting, perhaps, fisherman, c.f. Gothic 'nuta', meaning fisherman). Moreover, water symbolism does not appear to be primarily relevant when we consider the legends which have survived concerning Nodons and his Irish congener Nuadha. However, the temple complex at Lydney in Gloucestershire, which has inscriptions giving the god's name in the dative, also has bronze plaques depicting fishermen among other subjects. Carey concludes that Nodons is 'a god of multi-faceted but consistent character: a shining royal warrior presiding over the chaotic in nature, society and the Otherworld (water, war, the devils of Annwn)'.

R. S. Loomis argues (in *Celtic Myth and Arthurian Romance*, New York, 1927, pp. 178–83) that there is evidence to connect the Irish Manannán Mac Lir (Son of the Sea) and his Welsh near-counterpart Manawydan fab Llŷr with the Fisher King. They are both sea gods, and the Irish Manannán is well known for his connection with Other World visions. In the *Adventures of Cormac* (see Myles Dillon, *op. cit.*, pp. 110–12), Cormac comes upon Manannán in a palace with a beautiful maiden, and Manannán gives Cormac a gold cup which distinguishes truth from falsehood. In the *Voyage of Bran* (see note 38 to Chapter one), Manannán comes towards Bran over the sea and sings twenty-eight quatrains to him about the Other World, including the lines 'flowers pour forth a stream of honey / in the land of Manannán son of Ler' (this translation is from Proinsias MacCana, *Celtic Mythology*, London, 1970, p. 72). Loomis believes that a connection with the two sons of Llŷr — Manawydan and Brân (a god, while the Irish Bran is mortal) — led to the host's habitual appearance on water, and this puzzled the *conteurs*, leading them to invent the explanation that the infirm lord of the castle had taken to the sedentary occupation of fishing. The title 'Fisher King' then provoked the curiosity of Robert de Boron, and he concocted a fable that Bron caught a fish at the direction of a heavenly voice, thus acquiring the name of the Rich Fisher (*op. cit.*, p. 183).

37 One of these references, in the T text while not in the A text, is to the rich Fisher: 'Et del riche Pescheor croi / Qu'il est fix a icilui roi ...' (vv. 6417–18, T text). The A text reads: 'et del Riche Pescheor roi, / que filz est a celui ce croi ...' (vv. 6201–2).

38 Helen Adolf, *op. cit.*, p. 17.

39 D. D. R. Owen, in 'From Grail to Holy Grail', see note 20.

40 D. D. R. Owen, *The Evolution of the Grail Legend*, Edinburgh and London, 1968, pp. 153–64, and *Two Old French Gauvain Romances* (see note 43 to Chapter one), pp. 1–11. Owen suggests that Chrétien takes Gauvain 'down a peg or two' (p. 126, 'Burlesque tradition and *Sir Gawain and the Green Knight*', in *Forum for Modern Language Studies*, No. 4, 1968).

41 D. D. R. Owen, 'From Grail to Holy Grail', see note 20. Owen also says (p. 36) that, while it is true that all the MSS. include the hermit episode, at the same time all but four late or incomplete ones (B, C, F and H) contain one or more of the Continuations besides, Continuations of which the earliest copies themselves have passages commonly considered to be interpolations. Moreover, none of the MSS. appears to have been copied within a generation or so of Chrétien's death. Owen argues (pp. 44–5) that the hermit scene appears to have been inserted in the *Conte del Graal* after the composition of the First Continuation (see note 24).

42 *The Weddynge of Sir Gawen and Dame Ragnell*, edited by W. F. Bryan and G. Dempster, in *Sources and Analogues of Chaucer's Canterbury Tales*, Chicago, 1941, pp. 242–64. I discuss this story and other Loathly Lady stories in *Magical Thought in Creative Writing*, pp. 82–93.

43 I discuss the Hamlet plot in *Magical Thought in Creative Writing*, pp. 114–39.

44 Pauline Matarasso, in the Introduction to her translation of the *Queste del Saint Graal*, part of the Prose Lancelot, in *The Quest of the Holy Grail*, Harmondsworth 1969, p. 13.

CHAPTER THREE: SIR PERCEVAL OF GALLES

1 *Sir Perceval of Galles*, edited by W. H. French and C. B. Hale, in *Middle English Metrical Romances*, New York, 1930, vol. 2, p. 531.

CHAPTER FOUR: PARZIVAL

1 Margaret Fitzgerald Richey, *Studies of Wolfram von Eschenbach*, London, 1957, p. 53.

2 See note 6 to the Introduction.

3 Wolfram von Eschenbach, *Parzival*, Studienausgabe, Berlin, 1965. The translation used in this chapter is that of A. T. Hatto, *Wolfram von Eschenbach: Parzival*, Harmondsworth, 1980, except where otherwise stated.

4 Linda B. Parshall, *The Art of Narration in Wolfram's 'Parzival' and Albrecht's 'Jingerer Titurel'*, Cambridge, 1981, pp. 47–8.

5 Margaret Fitzgerald Richey, *op. cit.*, p. 54.

6 Linda B. Parshall, *op. cit.*, p. 45.

7 *Ibid.*, p. 46.

8 Margaret Fitzgerald Richey, *op. cit.*, p. 149. Dr Richey agrees with E. von Karg Gasterstädt that this passage is a later insertion on the part of Wolfram. There are, of course, other references to Lähelin — notably Sigune's, where she links Lähelin with Orilus, husband of the tent lady, declaring them brothers; they are both aggressors against Parzival, who is king of Norgals (140, 29), and Sigune's knight, killed by Orilus, was a vassal of Parzival's family. The Lähelin passage may well be a later insertion into the mother's advice: Sigune's reference, meanwhile, comes appropriately after Parzival's treatment of Jeschute, where any discussion of a thief would be relevant. Wolfram may have decided to give the information to the mother as well, as an afterthought. If so, Lähelin must have loomed quite largely in his mind — especially as he fails to see how inappropriate the passage is.

9 *Ibid.*, p. 57.

10 See Linda B. Parshall, *op. cit.*, p. 192.

11 *Ibid.*, p. 186.

12 Margaret Fitzgerald Richey, *op. cit.*, pp. 5, 62.

13 David Blamires, *Characterisation and Individuality in Wolfram's 'Parzival'*, Cambridge, 1966, p. 200.

14 David Blamires refers us to Peter Wepnewski, *Wolframs Parzival: Studien zu Religiosität und Form*, Heidelberg, 1955, for this point.

15 R. S. Loomis, *Arthurian Tradition and Chrétien de Troyes*, p. 395.

16 Hugh Sacker, *An Introduction to Wolfram's 'Parzival'*, Cambridge, 1963, p. 50.

17 Margaret Fitzgerald Richey, *op. cit.*, p. 47.

18 *Ibid.*, p. 59.

19 Jessie L. Weston, in her translation *Parsival: a Knightly Epic by*

Wolfram von Eschenbach, London, 1894, vol. 1, p. 312; she says Cunneware is derived from 'la pucele a la gonne vaire', that is, the maiden with the coloured robe.

20 David Blamires, *op. cit.*, p. 220.

21 R. S. Loomis, *op. cit.*, p. 394.

22 A striking alteration is that the grail is a jacinth stone with many magical powers. The sight of it creates abundant food and drink for the living and gives life to the dying. All who live in its presence are radiantly and permanently beautiful and young-looking. Many of these details we learn later, including Trevrizent's explanation that the grail's miraculous powers are renewed every Good Friday, when a dove from heaven lays a sacramental wafer on it, thus enabling it to provide all that Eden once provided (470, 1–20). Its mystery is enhanced by its being described in such terms as 'erden wunsches überwal' (235, 24), translated by Margaret Richey as 'the supreme choice of earth's desire' (*op. cit.*, p. 134). From time to time inscriptions appear on it, the letters fading away after they have been read. These give the laws of the order of knights which has grown up round the grail. They also make known the names of the elect, who are to be ministers of the grail. One particular day an inscription shows that a knight will arrive, and, if he asks a certain question on the night he comes, he will by virtue of that question take away the curse and bring healing to the wounded grail king. No one is to warn him or give him a hint of that question: it must come from his own heart. If it does not it will have no power to heal. The knight who asks the question will succeed the grail king immediately; the king has hitherto struggled to live — this made possible by his living in sight of the grail — in long agony, so that his people will not be left without a king.

It is Wolfram — not Chrétien — who develops the theme of the king's dominion as a waste land. His source may well be the Loathly Lady's description of lands being laid waste in Chrétien's version (T text, vv. 4675–83; ' "Ladies will lose their husbands, lands will be laid waste, girls will be left in distress and orphaned, and many knights will die" ', p. 51). Chrétien has himself used some realism in his description, but the fundamental idea may have been conceived magically, expressing the hero's vision of a wounded land as well as a wounded king.

23 See Margaret Fitzgerald Richey, *op. cit.*, p. 62.

24 Hugh Sacker, *op. cit.*, p. 56. Margaret Richey points out that Wolfram's explanation of the lack of 'triuwe' replaces Chrétien's that the hero's failure to ask the questions has come

upon him because of his sin against his mother. She says (*op. cit.*, pp. 63–4), 'There is no trace of this irrational ground in Wolfram's story, although ultimately, grown wise in the harsh school of experience, Parzival confronts with profound remorse his past responsibility for the death of his mother, for the death of Ither, and for the unrelieved suffering of Anfortas'. She describes Chrétien's two reasons for Perceval's fatal silence as 'the one irrational and primitive' (the sin against the mother) and the other a 'rational' result of the teaching of Gorneman (*op. cit.*, p. 68). I would add a caution here that the irrational reason is one of great power while the 'rational' one is comparatively trivial and irrelevant. Wolfram has used the 'rational' one well for a criticism of courtly society, but it may prove that he more powerfully develops Chrétien's theme of the sin against the mother in his portrayal of the suffering of Sigune and Jeschute.

25 Edwin H. Zeydel, trans., *The Parzival of Wolfram von Eschenbach*, Chapel Hill, 1951, p. 224. Margaret Richey, *op. cit.*, p. 137, translates the question as 'Sir, in what way do you suffer?'.

26 *Ibid.*, p. 328. Margaret Richey, *op. cit.*, p. 158, translates the question as 'Uncle, what ails thee?'.

27 Margaret Fitzgerald Richey, *op. cit.*, p. 71.

28 Linda B. Parshall, *op. cit.*, p. 132.

29 Ruth K. Angress, in her 'Interrogation in Wolfram's *Parzival*', *The German Quarterly*, LXII, 1969, pp. 1–10, evades these matters by saying, 'The question must be asked because it embodies man's readiness for God's grace, not because the words themselves have inherent power, as they do in primitive rites'. She continues that Parzival makes the question 'his own, his personal question', and that he makes it 'more intimate' (p. 9).

30 See Hugh Sacker, *op. cit.*, pp. 166–72.

31 Linda B. Parshall, *op. cit.*, p. 131.

32 See Margaret Fitzgerald Richey, *op. cit.*, pp. 52–3.

33 However, it is interesting to note in Book Two Herzeloyde's concern with her breasts and their (premature) production of milk. This may be linked with the motif of food in connection with women which seems to be present in the versions of both Chrétien and Wolfram; in particular, Wolfram's tent lady, Jeschute, tells the hungry Parzival not to eat her (131, 24). See note 26 to Chapter two.

34 Wolfram's text provides an opportunity to discuss the meaning of the name 'Perceval'. Sigune tells Parzival that his name means 'to pierce through', because great love cut a furrow in

the heart of his faithful mother, when she had to part from the
hero's father:

'deiswâr du heizest Parzivâl.
der nam ist rehte enmitten durch.
grôz liebe ier solch herzen furch
mit dîner muoter triuwe:
dîn vater liez ir riuwe ...' (140, 16–20)

Jessie Weston comments (*op. cit.*, vol. 1, p. 309) that the idea of
the furrow probably originates in Wolfram's understanding of
the 'val' in the French 'Perce-val' as meaning furrow; in Hein-
rich von dem Türlin's *Diu Krône*, 'val' is explained as 'Tal',
meaning valley, or 'Furche', meaning furrow. Jessie Weston
sees Wolfram as having given the name a symbolic meaning
peculiar to himself. W. A. Nitze and H. F. Williams (in *Arthurian Names in the 'Perceval' of Chrétien de Troyes*, University of
California Publications, Berkeley and Los Angeles, XXXVIII,
1955, p. 287) comment that a similar formation to 'Perceval' is
the name 'Percehaie', meaning 'Pierce-hedge', in the Norman
Domesday Book. Jean Marx, writing on *Peredur* and reflecting
that Chrétien's *Perceval* is a 'conte français d'aventure' by contrast with the Welsh version, which he describes as 'un témoig-
nage de haute valeur sur la forme ancienne du récit', comments that 'Peredur' is the name of an authentic British hero,
while 'Perceval est un nom inspiré par l'aventure (il perce le
secret du val où est le château)' (Jean Marx, 'Le Cortège du
Château des Merveilles dans le Roman Gallois de Peredur',
Études Celtiques, No. 9, Paris, 1960–1, pp. 92–105; I have
quoted from pp. 92–3). Rachel Bromwich regards 'Perceval' as
a loose approximation to 'Peredur', after the pattern apparent
in borrowings from Welsh names (for example, 'Merlin' from
'Myrddin' and 'Gauvain' from 'Gwalchmai'; p. 44, 'Celtic elements in Arthurian romance', in *The Legend of Arthur in the
Middle Ages*, Woodbridge, 1983). Chretien gives no derivation or
interpretation of the name, and Perceval 'guesses' his name
(when with his cousin) — by contrast with Parzival, who is
apprised of it by Sigune (Parzival's being informed of his name
is perhaps correctly deemed a rationalisation by W. A. Nitze
and H. F. Williams, *op. cit.*, p. 286). It is possible that the name
has a magical, sexual meaning, as has the aggressive, and
probably sexual, name 'Horn' in *King Horn*. However, there is
no convincing evidence in the text for this possibility, as there
is in the case of the name 'Horn'. It would not make good
magical sense for the hero to bring a sexually aggressive name

into being in his move with the cousin — his previous name having been 'Biax Filz' (A text, vv. 345 and 371–2; T text, vv. 373–4) or 'Biau Frere' (A text, v. 347) — unless he were declaring guilt to the cousin. In this move the hero is concerned with his guilt, but it would still be odd if he were declaring his aggression, sexual or otherwise, at this stage, when he has been aggressive hitherto and is now bent on establishing himself as an innocent 'Biax Filz'. In *King Horn*, the hero is 'Horn' when he is being aggressive and 'Goodmind' when he is being good. So the name of the acknowledged hero remains a mystery.

CHAPTER FIVE: PEREDUR

1 I have used the translation of *Peredur* by Gwyn Jones and Thomas Jones in *The Mabinogion*, London, 1949 and 1974. There are also translations by Lady Charlotte Guest and by T. P. Ellis and John Lloyd, see note 60 to Chapter one. There are editions by K. Meyer (1884) and by G. W. Goetinck, *Historia Peredur vab Efrawc* (1976).

2 Doris Edel, in 'Rhai sylwadau ar arddull *Peredur* a pherthynas y chwedl Gymraeg â *Perceval* Chrétien', *Llén Cymru*, Cardiff, XIV, 1981–2 (1983), pp. 52–63, argues that the Welsh storyteller knew the tale through Chrétien, but re-created it according to the material already in his possession.

3 See Thurneysen's examination of Mary Williams's book on *Peredur*, *Zeitschrift für celtische Philologie*, No. 8, 1912, pp. 185–9. I. C. Lovecy includes an investigation of Thurneysen's analysis in his 'The Celtic sovereignty theme and the structure of *Peredur*', *Studia Celtica*, Nos. 12–13, 1977–8, pp. 133–46.

4 See Ceridwen Lloyd-Morgan, 'Narrative structure in *Peredur*', in *Zeitschrift für celtische Philologie*, No. 38, 1981, pp. 187–231, and Glenys Goetinck, *'Peredur': a Study of Welsh Tradition in the Grail Legends*, Cardiff, 1975.

5 See Glenys Goetinck, *op. cit.*, note 4 above. This view is examined by I. C. Lovecy, *op. cit.*, note 3 above. For the Welsh sovereignty theme, see also Catherine A. McKenna, 'The theme of sovereignty in *Pwyll*', *The Bulletin of the Board of Celtic Studies*, XXIX, 1982, pp. 35–52.

6 Ceridwen Lloyd-Morgan discusses this comment of Jean Marx in *op. cit.*, note 4 above, pointing out that, if the material before us fails to conform to our present-day European concepts of logic and unity, perhaps we should reject the logic and find a new one.

7   Glenys Goetinck, *op. cit.*, note 4 above, p. 177.

8   By contrast with sections I(*b*) and II, section III has the appearance of being a miscellany of additions, including, on the face of it, some of Chrétien's Gawain material in his *Conte du Graal*, even a few lines inspired by the hermit episode, and also material found in the Second Continuation of Chrétien's *Conte du Graal*. .

CHAPTER SIX: GAWAIN AND THE GREEN KNIGHT

1   The edition of J. R. R. Tolkien and E. V. Gordon, revised by Norman Davis, *Sir Gawain and the Green Knight*, Oxford, 1967, has been used for this discussion. There is a good translation by Brian Stone, *Sir Gawain and the Green Knight*, Harmondsworth, 1959. R. T. Jones has made the original more accessible to non-specialists by regularising the spelling, in his *Sir Gawain and the Grene Gome*, London, 1972, and so has J. A. Burrow, by modernising some obsolete characters and usages, in his edition, Harmondsworth, 1972.

2   I discuss 'Sir Gawain and the Green Knight' in *Traditional Romance and Tale*, pp. 80–2, 96–107, and in *Magical Thought in Creative Writing*, pp. 94–107 (in conjunction with 'The Grene Knight') and pp. 107–13 (in conjunction with *The Lord of the Rings*).

3   See my discussion of *Wuthering Heights* in the Introduction, and in note 31 to the Introduction.

4   G. V. Smithers, 'What *Sir Gawain and the Green Knight* is about', *Medium Ævum*, XXXII, No. 3, 1963, p. 187.

5   J. A. Burrow, *A Reading of 'Sir Gawain and the Green Knight'*, London, 1965, p. 165.

6   Norman Davis, *op. cit.*, p. xxi.

7   P. M. Kean, in a review of J. A. Burrow, *op. cit.*, *Medium Ævum*, XXXVI, No. 1, 1967, pp. 92–3.

8   Norman Davis, *op. cit.*, p. xxi.

9   J. A. Burrow, *op. cit.*, pp. 178–9.

10 G. V. Smithers, *op. cit.*, p. 187.

11 *Ibid.*, p. 189.

12 J. A. Burrow, *op. cit.*, pp. 125–6.

13 Marjory Rigby, '*Sir Gawain and the Green Knight* and the Vulgate *Lancelot*', *The Modern Language Review*, LXXVIII, Part 2, April 1983, p. 265.

14 G. V. Smithers, *op. cit.*, pp. 180–3. The analogues discussed by Smithers are the MHG *Lanzelet, Hunbaut, Yder* and *Le Chevalier à l'Épée*.

15 J. A. Burrow, *op. cit.*, pp. 93–4.
16 Marjory Rigby, *op. cit.*, pp. 264–5.
17 Norman Davis, *op. cit.*, p. 110.
18 G. V. Smithers, *op. cit.*, p. 179.
19 *Ibid.*, pp. 171–4, 177.
20 *Ibid.*, pp. 171, 178, 183.
21 *Ibid.*, pp. 171, 183, 184.
22 J. A. Burrow, *op. cit.*, pp. 105–10.
23 Norman Davis, *op. cit.*, p. 128.
24 G. V. Smithers, *op. cit.*, p. 174.
25 *Ibid.*, p. 189.
26 A study of *Bricriu's Feast* involves establishing a text free of all
    the interpolations of 'H', the thirteenth-century interpolator of
    the Book of the Dun Cow. The problems are discussed by
    Edgar M. Slotkin, in 'The structure of *Fled Bricrenn* before and
    after the *Lebor na hUidre* interpolations', *in Ériu*, XXIX, 1978,
    pp. 64–77. A good translation of the text, in its interpolated
    state, is available in *Early Irish Myths and Sagas*, by Jeffrey
    Gantz, Harmondsworth, 1981, pp. 221–55. For editions, see
    George Henderson, *Fled Bricrend*, Irish Texts Society, London,
    1899; R. I. Best and Osborn Bergin, *Lebor na Huidre: Book of
    the Dun Cow*, Dublin, 1929 (which distinguishes the work of
    the interpolator in the print), and Kuno Meyer, 'The Edin-
    burgh version of the *Cennach ind Rúanado*', *Revue Celtique*,
    XIV, 1893, pp. 450–9.
27 The plot seems to have four parts: the quarrel in Bricriu's hall
    over who should receive the champion's portion; the tests of
    the Crúachan cats, set by Ailill and Medb, in which Cúchulainn
    emerges champion but the two other contestants do not accept
    this; the tests at Cú Roí's stronghold, in which Cúchulainn is
    again champion while the two other contestants deny this;
    and, finally, the beheading exchange with Cú Roí at Emain
    Macha, after which Cú Roí once more proclaims Cúchulainn
    the champion, and this is accepted. I have investigated the
    possibility that the third part of this narrative, where Cúchu-
    lainn is in Cú Roí's stronghold with Cú Roí's wife, in the
    absence of Cú Roí, may have links with the scenes between
    Gawain and Bertilak's lady, and have found no evidence for
    this. In the separate story of the Death of Cú Roí, Cúchulainn
    kills Cú Roí in order to take his wife (Blathnat), but there is no
    suggestion of this material in *Bricriu's Feast*. There are two
    texts of the Death of Cú Roí: 'Aided I', preserved in the
    sixteenth-century Egerton MS., and edited and translated by
    R. Thurneysen, in *Zeitschrift für celtische Philologie*, No. 9,

1913, pp. 190–6; and 'Aided II', preserved in the fourteenth-century Yellow Book of Lecan, and edited and translated by R. I. Best, in *Ériu*, II, 1905, pp. 18–31.

28 *Early Irish Myths and Sagas*, see note 26 above, p. 254.

29 *Ibid.*, pp. 254–5.

30 There is a useful discussion of the relationship between the hunting and bedchamber scenes — in spite of its legal-historical approach to the problem of the treason — in W. R. J. Barron's *'Trawthe' and Treason*, Manchester, 1980.

31 The tail-rhyme treatment of the Green Knight story, *The Grene Knight*, appears to be a light version of the *Gawain*-poet's romance, without much fear, but it does throw some light on the status of the testing theme in this plot. In *The Grene Knight*, the witch's purpose in enchanting the knight and sending him to Arthur's court is entirely to do with love, while it is the Green Knight who speaks of testing, and there is confusion throughout as to what he is testing. I discuss *The Grene Knight* in *Magical Thought in Creative Writing*, pp. 98–107. The witch's purpose, and the Green Knight's, are revealed in ll. 58–72:

> shee said, 'thou shalt to Arthurs hall;
> for there great aduentures shall befall
>   That euer saw King or Knight.'
> all was for her daughters sake,
> that which she soe sadlye spake
>   to her sonne-in-law the Knight,
> because Sir Gawaine was bold and hardye,
> & thereto full of curtesye,
>
>   to bring him into her sight.
> the knight said 'soe mote I thee,
> to Arthurs court will I mee hye
>   for to praise thee right,
> & to proue Gawaines points 3;
> & that be true that men tell me,
>   by Mary Most of Might.'

There is confusion in the text as to whether the 'points 3' are bravery, toughness and courtesy (ll. 64–5) or courtesy, nobility and loyalty (ll. 469–80), the first points being the qualities which attract the witch's daughter (the knight's wife) and the second being those listed at the tryst as the qualities Gawain has forfeited by keeping the lace. At Arthur's court, the Green Knight tells Arthur that he has come to prove points which belong to manhood (ll. 116–19), and the beheading game then ensues, as if it is to be this test. *The Grene Knight* is to be found in Bishop Percy's Folio MS., *Ballads and Romances*, vol. 2, edited by J. W. Hales and F. J. Furnivall, London, 1868, pp. 58–77. There is a translation of *The Grene Knight* by Elisabeth Brewer in *From Cuchulainn to Gawain: Sources and Analogues of 'Sir Gawain and the Green Knight'*, Cambridge, 1973, pp. 83–91.

32   My hunch that the designation 'chapel' may express taboo is prompted by the data in Roger Frétigny and André Virel, *L'Imagerie Mentale*, Geneva, 1968, a study of the use of the guided day-dream in psychiatric treatment. In the day-dreams cited, a woman seen as taboo frequently appears as a nun, the Virgin or a veiled woman. The use of the word 'chapel', even with the word 'green' to describe it, appears with reference to the vagina in Norman Mailer, *An American Dream*. The passage is quoted and discussed in Kate Millett, *Sexual Politics*, London, 1971, Abacus edition, 1972, pp. 9–16. The context is so entirely different that it provides no useful information for the Green Knight plot except that a woman's sexual parts can be referred to in terms of a surprising number of public buildings. Where the adjective 'green' is concerned, I have not returned to the discussion of this colour conducted in my first study, because I do not feel there is sufficient evidence in the text for a useful exploration of it.

INDEX